THE ART OF THE LOOPHOLE

Nick Freeman

with

Angela Epstein

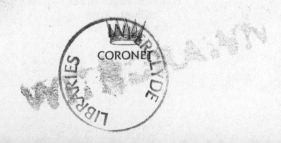

First published in Great Britain in 2012 by Coronet
An imprint of Hodder & Stoughton
An Hachette UK company

First published in paperback in 2013

1

A CIP catalogue record for this title is available from the British Library

ISBN 978 1 444 73408 9

Typeset by Hewer Text UK Ltd, Edinburgh

Printed and bound by CPI Group (UK) Ltd, Croydon, CR0 4YY

Hodder & Stoughton policy is to use papers that are natural, renewable
and recyclable products and made from wood grown in sustainable
forests. The logging and manufacturing processes are expected to
conform to the environmental regulations of the country of origin.

Hodder & Stoughton Ltd
338 Euston Road
London NW1 3BH

www.hodder.co.u

*In honour of my mum, Pat, and honoured
memory of my dad, Keith*

ACKNOWLEDGEMENTS

Though the contents of this book have been drawn from a thirty year career in the law, it would never have come to pass without the help of some remarkable people.

I'd like to thank my editor, Mark Booth, one of life's true gentlemen, whose vision, guidance, faith, and clarity of thought were a constant source of support. My agent, Heather Holden-Brown demonstrated bountiful enthusiasm and endless patience.

I also salute barrister, Dean George, a huge legal talent, whose constructive criticism and painstaking proofreading played a vital part in the evolution of this book.

On a personal note I'd like to thank my great friend and sparring partner, barrister Gary Bell for always fighting my corner. Thanks too, to my staff at Freeman & Co and Freeman Keep on Driving Ltd, who are unwavering in their loyalty and affection.

Finally, I'd like to say a special thank you to my ghost writer, Angela Epstein. A fine journalist and fellow perfectionist, who has lived and breathed this book since we first hatched this project together and embarked on our joint writing partnership. I know I'm a difficult task master so thank you for keeping your warmth and humour. I've really enjoyed our journey.

CONTENTS

1 How it all began   1

2 Honing the technique   17

3 Loophole: eureka instinct!   40

4 Loophole: in sickness and in health   76

5 Loophole: identification   113

6 Loophole: don't talk unless you can improve the
   silence – or the defence   148

7 Loophole: crown cock-ups   179

8 Loophole: check the small print   216

9 Tying up loose ends and loose loopholes   245

I

How it all began

I was seven years old when I realised that I wanted to be a lawyer. A relatively tender age to make such a weighty career decision, especially as I didn't even know what the word 'lawyer' meant. But my choice was an entirely practical one. I'd been put on the spot by my father and needed a quick answer.

Dad was walking me back from Sunday school one crisp autumn morning when, without warning, he suddenly decided to cross-examine me about my long-term career plans.

'What are you going to do when you grow up?' he demanded as we marched – at his pace – through the quiet streets near our home in suburban Nottingham.

Trotting to keep up, I stole a look at the sober expression on his face. As a young boy who was slightly in awe of his father, I could tell this wasn't a game. Or even a trick question. Dad really wanted to know what I was going to do. As the eldest of his three sons, I was the prototype. Clearly he didn't feel it premature to discuss my future even though I still had scuffed knees and wore short trousers.

In his defence, I must explain that Dad wasn't some pushy parent, keen to hothouse a precocious son. His motive was far more honourable. He wanted me to make something of my life, and had a staunch belief that education was the only way forward. That's why my name had been put down for Uppingham, a public school in Rutland, the day I was born.

And it's probably also why my childhood memories are speckled with images of a threatened stroke of the hair-brush or riding crop if my school work was poor, along with recollections of being force-fed Dickens novels on a Sunday afternoon.

But love and discipline weren't mutually exclusive in the Freeman household. Dad's motives were certainly a world away from those of fathers who'd swagger home after tumbling out of the pub, then lash their kids to prove who was in charge. Instead, the threat of punishment and early enquiries about my future were Dad's way of making sure I worked hard in order to make something of myself. Though I've never raised a hand to my own children, look-ing back, I think in many ways he set me on the path to becoming Mr Loophole.

Reflecting on all those childhood memories, one turning point stands out. It happened when, at junior school, our teacher began to set fortnightly tests of our grasp of multi-plication. My performance in the first 'times tables' test netted a magnificent nought out of twenty. Two weeks later I scored another 'nul point'. When Dad found out he went mad, shouting, 'I'm not spending all this money on you just so that you can mess about with your education.' If I didn't study hard for these tests, he added, he was going to wallop me for every answer I got wrong. Some may disagree with his admittedly Victorian methodology, but it forced me to knuckle down and study.

In the next test I scored thirteen and came home ner-vously, expecting to get whacked seven times. Actually Dad let me off. He could see how hard I'd tried and he never relished punishing me.

But I was on a roll and I could already see – as I would also see in my legal career – how hard graft and intricate knowledge can bring success.

Two weeks later my teacher returned my test paper with a beaming smile. Turning it over slowly, I couldn't believe my eyes. I'd scored full marks. I was euphoric. I remember looking down at the marked test paper on my desk and thinking, this is amazing. I don't ever want to be anywhere other than the top. This wasn't arrogance: it was a desire to be at the top of my game.

It's clear to me now that as Dad had instilled the work ethic in me even earlier, it was not unreasonable for him to discuss my career plans when I was only seven. He wanted to nudge my green and impressionable mind into thinking about the future. But how can a boy of that age have any idea what he's going to do with his life?

As we continued our march home, my stomach rumbling because I wanted my lunch, I knew better than to offer Dad a flippant reply, to tell him I wanted to be an astronaut or a footballer. When my father was serious, I knew he meant what he said. How then to answer his question about my career plans? Under his penetrating gaze, I thought quickly. I yearned to please him but also wanted to say something meaningful. In the end a boyish impulse kicked in, and out tumbled the words, 'What job will make me the most money, Dad?'

My father conceded an indulgent smile at my commercial instinct. 'That has to be lawyers,' he replied, without missing a beat. 'They earn about £4000 a year.'

My eyes widened. Four thousand! That's a year, by the way, not an hour, as this was 1963. I couldn't believe what I was hearing. My childish imagination conjured up a Himalayan heap of bank notes. Piles and piles of them. It sounded too good to be true.

I repeated the word 'lawyer' under my breath, rolling those two syllables round my mouth with tasty satisfaction. It sounded impressive. And the prospect of such riches was irresistible. I ventured a further question.

'What exactly do lawyers do, Dad?'

'Well,' my father replied solemnly, 'they argue for a living. And they use the law any way they can because they want to win.'

Unimaginable wealth? Tick. A licence to answer back (and not get a walloping)? Double tick. What more could a seven-year-old want to hear? I was hooked. Spool forward thirty years and as I stand in front of a courtroom, a nervous defendant at my side, the prosecutor spoiling for a legal fight, the atmosphere crackling with tension, I still am.

I live for these moments. On every side, eyes are boring into you: the ushers with their raven-black robes, the legal adviser, the public waiting restlessly in the gallery, the members of the press, chewing their pens and agitating for a story. At times it feels as if the very air itself heaves under a leaden weight. Then the door swings open, the court rises, the magistrates or judge take their seats. My heart drums a tattoo in my chest as I ready myself to take aim with the only weapon I have: the law. Law that I make work for me.

That's why I'm still hooked. I probably always will be.

But why? For the money? Well, let's be honest, who wouldn't be? (Part of the seven-year-old lives on inside me.) For the chance to argue and to show that if I do my homework I can get twenty out of twenty? Certainly. And for the burning desire to win, to be the best I can be? Nearly five decades after my ordeal with the times tables test, yes, more than ever before.

Of course, there are times when I've thought, how on earth did I get here? In fact, sometimes, when I'm on my feet in court, chewing at the Crown's case with my legal arguments, I think of Dad's snappy appraisal of what a lawyer does: 'They use the law any way they can because they want to win.' He was so right.

But when he sowed a seed in my impressionable mind all those years ago, neither of us could ever have envisaged that I'd go on to be regarded as one of the most 'notorious' figures in the legal profession, a man who's complimented and castigated in equal measure for the work that he does. Being a legal pioneer was never part of my brief. I just wanted to win my cases – today, tomorrow and thereafter.

Yet my dad made a good call. And Mr Loophole and I have never looked back.

As a boy, it seemed to me that only heroes (and villains) had special names, like Spiderman, Batman or Superman. To my knowledge there was never a Loopholeman. And there definitely wasn't a Mr Loophole.

Reports of my courtroom behaviour sometimes imply that I'm something of a saviour. Not, unfortunately, of the future of mankind – I'll leave that to Spiderman – but rather of speeding celebrities. It's claimed that I'm a courtroom chancer, existing purely to redeem the unredeemable by digging out dark details of the law to net an undeserving acquittal. That with my courtroom antics I throw the keys back to a speeding soccer star or a boozing TV presenter.

Like many things in life, it isn't that simple. Sure, I've defended thousands of people and secured acquittals for the majority of them. But there's no magical ingredient that I've cooked up. It's simply the art of the loophole. It's making the law work for me. And it's a skill that – unlike Superman's fantastic powers – is open to anyone to explore and eventually master should they find themselves in a sticky situation.

The defences I've marshalled over the years for the likes of David Beckham and Jimmy Carr are there for any lawyer to use or for any member of the public to be made aware of. There isn't a special statute devoted to people who have scored a winning goal at Wembley or had a stint in the jungle courtesy of *I'm A Celebrity* . . .

OK, so some of my defences might seem quirky because they're buried deep in the gloomiest corners of the statute books. But they're 100 per cent based on the law and what has been set down by Parliament. The art is knowing where to look and how best to use what you find. That, I suppose, is why I'm the man they call Mr Loophole. When I say 'they', I mean the press, or rather, a *Daily Express* reporter called Paul Broster who coined the nickname back in the mid-1990s after it seemed to him that I was winning case after case by using what he termed loopholes.

When I first read such comments, I thought, OK, this is the media's view of what I do, but it's not a true reflection of my work. What's more, 'Mr Loophole' wasn't a name I particularly liked. It connoted something sinister and underhand. I'm neither.

It's not that I was touchy about having a nickname: at school I was rather charmingly known as the 'little Yid without a foreskin' (yes, I'm Jewish). But 'Mr Loophole' stung me for different reasons. When you're a kid, everyone picks on what they see as a distinguishing feature. A redhead becomes 'Ginger', an overweight child is cruelly dismissed as 'Fatso'. Believe me, as someone who is deeply revolted by prejudice, I don't draw such comparisons lightly. Yet nicknames like those, though deeply unpleasant and unnecessary, are at least based on accurate observation.

But at that time 'Mr Loophole' bothered me so much because it was a slight on my work. Then again, I thought, it was just some reporter being cute. How could a daft name have any impact? What I was too short-sighted to realise at first was that newspapers love a good nickname. So whenever the press reported on a successful case the headline would scream, 'Mr Loophole Wins Again!' Equally, newspapers would be quick to relay my failures, shouting, 'X Loses His Licence – Despite Mr Loophole.'

To begin with I just ignored it. In any case, the press attention was, on balance, quite positive and good for business. And I'd chuckle when prosecutors would slyly slip the word 'loophole' into their submissions as a kind of private gag.

But one morning I was reading the local paper over breakfast when my eyes drifted to a report about a solicitor from Ashton-under-Lyne in Greater Manchester who had just won a driving case for a client. The article referred to him as the 'local Mr Loophole'. That really hacked me off. I might not have liked my tag, but I certainly didn't want anyone else taking advantage of my success in court. I began to wonder who else was enjoying the party.

So when I got to work that day I asked my secretary, Denise, to look up Mr Loophole on the internet. (I'm a complete technical dinosaur and to this day don't know how to use a computer.) The search yielded countless shifty websites credited to a 'Mr Loophole' and offering what appeared to be wholly inaccurate advice. And anyone reading them might well have concluded that I was the one dishing it all up.

I need to protect myself here, I decided. And I need to protect ordinary people from being ripped off by cowboy 'lawyers' – or just plain cowboys. (Even now I can feel a red mist descending when I hear of cases where the client has had poor guidance from their solicitor.) I felt I had no choice but to trademark 'Mr Loophole', an unprecedented move by a lawyer with regard to a nickname. Several months and £2000 later, the trademark was registered. It was official. I was and will always be Mr Loophole. Possession may be nine-tenths of the law. A trademark makes it a perfect ten.

So here I am, Mr Loophole by name. But, as I've said already, loopholes are not really loopholes at all – at least not in terms of the law. They're simply the law. And in this book I'll show you how the law can work for you. Look in the dictionary and you'll find a loophole is defined as a dodge, an excuse, a get-out clause. If that's what loopholes are, then I'm afraid that's not how I win my cases.

I don't use loopholes, I just use the law, though it might be a way of applying the law that hasn't been spotted or deployed before. Calling my defences loopholes suggests that I'm bucking the system. Well, I suppose I do sometimes buck the system. But if I do it's only because the system has itself failed because a magistrate, defence lawyer, police officer or prosecutor has failed to do their job properly.

That, in short, is the art of it all. And the truth of this will be evident again and again throughout this book. It's only thanks to a combination of the mistakes made by those in the prosecuting process and my own slightly – well, seriously – obsessive interest in regulations and procedures that it appears as if I'm using loopholes.

I'm not alone. Every day the law dishes up what seem to be loopholes. And it's not just in road-traffic cases. Convicted criminals can walk free because of 'human rights' issues. Sexually incontinent celebrities keep their infidelity out of the papers thanks to super-injunctions. It's not that the courts are powerless. But they are governed, or even limited, by the law; that is, by what is set down in statute by Parliament and how it is applied by the judicial system. If it's the law, then it's the law.

That's why, even though I'm frequently challenged about the way I work, I don't have a problem with what I do. By focusing solely on my legal obligation I suppose I sometimes attempt to isolate myself from the emotional aspects of my cases. I have to, otherwise I simply couldn't defend my clients. It sounds harsh, bloodless and unfeeling, I know. But when I trained to be a defence lawyer, I knew what I was signing up for, what the rules of engagement would be. If I stray from those rules, and instead ponder the ethical rights and wrongs of whether a defendant should go free, then I'm of no use to my client or indeed to the legal profession.

I've only once let my heart rule my head. I remember defending a lady on a drink-driving allegation where the legal arguments became so absorbing that the prosecution forgot to slide in a vital piece of evidence, namely the statutory warning. Now this prosecutor was a really lovely chap who had been very fair with me and I immediately spotted the error he'd made.

I suppose I wanted to salve my conscience because he'd been so decent to deal with. So I alerted him to his mistake, though I did so when I thought that it would probably be too late in the case for him to do anything about it. (I'd finished calling all my witnesses and was about to make a closing speech. It would be unusual for the court to allow the prosecution to call any further evidence at this stage). Anyway, even if he did rectify his mistake, I had plenty of defences which I thought would nail my case.

It was a fatal error.

The prosecutor thanked me for the tip-off, then immediately applied to the judge to get the evidence belatedly included. Astonishingly, he was allowed to do this, and my client was convicted. So much for being Mr Nice Guy. I was hoist with my own petard. Little wonder I've resisted ever doing anything like this again.

On the other hand there are cases in which I'm only too glad not to be involved.

When footballer Luke McCormick smashed into a car and killed two young children I felt an overwhelming sense of revulsion at what he'd done. The Plymouth Argyle goalkeeper went on to be jailed in October 2008 after admitting causing death by dangerous driving and drink-driving. Of course, it's both inconsistent and hypocritical for me to feel this way. As a lawyer, it's vital to park your emotions. Your primary duty is to defend your client. But this was a terrible, needless tragedy. Defending McCormick would have posed a very serious moral struggle because of the way I felt about what had happened. I knew that being asked to take that case would have tested me and I prayed that he wouldn't contact me. If there was a loophole in that harrowing case, well, I was hoping I wouldn't be called upon to find it. Though if I got the call, I knew I had a professional duty to this man. Fortunately, on that occasion the phone didn't ring.

In fact there are times when I almost hold my breath after learning about a particularly gut-wrenching and tragic case such as the killing of Baby P. Cases like this make my insides churn with disgust. Yet, as a lawyer, I'd have to set such feelings aside and fulfil my professional obligation to defend my client, test the prosecution case and find the flaw. The loophole.

And there may well have been a loophole in either of the cases I've mentioned. In most cases there usually is. But you have to know how to find it. To defend a case with a loophole argument, a lawyer has to look forensically through the court papers before forming an opinion and arming his client with all the information they need so that they can decide how to plead.

So, you might think, if it's that simple, why don't more people walk free? Why don't more Crown cases fold? For some lawyers, the temptation is to take what might appear to be the easier option, and plead guilty. If the client was stopped with more booze sloshing round his system than a barman's stag do, and the client assumes that because of this he is guilty, then, his counsel may well think, how can there possibly be a way out? To me, this is just giving the prosecution an easy ride, and as such is a foul betrayal of the profession. It's not for the defence to prove their client's innocence: it's for the Crown to prove that person's guilt. The art of the loophole means finding a way to stop the prosecution from being able to do that.

In fact I've probably entered a guilty plea in fewer than 1 per cent of my cases. But let me tell you about the one time I really wanted my client to enter a guilty plea and he wouldn't let me. And yet I still found a loophole.

The case involved an allegation of drink-driving and my client, a white-collar professional, was facing prison if convicted. Not only had he produced a high alcohol reading, but he also had four previous convictions. When I first looked over the papers I felt certain there was no defence. The Crown had done their job properly: all the documentation was in order and correct procedures had been followed. End of story. I couldn't see any way forward other than a guilty plea. But my client wasn't having any of it, storming at me that I was supposed to be a 'f*****g hotshot lawyer' and that there must be a way to 'get him off'. Having been blasted by his charm, I rasped out my response with barely concealed frustration. 'Well, that's very flattering of you to say so. Look, if you have a defence, you tell me what it is.' 'F*****g hotshot lawyer' or not, I couldn't see one. But my client insisted that it was his right to pay me to come to court to see if I could 'do something'. Perhaps this was the price I was paying for my growing reputation. It made people feel that I could wave a magic wand. But in this case I really couldn't see a way out and didn't feel comfortable taking the man's money. I even asked the Law Society to confirm that it was ethical. Overall, I didn't want to make a monkey of myself in court. But my client wouldn't let up and in the end I reluctantly agreed to defend him.

The day of the trial dawned and I felt myself bowing under the weight of unrealistic expectation. When the proceedings began all I could do was to listen intently as the prosecution established their case, praying that at some point they would trip up. It was such a ridiculous long shot it made me squirm in discomfort. I'd never been in court without having something that I could argue persuasively. What the hell was I going to do? The Crown's evidence was impeccable. I could feel my client's eyes drilling into me. I felt duty bound to turn to him and whisper, 'It isn't looking good.'

When it was my turn to cross-examine the prosecution witnesses I slowly got to my feet, thinking that I needed a miracle to win this one. The only thing I could do was to take the police officer in the witness box back through his evidence to explore it in greater detail. I began by asking about where, when and why he'd decided to stop my client. So far, so watertight.

And then, out of nowhere, something astonishing happened. As the officer described my client's first attempts at using a breathalyser, I asked what the screen on the machine displayed after he'd tried to blow into it.

'Well, sir, it showed the word "void",' said the copper.

I swallowed hard. 'Void' flashes up on that particular type of breathalyser when the machine has malfunctioned. In contrast, it shows 'voided' if the person being breathalysed hasn't provided enough breath to produce a reading. So the two words mean something entirely different.

How did I know this obscure bit of semantics? I'd read it once in one of the law books – a favourite holiday pastime that I'll come back to later. I remember being astonished how two little letters – 'e' and 'd' – could make such a difference to a case. Out of nowhere that nugget of information catapulted to the front of my mind, and suddenly a hopeless case was beginning to show a promise of victory.

Had the police officer used the wrong word by accident? Was it just a slip of the tongue? Possibly. But the court was reliant on the witness's evidence. And he had just dished up an answer which totally destroyed the prosecution case.

I didn't ask him to repeat it. When you spot a loophole, never give your opponent the chance to repair the damage. Instead, let the firework smoulder.

After the Crown had closed their case, I then made the submission that there was no case to answer. The whole court seemed to swivel their heads towards me in one united movement. What on earth could I mean? Now for the spelling lesson. Calmly, I explained how the prosecution's evidence showed the breathalysing machine hadn't been working.

Everyone looked slightly baffled. So I explained the difference in meaning of 'void' and 'voided' when they show up on this particular breathalyser. No one else had appreciated the significance of the two words. And what's more, I had a textbook to hand – I always takes stacks of them into court – to confirm the accuracy of what I was saying.

The case was adjourned so that the prosecution could consult an expert in order to establish the exact difference between 'void' and 'voided' in this situation. The expert confirmed that 'void' meant the machine wasn't working. The Crown conceded that as a consequence of the officer's evidence the court couldn't confirm whether or not the machine was working. So, instead of going to prison, my client was free to go. And I had wanted him to plead guilty.

What this episode so powerfully highlights is that there's almost always something that might lead to a crack in the prosecution case. You just have to know your stuff.

Knowing the law and how to use it is what lies at the heart of the art of the loophole. It's about finding failings in the prosecution's evidence that justify taking a case to court. Of course, it's for the client to decide how to plead. But, in my view, a client who is considering pleading guilty needs to do so on a properly informed basis. This means that as a lawyer you should turn over every single comma and full stop in evidence before deciding whether the prosecution can prove their case. All it sometimes takes is for the prosecuting authorities to make a slight slip and the case is over.

Yet still, as I've said, so many defence lawyers continue to err towards the guilty option.

I remember once waiting in Macclesfield Magistrates Court to do a speeding trial. As I sat in the court, another solicitor came in and slid down next to me, his client hovering just out of earshot. This chap was defending a speeding case – his client had been doing 105mph – and, since he wasn't local to the area, this lawyer wanted to know if I knew what the magistrates were like that day and therefore what kind of penalty he could expect from the bench.

I looked at him for a moment. 'So you're pleading guilty?' I asked, frowning.

He shrugged. 'Of course, what else is there to do?'

I tried to conceal my distaste, and asked, 'Well, what sort of device did the police use to catch your client?'

Another shrug. He hadn't got a clue. It's against every rule of professional etiquette to dress down a peer. But since his client couldn't hear us I couldn't contain my contempt. 'Is your client paying for your advice?' I hissed.

'Of course,' he said, grinning. 'Five hundred pounds.' I bit my tongue. This was manifest laziness and pure courtroom robbery. A total dereliction of duty. There was no attempt to find out anything about the prosecution case.

I said, 'You know what? I'm about to do a speeding trial ahead of you. Why don't you stay and watch. It'll give you a feel for the magistrates.' Palpably arrogant, I know, but my blood was boiling. My slightly baffled colleague went back to his client to tell him that they would be staying in court until their case was called. I went on to win mine.

Afterwards the other lawyer's client came over to me as I prepared to leave. Shooting his own counsel a withering glance, he asked, 'Why am I pleading guilty? Can't you defend me instead?' It would have been inappropriate to filch the case from my peer, much as I'd have liked to. So I had to decline. To this day I wonder what the bench threw at this poor chap.

This kind of scenario happens day in, day out. But it doesn't have to. There's nothing to stop a defence lawyer working in any area of the law finding things that justify the case going to trial. Nothing to stop that lawyer excavating these so-called loopholes. I don't understand why more don't do it. Let's face it. Law courts may appear to some to be no more than sophisticated places to have a stylish street fight. To be a good lawyer means having to summon a watertight argument to smash the prosecution case to pieces and knuckle the Crown. You have to be focused, relentless, firing through the opposition's evidence like a heat-seeking missile, until you find their weakness.

And, in truth, that weakness can be tiny. I always think of those fabled stories about jet engines which are brought down by an errant screw or a loose rivet. It only takes a wayward bolt or wobbly pin to unravel even the greatest feat of engineering and cause it to crash.

So too in the law. It might be a phrase, a date, a spelling mistake. But it might be all that's needed.

Of course, mastering the art of the loophole takes both time and an unstoppable devotion to the quest. I'm still learning, still in pursuit. But it can be done.

2

Honing the technique

One of the things I get asked most frequently is, 'How do you do it?' It's a flattering question, since built into it is the implication that I'm a practitioner of some kind of mystical technique. I wish.

In truth, there's no single strategy. In fact – as the armchair psychologist in me would reluctantly admit – a lot of how I work is rooted in my background. I had it instilled in me from a young age that I must work hard. (Which made me want to play harder, but that's another story.) And, after the times tables incident, I wanted to be the best I could.

But I've also always been prepared to fight my corner, forensically examining the finer details to ensure a victory – regardless of how formidable the opponent. In fact one of the first times I took on a David and Goliath tussle with authority was back in 1975, when I was a first-year law student at Trent Polytechnic. I'd driven to a lecture in my prized motor – a little red Triumph 1360 convertible with a brown leather steering wheel, a Motorola radio and plastic 'sportif' wheel rims – which I'd bought with my gap-year earnings, and parked on Chaucer Street in the centre of Nottingham. As I peeled off my leather driving gloves (this was 1975), I studied the parking sign displayed overhead. It said, 'Parking for an hour. No return within an hour of leaving.' This seemed rather ambiguous since it didn't specify where exactly one shouldn't return to. To me, though, it implied a driver couldn't come back to where they had just parked once they vacated the slot.

I went off to my lecture and just before the hour was up, I came out, moved the car a few hundred yards down the road and then went back into college. When I came out of the lecture about half an hour later, I was horrified to discover a parking ticket flapping under my wipers. The penalty, as I remember, was £14. No one relishes getting a ticket, but to me this was more than a king's ransom. Cash was really tight as all my money went on rent, food and running my car. I was doing bar work as well as manning the door of the Hot Brick café, showing people to their tables and sorting out fights. I simply couldn't afford it. And it was then that the injustice of the situation began to gnaw away at me.

In fury I strode over to the sign and studied it again. This sign was definitely ambiguous. I'd moved my car but I hadn't returned to the same spot – as the sign seemed to suggest I shouldn't – so why was I being punished?

Back home, I dashed off a letter to the local council pleading my case, pointing out that I was a law student and that the sign was clearly open to misinterpretation. A few days later I received a reply. The local authority conceded my point and cancelled my ticket. I was absolutely euphoric. It was a very early lesson in fighting for what you believe is right.

So you could say that loophole hunting suits my personality.

But, as well as being intolerant of injustice, I'm also one of those irritating people who seem to be hard-wired with a relentless eye for detail. I notice tiny flaws and blemishes everywhere I look and can't stop myself from registering the most insignificant of details.

Only the other morning I was driving to the office when I noticed a bit of mud on the mat below the passenger seat. I had to pull in and pick it up! When I sit down to work, my desk has to be completely clear – I just can't do clutter. Some of my pals suggest I've got a touch of obsessive–compulsive disorder (though others maintain I'm simply a fussy sod). When I get back from a day in court my trousers hit the trouser press and my shoes are polished even before I've put down my briefcase! Maybe I should hop on the therapy couch and find out what's behind all this. But I doubt the perfectionist in me would allow me to go through with it.

I do admit, though, that being a perfectionist has turned me into a borderline obsessive where work is concerned. When I'm doing a case I think about it all the time. It churns round and round in my mind – regardless of where I am or what else I'm doing. I'm an avid golfer and only the other week I was playing in a club championship when suddenly I had a brainwave about a case. I fumbled around in my pocket for the score card, dawdling at the ninth hole as I scribbled down my thoughts on the back of it.

'What on earth are you doing?' my golfing partner, Martin, remonstrated. 'There are people coming up behind us. We have to move on.'

'Sorry,' I said. 'I'm just making notes on a case.'

'See this green, Nick. It's called a golf course. It's not an office,' Martin replied, exasperated now as he left me to do more frantic scribbling before I raced after him.

So I suppose the first principle in the art of the loophole is: *keep looking at your situation from every single angle until you find a solution.*

Sometimes I have eureka moments: unexpected opportunities to nail the case, driven by a hunch. I think that having this instinct is vital for finding legal arguments. When you get that gut feeling, you need to be ready to fly with it. I'll discuss how valuable this has been to me in the next chapter. But just to give you a flavour, let me tell you about one particularly memorable defence. It was one I hadn't actually spent any time chewing over. Yet, funnily enough, it revolved around a piece of gum.

The case involved a client accused of drink-driving – the chap, though admittedly over the limit, claimed he had been sleeping in his car and hadn't actually been driving it. At the trial, proceedings had barely started when I noticed that the main police officer who would be giving evidence was chewing gum. He went on chewing right through the prosecution case, his mouth rotating like a washing machine on final spin. And he continued to chew when I began to cross-examine him. Being a bit of a stickler for common courtesy, I thought, you shouldn't be doing this in court. And, without a specific game plan, I decided I'd ask the officer to explain on oath why he was doing so.

I don't exactly know why I did this. I suppose it's a bit like fencing: you're probing and testing the witness. I just wondered if there was some way I could make use of the fact that the officer was chewing to highlight his lack of respect for the court. Maybe I'd make him apologise to the magistrates, which would showcase his bad manners and cast him in a poor light. All of these things ran through my mind as I lobbed my opening question:

'Are you chewing gum, Officer?'

'No,' the witness batted back, rather defensively, startled by the direction of my interrogation.

Bingo! Out of nowhere I suddenly had an officer lying on oath! Yes, about something irrelevant – namely, chewing gum. But it was still a lie. Incredible.

'Officer, what's in your mouth?' I persisted.

'Well, it's medicinal. I've had a cold,' he replied huffily.

'OK,' I continued, with a faux-sympathetic tone. 'Well, what are you chewing now? You told us a moment ago you weren't chewing anything. Now you say it's medicinal, so what is it?'

It turned out he was chewing Airwaves mentholated gum. Good for clearing your head perhaps, but neither medicinal nor a prescribed drug. In other words, he'd lied – again.

'So, Officer, when you said on oath that you weren't chewing gum, you weren't telling the truth, were you?'

'No,' he mumbled

'So why did you lie on oath?' I persevered.

He shook his head, blindsided by the cross-examination. 'I-I-I don't know,' he stammered.

It didn't take long to persuade the magistrates that if this officer could lie on oath under the full scrutiny of the court, how could we trust his uncorroborated account of a 3am arrest in a darkened car park with my intoxicated client? Lying about chewing gum smashed his credibility.

The court spat the case out. Which was more than this copper had done with his gum.

So a key rule in the art of the loophole is: *expect the unexpected and be ready to turn it to your advantage.*

I think another ingredient in my successful loophole hunting – at least in road-traffic law – is that I absolutely love cars. I always have done. I love the driving experience and I read car magazines whenever I can. And being enthusiastic about cars is a fantastic source of knowledge. If I'm doing a speeding case I'll know about acceleration. I understand the performance of cars, how they operate, their braking systems. Often it's very useful because you can be chatting to a prosecutor who hasn't got a clue about the vehicles involved. That must be a huge disadvantage for them, and so a big plus for me.

I remember two Crown witnesses in one of my driving-without-due-care-and-attention cases who totally misjudged the speed at which my client was travelling. They were very nice elderly ladies who enthusiastically told the court how my client had zoomed past their car in his Porsche even though the speed limit was only 30mph. What they hadn't realised was that, at the point on the road at which they'd spotted him, the limit had been lifted from 30mph to 60mph. (I knew this because in preparation for the case I'd done a 'recce' of the road, driving along the stretch in question as I would do in many of my cases.) Unaware of this, the two ladies had continued to pootle along at 30mph. No wonder that, relative to their leisurely progress, my chap seemed to be racing like a lunatic.

I immediately realised the two women had a skewed perception of speed and my client was acquitted. (Had I been feeling mean-spirited I could have suggested in my closing speech that these two ladies should have been prosecuted for driving too slowly. But I couldn't do that, as I'm a softy at heart.) However, loving everything about cars really does help.

Which brings us to another key to loophole hunting: *know the rules far better than your opponent and read around the subject.*

However, if there is really one critical component that lies at the heart of loophole hunting, it's simply this: *knowledge.*

Some things in life can be handed to you on a plate. Understanding the law, alas, isn't one of them. If you want to find the technicalities that can expose flaws in the prosecution case, you have to dig, and read and research, until you find them.

★ ★ ★

Although I'd hatched my career plans at just seven years of age, when I left law school to take up articles (a solicitor's training contract) with a local Nottingham law firm fifteen years later, I didn't have any specific idea of where my career might take me. I had some vague notion of perhaps becoming a hotshot commercial lawyer, wheeling and dealing for blue-chip companies. I imagined taking up residence at some white-hot law firm where my office would be so big I'd be able to practise my putting shots.

Of course, there would be all the trappings too: the designer suit, the flash car, the multimillion-pound contracts. The cult of the yuppie was beginning to mushroom and as a green and hungry articled clerk I wanted some of the action.

Most of all, I had big ideas. It wasn't just about the money – that fabled £4000 a year, a month, a week or even an hour. I wanted to be Mr Big. That's why, when I left law school, being a criminal lawyer had no appeal: the last thing I wanted was to be in court every day trying to get a succession of clients out of a hole. It sounded far too stressful. Who'd want to do such a thing when you could be up in the penthouse suite of some futuristic office building, ruling the world?

However, my plans to become some kind of heavyweight commercial lawyer changed when a solicitor that I worked with during my training contract entered me – without my knowledge – for a local advocacy competition. When he told me what he'd done, I refused to take part. It simply wasn't my thing. Then he told me about the prize money. With a salary that barely covered my living expenses, I was seduced by the £50 on offer – a lot of money back in 1980.

So I took part and to my amazement not only did I win,

but I absolutely loved it: the adrenalin rush, the verbal jousting, the digging around for the killer defence. At that moment the scales – or rather images of sharp suits and a key to the executive washroom – fell from my eyes. I completely changed my plans. I wanted to be out there, on the shop floor. I wanted to be on my feet in the courtroom, duelling with my opponent and crushing him or her with a winning argument.

So, after qualifying, I left Nottingham in 1981 to take up a job as a prosecutor with Greater Manchester Police. A prosecutor's salary back then was twice that of a newly qualified solicitor. Dad's words were obviously ringing in my ears. But what most attracted me to the job was that I knew I'd be thrown in at the deep end. That I'd spend day after day on my feet, and being kept on my toes, arguing in court.

And I was. Another key factor in the evolution of Mr Loophole.

I spent my first day observing how prosecutors worked. After that I was on my own, travelling from court to court across Greater Manchester to do battle on behalf of the Crown. As a young prosecutor I had an insatiable desire to learn. Sometimes, when there were no cases for me, I'd go off to watch seasoned and talented lawyers at work. The very best would present their cases like an irresistible sales pitch. It reminded me of Voltaire's famous saying: 'The best is the enemy of the [merely] good.' Those who combined their advocacy skills with intricate legal knowledge – loophole knowledge – together with instinct, really were the best.

Though I was prosecuting a wide range of criminal cases, what soon became clear to me was that road-traffic work was deeply unpopular within the legal profession. Back then lawyers from both sides of the fence shied away from this profoundly complex area of law. It was regarded as the gutter end of the job, the province of the white van man, a grubby tussle embarked on to enable speeders and drunks to try and cling onto their licences. Lawyers can be quite snooty about the work they do. Or at least they were all those years ago: today's brutal economic climate doesn't always allow the luxury of such snobbery. But in the early 1980s no one wanted to get their hands dirty with motoring cases.

Meanwhile I loved my job, but I'll admit that I was a bit of a cheeky thing around the office. So handling road-traffic cases was regarded as some kind of comeuppance for both my cocky tongue and obvious inexperience. As the junior whippersnapper, I'd find a tall pile of motoring cases dumped on my desk most afternoons. Sometimes I'd come back from lunch deliberately late to see if someone else had received the blow. But the chief clerk would always be circling. 'Had a good feed, Freeman?' he'd invariably smirk. 'I hope so, because that'll keep you busy for a few hours.' Ironically, in his bid to bring me down a peg or two, he was actually giving me a leg-up – though neither of us knew it at the time.

I had no choice but to plough through motoring case after motoring case. And I did have my fair share of success batting for the Crown.

But then came my epiphany – the moment that set Mr Loophole on his way. It happened one morning while prosecuting what appeared to be a straightforward drink-driving case at Altrincham Magistrates Court. It was a warm day, everyone felt a little languid in the heat and my opponent, a smooth, suave and seasoned defence lawyer, seemed to be making only minimal effort at cross-examination. As I listened to the rich timbre of his voice, I thought to myself, this isn't going anywhere, I've got this one in the bag. My mind drifted off to what I fancied for lunch, and who I fancied having it with. The proceedings certainly didn't need my full attention. I knew that I could prove the defendant was driving and that we had evidence to show he was over the limit. In my mind, the case was already over. I'd nailed it with very little effort. Mm, sandwiches or pasta?

And then, just as we got to half-time, my opponent slowly rose in one fluid movement, cleared his throat and said, 'Your Worships, there is no admissible evidence that the device is working correctly.'

I sat bolt upright in my seat. Had I misheard him? What on earth was he talking about?

'The prosecution has not submitted written proof of the calibration checks on the breathalyser,' he continued calmly.

The impact of his words slammed into me with brute force. It was true: I hadn't produced the relevant printout. But this was only because I had an officer giving evidence on oath of what that reading was. I thought that was all I would need. I started to panic, floundering to find a way out of the hole I'd dug myself. I couldn't. In a heartbeat, the case had been pulled from under my feet and tossed out of court.

As the trial finished, the defence lawyer turned to me and shook my hand, his head inclining with a cautionary nod.

'Better luck next time,' he said, leaving me shell-shocked by the skill of his advocacy and the intricacy of his knowledge. *Knowledge – the art of the loophole and the heart of all areas of law.*

In private I've always been very hard on myself when I don't succeed. I really don't like losing. (I give myself hell if I lose a round of golf or a game of squash.) But that loss really, really hurt.

The events of that morning marinated in my thoughts for

weeks, as I replayed the defence lawyer's manoeuvre again and again. I thought I was a decent chess player. But this had been a neat, easy checkmate. I'd screwed up because I hadn't anticipated the moves and didn't know the law. I felt irritated and angry at having been ill prepared for my case.

I continued to beat myself up but, as I did so, a parallel thought took root. Road-traffic law might well be grubby. But I realised what a huge advantage it was to know every corner of this tangled and complicated web. I wanted to be back on top, to reclaim that feeling of scoring full marks in my times table test.

At that moment I vowed I'd never get caught out again. I just needed to work out how I was going to do that. By the time I quit my prosecutor's job in 1983 to take up a position as a criminal defence lawyer with a leading firm in Manchester, I'd come up with a plan. I realised what I needed was to amass as much knowledge as possible. So I spent the final weekend before I left my job as a police prosecutor digging out every motoring case that I could find in the textbooks piled up in the police law library.

Slowly, in painstaking long hand, I copied out the title of each case, the details of the offence and the court's ruling. By the end of my two-day stint my hand was throbbing but my heart was racing.

While I scribbled away among those dusty books, a pattern had started to take shape. I realised that with this kind of knowledge of the law there was every chance a defence could leap out to trample on any prosecution argument. Sure, motoring law was intricate – stacked with anomalies, ambiguities, technical points and other potential loopholes. But a solicitor who knew his stuff could be invincible in court. I wanted to be invincible. I wanted to give my clients the best representation they could get so that they would turn to me afterwards and say, 'Mr Freeman, that was a fantastic job.' I maintain to this day that these should be the driving principles of any decent lawyer.

I started my new job with the broad description of criminal lawyer but I ended up doing increasing amounts of motoring law. No one else in my firm wanted to get involved in that field. It didn't bother me. Having spent that long weekend in the police law library, I was already drawing on rich reserves of case law and defences that were earning me success. As I say, if you have enough law, enough knowledge, on your side, you'll always – or nearly always – find an answer.

Actually it's true of all areas of law. For example, as I was building up my motoring clients my firm also brought in a lot of cases involving brothels, an area which is also full of complex law. (Did you know that there have to be at least two women working there for the premises to be defined as a brothel?) But many of my peers couldn't be bothered to read it, let alone understand and learn it. Again, by doing my homework – not, in this instance, literally – I was in a prime position to win countless cases.

Brothels aside, I soon started to make a name for myself as a road-traffic specialist and began to attract some local celebrities, including Shaun Ryder from the Manchester group the Happy Mondays and Simon Gregson from *Coronation Street*.

However, it was clear that working in a large practice, ring-fenced by partners who were senior to me in age if not knowledge, was going to stymie my ambition. I felt I'd created a niche and I wanted to steward my own ship. I couldn't have cared less about big offices or partnership meetings. I didn't want to be ruled by majority or seniority decisions. I wanted to break free and have my own name above the door. I took advice from friends, fellow professionals, indeed anyone whose opinion I valued, and the verdict was overwhelmingly positive: I should seize the day and take a leap. So in 1999, after six long years of reflection, I uprooted, along with my loyal secretary Denise, set up on my own and opened the doors of Freeman & Co. Then all I had to do was wait for the phone to ring.

When I began working for myself, my ambitions stretched no further than winning my cases and matching the comfortable six-figure salary I'd been drawing from my previous firm (with two kids in private school and, by now, a lovely home in Cheshire, I had little choice). Luckily, as soon as I opened for business, the work began to flood in.

As well as the fact that every single one of my clients from my previous firm transferred their cases to my new practice, work continued to flow in, as it always had done, through personal recommendations. And alongside road-traffic cases, I continued to do a large number of criminal cases too. One such case involved Leeds United and England player Jonathan Woodgate, who was convicted of affray but cleared of the more serious charge of causing grievous bodily harm with intent. The case lasted six months and he was given 100 hours of community service.

This was nothing to do with my being known as Mr Loophole – I'd yet to be christened with my nickname – but my successes were based on the fundamental strategy of tracking down technical errors in the Crown's case. But, thankfully, business boomed.

And this wasn't just in Manchester where my office was based. My case load stretched like a piece of elastic from the Scottish borders down to Land's End. I didn't mind. I was utterly single-minded. To me, geography was no obstacle: I simply followed the work. A typical week's diary would read: 'Monday, Bow Street Magistrates Court, London; Tuesday, Teesside Magistrates Court; Thursday, Cheltenham Magistrates Court; Friday, Birmingham Magistrates Court.' I kept Wednesdays free – not for respite, but to nip back to Manchester to catch up with what was going on in the office.

The way I structured my working week was tantamount to sheer lunacy. I'd spend most of Saturday and Sunday at my office at home, preparing for my trials for the week ahead. (I'm ashamed to say that my wife and children often only saw my back for the entire weekend.) By the end of my work on Sunday, I'd made sure I'd structured several legal arguments for each of the cases I had scheduled in the week ahead.

Then, that evening, I would jump in my car, book into a hotel near the court where my first trial of the week would be, do a little more work over a room-service supper and then sleep on it. On Monday morning I'd be up at 6am for a run, then have a shower and grab some breakfast before setting off to get to court early. As soon as the trial was over I'd leap back in the car and drive to my next case, repeating this madcap working practice all over again. (My mushrooming legal knowledge aside, I'm sure I could have also written a definitive guide to Britain's mid-market hotel industry.)

Meanwhile my car became my office as I fielded work calls while I was on the road. Most days my mum would ring too. I remember telling her one day that I was on my way to Cardiff.

'Cardiff? I thought you were in London.'

'That was yesterday, Mum.'

All the time I was gaining vital experience. Trying cases became as natural to me as breathing. It wasn't unusual for me to clock up over 1000 miles a week and I'd spend those long hours behind the wheel mentally working out how to argue the next case. *If you're going to find a loophole, you have to be forensic about it.*

I'd think, well, if I ask a police officer this question, where might it lead to? Where am I going with all these points? This enabled me to move fluidly during the course of the trial, so that every time the prosecution set off in one direction, I could claw back the situation to my advantage.

Being on the road was a pretty lonely existence and, looking back, I regret how much time I spent away from my family. Yet even with the benefit of hindsight, I don't think my personality and my desire to win would have allowed me to do things any differently. I was totally consumed with what I was doing, and galvanised by the fact that my legal arguments were starting to cause mayhem in courtrooms. I was trapped by my own success.

One wintry February day in 2004 really sticks in my memory. My dad had been battling brain cancer and was having a huge and complex operation in Nottingham to remove a malignant tumour. The same day I'd driven to Richmond in Surrey for a case. I also had a speeding trial in North Yorkshire the following day, but I was desperate to see my father. This was the man whose ideas had sent me spinning into the legal stratosphere, who was the architect of my career. Ironically, it was this same career that was threatening to keep me away from him at the time I most wanted to be by his side.

My case in the south didn't get started until 4.30pm and, unusually, the court, which normally retires around that time for the day, decided to press on. The case didn't finish until 6.30pm. While I was doing the trial snow had started to fall. By the time I came out of court the landscape was white and eerily quiet. Limping around the M25 at 25mph, stewarding my recalcitrant Aston Martin DB7 Volante carefully, to avoid skidding, I didn't reach my parents' home until 3am.

After snatching a few hours' sleep I went to see Dad in hospital. Though he was out for the count, to my enormous relief I was told that the surgery had been successful.

Once I was there, I didn't want to leave. I just wanted to cancel my next case and stay. My mum wouldn't have any of it. 'Do you think your father would want you to sit around here when you've worked so hard and got this far?' she stormed at me. 'Don't you dare let either of us down. Now go back to work. And make sure you win.' I drove to Yorkshire and I won. The seven-year-old had fulfilled his father's prophecy. To this day it remains one of the most significant days of my life.

And so the phone continued to ring and I carried on chasing around the country on behalf on my clients. With every case I stockpiled more knowledge, more experience. Indeed, as word of my success spread, I found that law students or young barristers would come in and watch me, which I admit was very flattering. All my work was trial work – rather than in busy remand courts, where quick decisions are made about matters such as bail and sentences for guilty pleas – so I tended to occupy the spotlight.

I suppose it was a case of practice making perfect.

With every trial I did, I was dealing with legal arguments. The learning curve was steep and open-ended. It still is. It was like training your brain for a marathon, constantly working to beat your last performance. No other lawyer at that time – or indeed since – would lead such a crazily nomadic professional life. But by working this way I wasn't just perfecting my trade. Batting away from home enabled me to learn how to cope with the different characters and diverse views of law that permeate the courtroom. The clerk in one court may have very different ideas to the clerk down the road in the next town. Travelling from court to court taught me how to be fluid and adaptable, to anticipate the clerks' interpretations and to be ready to deal with negative or challenging situations.

Though I did win case after case, there were times when things didn't go my way. But even that was part of the way I honed my technique. If I did lose, unlike many other lawyers I'd work on the appeal that same night, my preparations fuelled by the white-hot anger of losing my case. There are advantages to this. Your mind is still crammed with every shred of evidence from that day's trial. What I do is get all that evidence down on tape and record all my thoughts that very evening. Then the entire brief is ready, even if the appeal isn't going to be heard for months. The moment you do another case you invariably lose some of that knowledge. Forging ahead with appeal preparations the same day is also a great way to unload and mitigate the tension that comes with losing in court. It's also much healthier than hitting the bottle.

As my practice continued to flourish and more celebrities came knocking on my door, media commentators started to mutter about the 'questionable morality' of my putting suspected speeders and drunks back on the road. That's something I'll return to later in this book. In short, I simply couldn't be a defence lawyer if I was preoccupied with the morality of each case, or burdened by what could be termed a social conscience. As a lawyer it is a dereliction of your duty to look at anything other than how the law allows you to win your case. That needs to be the focus of your attention if you're going to find that loophole.

Of course, as I've mentioned before, there are many occasions when humanity and legality jostle in my mind. It might not be comfortable and sometimes it feels deeply unpleasant. But if it hurts, which sometimes it really does, that's my private battle. As a lawyer, I always, always side with the law.

As well as getting lots of shop-floor experience by trying so many cases, I also read voraciously on the subject – from law books to the riveting contents of a speed camera's instruction manual. I did this whenever I had a spare moment. On holiday, I'd lie on the beach under my umbrella, oblivious to my children's pleas to go for a swim with them, the scenery, even the pretty women walking by. I was totally absorbed.

Of course, it's one thing having knowledge, but another knowing how to use it. And I learnt very quickly that when you are cross-examining a witness, knowledge can be very intimidating. Prosecutors used to say to me they couldn't believe what happened to police officers when I questioned them. This was flattering, of course, but I never really took it to heart. As any advocate could testify, there is a certain amount of theatricality in cross-examination. I like to ask a question, let the witness answer, hold their gaze for a few moments before sliding a surreptitious glance to the magistrates' pens to check they've finished writing everything down. Then I move on to my next point. I never rush or show aggression. I wait for the perfect moment to light the loophole's touch-paper and ignite the witness's testimony.

I still chuckle over what happened during the case of a Sheffield solicitor I represented who was accused of speeding. During the trial the policeman giving evidence kept getting the time of the incident hopelessly wrong. The prosecution tried to help him by handing him his pocket notebook, which had the correct time in it. But the poor man couldn't get the time right. I was watching him *intently*, as I always do. Eventually the officer tied himself in knots and the judge intervened and said, 'Officer, you've been asked a very simple question and you've got your notebook. Why do you insist on telling us that this incident happened at a time when it clearly didn't?'

'It's that Mr Freeman, sir,' the policeman replied. 'He's hypnotised me.'

I don't know where he got that from. I've tried plenty of defences in my time but hypnosis certainly hasn't been one of them. That was the end of the case. I'd have loved to know what that was about. But when I saw the witness in the corridor afterwards, he raced off as soon as he caught sight of me. It could, of course, have been embarrassment. The copper was big and brawny and I'm a bit on the short side to be intimidating. After all, what could be worse than being shown up like that in open court? Anyway, it's much simpler than hypnosis. My textbooks are my spell books. I get the evidence in, evidence which the opposition fail to appreciate. I don't let them know where I am going and then I hit them with it. By which time it's too late. It's a fundamental loophole principle.

As well as the hypnosis charge, I'm often accused of dreaming up my defences. My detractors point the finger at the novelty, quirkiness or what appears to them to be the sheer nonsensicality of my arguments. I take all that as a compliment! My arguments only seem that way because no one else has spotted them.

(Actually, I once did represent a hypnotist who had been

accused of driving at 105mph in Yorkshire. I did jokingly wonder if it would be possible to hypnotise the bench - though obviously discounted the thought!! But despite this my client still hung onto his licence.)

It helps that I have a lot of friends who are lawyers. As an argument grows and develops I run it by them. I need a legal argument that has every prospect of winning. Fortunately the response is frequently encouraging. As my barrister pal Gary routinely comments, 'Bloody hell, Freeman, that's a cracker. How on earth did you come up with that one?'

Working the way I have done over the years has undoubtedly enabled me to gain an intimacy with the law – particularly road-traffic law – that many of my colleagues and peers have failed to acquire.

But is there a talent in what I do? My ego would love me to believe that I was uniquely gifted. But the truth is far more brutal. Remember it took hard graft to work my way up from zero to full marks in that seminal test at school. We lawyers all have the same textbooks at our fingertips. The same evidence is available to all of us. What you have to do is use that evidence and appreciate its significance. To know how to hit the opposition with the law. If there is any question of talent, I suppose it lies here.

I hate the idea of people being badly advised and ripped off, and that also drives me on. Lawyers have a bad enough reputation for 'setting the meter'. Certainly the spate of super-injunction cases involving actors, footballers and others in the public eye which rippled across the British press last summer was seen by many as a money-making exercise by greedy lawyers.

You'd also think that by now the police would realise that when I first receive the prosecution statements, I check the

details with a fine-tooth comb to assess whether all procedures have been carried out properly. Have they got the
right dates and the right days? Have they got the right road,
the right car, name, number plate? Have they added up the
pages in their statements correctly? For example, an officer
could write at the top of the statement that it's four pages
long when in fact it is five. I'm searching for any errors to
attack a witness's credibility. I suppose that if they can't be
bothered to do this, then why would they think someone
else would take such an anal approach?

I mentioned earlier that it was never in my game plan to
forge ahead as some kind of courtroom pioneer. But I would
like to think that other lawyers will take my methods on
board and realise the importance of rigorously putting the
prosecution to proof in order to win their cases. Some do,
but there are plenty who still don't. They don't want to
spend years, as I once did, with their heads in books, trying
to process case law or long, wordy statutes. They want the
gain but not the pain.

There are times when I feel irritated, others when I feel
disheartened, by the paucity of enthusiasm among my
peers. And what I find most dispiriting of all is the misery
of the luckless, vulnerable motorists who suffer as a consequence of this. I hope this book will help to change this state
of affairs. Often I sit in court watching other lawyers when
I'm waiting for my case to go ahead, and it takes every fibre
of self-control not to butt in when I feel they're simply dishing up a paint-by-numbers defence without any thought of
the implications for their client.

In fact there was one occasion when I couldn't help but
step in. I was waiting to do a speeding trial in Middlesbrough
and the solicitor ahead of me was making an application for
an adjournment. His client had been charged with

drink-driving but was unable to attend to court because, after being out of work for nearly two years, he'd finally got a job.

Unfortunately the lawyer made what seemed to me to be an extremely weak application for an adjournment. Not surprisingly, he didn't get it. The solicitor then asked for the court's permission to be excused from the hearing, leaving his absent client like a lamb to the slaughter, since he had no representation. Or so the solicitor thought.

I sat back watching the scene unfold, my knuckles clenched white with frustration. How could a lawyer behave this way, dropping his unsuspecting client in it? Meanwhile the trial went ahead, without the defendant or his lawyer. The prosecution, feeling they were being unchecked, hot-footed it through the case. The pressure was off. There was no defence lawyer to challenge them and hold them to account.

However, as I listened intently to this high-speed race I realised there was no evidence of the police having read to the defendant what is known as the statutory warning before breathalysing him. There's a legal requirement to do this – it's mandatory. Without it, the reading is inadmissible.

Just before the magistrates were about to retire I jumped to my feet and, putting on my most helpful face, described myself as a quasi 'McKenzie Friend' (a person who goes with a defendant to a court hearing in order to offer support such as taking notes or quietly making suggestions such as questions to put to a witness – it's not usually a lawyer – thus the quasi bit!).

I then pointed out the omission.

The prosecutor looked at me in astonishment, clearly baffled by the appearance of this legal fairy godmother. I turned and gave him a wink, then explained that to the court this meant the case was fatally flawed. The loophole worked and the client was acquitted.

If you know your law, you'll know your loopholes. So let me show you how the art of the loophole can make the law work for you.

3

Loophole: eureka instinct!

Around seventy years ago, a Swiss electrical engineer called Georges de Mestral came back one evening from a hunting trip to find countless burrs had caught onto his clothes. What's more, it took a lot of effort to remove them, as each bristly bit clung with great resolve to his coat and trousers. The task done, de Mestral could have simply slung his clothes in the laundry basket and relaxed with a foaming tankard of beer. That's what I would probably have done. But instead he decided to look at the burrs under a microscope. His instinct told him that this prickly nuisance could be cradling something far more interesting.

What de Mestral discovered was that the burrs were covered with tiny hooks, which is why they sank so enthusiastically into his coat and pants. For him, this was a 'eureka moment' – a chance discovery that would lead to his development of one of modern culture's most useful inventions: Velcro. And where would we be without Velcro?

History is littered with eureka, or 'light bulb', moments like this. They've brought us everything from bagless vacuum cleaners to Viagra. (Initially trailed as a drug to treat hypertension, Viagra was noted to also cause a rise in the tester's manhood!) That's why, as famous scientist Louis Pasteur stated, and as I truly believe, 'Chance favours a prepared mind.' If you set your dial in anticipation of an opportunity, then you're in pole position to grab it when it comes along.

But there is an additional ingredient that you need to have too: it's called instinct. That way, even if you seem to be in what Sir Alex Ferguson once famously called 'a squeaky bum' situation (the sound made by squirming in your seat when all seems lost), you may feel a growling hunch that might just turn your fortune around.

Placing the law, like those burrs, under the microscope and trusting my instinct has, I think, helped win countless cases that would otherwise have appeared almost impossible to defend.

Of course, you can't legislate for when you'll get these moments. That's the eureka bit. Like Archimedes, who uttered the word when he stepped into a bath, I also have mine when I least expect them: perhaps washing the dog or sitting in the dentist's chair having a scale and polish. What stops me from dismissing them as nonsense or whimsy is instinct: a pure, almost unapologetic belief that I could be in sniffing distance of something that could win me my case.

Perhaps the first time I really understood this was when I defended Manchester United and England star David Beckham. At the time, I was still basking in the afterglow of getting Sir Alex Ferguson acquitted – a case we'll come to later in this book. Having just set up my own law practice, I was especially hungry and wanted to capitalise on that success. It's that hunger that keeps your instinct sharp and your hunches even sharper. Though I was getting plenty of work and winning my cases, I did wonder if more big names would follow the Reds manager to my door. And then it happened.

A few days after winning Fergie's case, I was ploughing through a pile of papers in my office one afternoon when the phone rang. It was the super-powerful football agent Tony Stephens, who had an impressive portfolio of top-flight talent on his books, including one of the biggest names in the game, David Beckham. It was Beckham that Tony wanted to talk about. I straightened up in anticipation. Getting within sniffing distance of a big case did wonders for my posture – and continues to do so to this day.

This was 1999, and the United midfielder and England star was already headline news: not only for his breathtaking skills on the pitch but because of his marriage to Victoria Adams, who at that time was enjoying global success in one of the most successful girl groups of all time, the Spice Girls. Together they were the celebrity couple *du jour*, with a press following unprecedented in football. However, Beckham was about to make the papers for an altogether different reason. As would later come out in court, he had allegedly been caught by the police driving his £150,000 Ferrari at 76mph in a 50mph zone. What's more, the football star already had nine penalty points on his licence. If the courts found him guilty, a ban was inevitable.

Now it would be undignified to say I rubbed my hands with so much glee there were sparks flying off my palms. But, frankly, I couldn't believe my luck. First Sir Alex Ferguson, now David Beckham. I was disgustingly pleased with myself. In fact I was ecstatic. To me, Beckham was the ultimate golden opportunity, and to land him so soon after setting up on my own was unbelievable. I've always felt that your clients are like your trophies. It's not about money, it's about prestige. Beckham was my Oscar.

But first there was the small matter of actually having to win the case. So, following the agent's call, I went down to United's training ground to meet 'Becks' himself and find out just what had happened on that fateful day.

I have to admit, I've never had the time to get to football matches, and anyway, I'm not even a Reds fan. My home team is Nottingham Forest. But when I pulled up outside the Reds' training ground I was buzzing. I felt I was on my way to being the new United defender. Sad perhaps for a lawyer who was the wrong side of forty. Unspeakably arrogant too. But the boy inside me was doing cartwheels.

When I arrived I bumped into a member of the ground staff whom I'd met before. He shook my hand and immediately I felt at ease.

Client privilege prevents me relaying what David told me as we met in the coffee bar next to the pitch. However, as came out in court, it seemed that on the day of the incident the United star had set off from his Cheshire home for a pre-season friendly when he spotted a paparazzo sitting in a stationary white car near his driveway. As Beckham drove past, the snapper eased into the road and began to follow him, tailing the footballer for ten miles. At first this was just an annoyance. Then an increasing nuisance. And finally pure danger as the photographer veered into David's lane and forced him to swerve his silver S-reg Ferrari 550 Maranello. As David would tell the court, 'I decided to get away from him because if not there was going to be a serious accident, if not to me, then to other people.'

Another thing to consider is that by this stage in his life Becks was a family man. He and Victoria had a young son. The last thing he was likely to be doing was playing keepy-uppy with the traffic. He just wanted to get away from the guy on his tail.

It reminded me of those high-speed car chases I used to love watching on television as a boy, with highly tuned motors hurtling down the highway (well, in this case the not-so-glamorous A34 in Cheshire as a predatory photographer tries to land a shot of the nation's most famous footballer). But, looking at the facts through the prism of the law, I realised the turn of events had the kind of ingredients that ratchet up a speeding case into a legendary piece of litigation. The eureka moment! This was a unique situation and, to my mind, unique situations in law demand unique arguments. My reason briefly cautioned me that what I had in mind might not work but my gut instinct powered me forward with the belief that it was bound to.

To put it simply, David was an icon. Ruthless photographers, chancing to make a buck, would do anything to grab the prized shot that could net a lucrative fee. And though it had happened two years before, a grieving nation was still reeling from the late Princess Diana's tragic and untimely death after being chased by paparazzi in a Parisian underpass. Pitiless pursuit of celebrity prey was very much imprinted on the nation's consciousness, mine included. Not that I would ever have been so crass as to make the connection in court. It would have cheapened what had happened to the Princess of Wales.

But I knew there was a comparison to be made there – even if I didn't say so to anyone. As soon as I learnt what had happened to Beckham, I knew exactly how I was going to defend him. I was going to rely on an obscure legal argument. One I'd never used before and have since used only used twice in over 2000 trials. And the defence? Duress of circumstance. And I was going to argue this to defend my prized client and, hopefully, get him acquitted.

In simple terms, duress of circumstance means that a person has been impelled to break the law in order to avoid death or serious injury. In this sort of situation there's not much of a choice really: it's like a form of necessity. What's 'necessary' will often be gauged by the situation the defendant was seeking to avoid. In cases involving driving (such as dangerous or reckless driving) it usually means the driver acted the way he did to avoid death or serious injury so, in Beckham's case, to avoid having a huge smash as a result of being chased by papparazzo. But as a defence in court, duress of circumstance is rarely used. I didn't even learn about it during my law studies. I only discovered it on one of my innumerable for-the-hell-of-it outings into the legal textbooks. In fact when I first read about it – probably under a parasol on holiday – I was thinking, when on earth will I ever have to use this one?

The reason duress of circumstance is so rarely used is because the circumstances which would place a defendant in this position have to be exceptional. How often do people find the need to break the law to avoid death or serious injury? Hardly ever in normal, everyday life. It was a defence very unlikely to be at a lawyer's fingertips. Unless you're an anorak like me. Before I could shout, 'Eureka', it had flashed into my mind.

In David Beckham's case there was no disputing that he'd been speeding. His car had been snapped by a speed camera. Yet he'd also dialled 999 three times in ninety seconds – hardly the actions of a hapless soccer star punch-drunk with the velocity of his motor. Indeed David explained in court how raw, naked terror made him instinctively and repeatedly dial for help. This was clearly the knee-jerk reaction of a terrified driver who was being chased at top speed and who feared he might have a terrible accident. Or even end up dead.

I could, of course, advise my client to plead guilty, using instead the facts as mitigation to try to net him a lighter sentence. But that eureka moment brushed aside any such tactics. Sure, I was dealing with a remote and obscure point of law which I would have to argue in the full glare of the media spotlight. But I remained utterly convinced that I could conquer this legal Everest.

I began preparing my case by repeatedly returning to the scene of the incident. Habitual users of the A34 may have wondered why a British Racing Green Aston Martin could frequently be spotted driving endlessly up and down this fairly unexceptional tract of dual carriageway. But, to me, doing so was vital. You can pick up so many things if you take the time and trouble to look at the setting of a case. It meant I could work out whether there had been any side roads my client could have taken, whether he'd had the option to double back. I wanted to understand Beckham's manoeuvres in the context of the road. I wanted to know how the proximity of the photographer at various stages of the route would have affected his driving. Not all lawyers could make the time to do this.

Aside from getting forensically acquainted with the route, I also spent some time at David's plush penthouse apartment. As I was fielding an exceptional defence, I needed to spend more time with the client than I would ordinarily need. And it was on one of these occasions that I met Victoria for the first time. She was lovely. But I thought it would be a bad idea for her to come to court, as much as she might want to support her husband. Her appearance could quite possibly crank an already high-octane situation into an all-out media circus. But even without the presence of a Spice Girl, when we arrived at Stockport Magistrates Court on the day of the trial, the place was still a circus.

I was driven to court, along with David, by United's head of security and former SAS man Ned Kelly (who had also chauffeured me to the Alex Ferguson trial). I'm a dreadful passenger even on short distances so I hopped into the front of the black Mercedes, hoping to avoid any crashing waves of nausea.

When we arrived the press were like a tsunami, surging forward with an unstoppable force the moment we opened the car door. I'd never seen a scrum like it. In fact I got punched in the stomach and winded – not an ideal way to start the most important trial of your career to date.

As I was tossed around among the heaving bodies, the irony was palpable. Here was my client, whose defence was that he had been speeding to get away from the ruthless pursuit of a paparazzo. And here were the massed ranks of the media, demonstrating exactly why they could pose such a threat. It felt like an eternity, but with all my force I managed to shove through them and get up the steps into the court, breathless and shaken. David's expression was unreadable.

Predictably, the courtroom was packed, and you could almost taste the expectation from the public gallery and press benches. I forced myself to ignore it all.

David appeared outwardly calm as he sat beside his agent. We shook hands briefly and then it was down to business. The prosecutor outlined his case, then I was on my feet putting forward my eureka argument.

As usual I scanned the faces of the magistrates for any clues to their thought processes. The signs weren't good. In my view, the chairman of the bench seemed to relish the fact that he was involved in such a show-stopping trial. Like some hammy B-movie actor, he kept making dramatic expressions of disbelief by rolling his eyes and raising his eyebrows, his facial semaphore clearly stating that whatever my guy was accused of, he wasn't going to get away with it. As the magistrate continued his floor show, he seemed energised by the sense of occasion. He seemed, to me anyway, to be doing that nauseating thing people do when they find themselves hurled into an unexpected position of power. They play to the gallery.

I ignored what was going on and called David to the witness box, asking him what was going through his mind as the other car pursued him at breakneck speed. He said, 'I was uncomfortable because it was at least a car's length away and I thought it was very dangerous. There's no doubt that if I had stopped he would have gone into the back of me.'

Though listening intently I cast a covert glance around the court and could see people nodding in sympathy. Surely the magistrates would also take this view? Even the chairman, despite behaving, as it seemed to me, like a contestant on *Britain's Got Talent*. Unfortunately they didn't. They returned a guilty verdict. The magistrate said, 'Our conclusions are that Mr Beckham's responses were unreasonable in the situation he faced. We consider that there were other alternative courses of action open to him other than exceeding the speed limit by 26mph.'

I was angry and disappointed, but, frankly, not surprised. The chairman's behaviour had pretty much given me a heads-up on how things might go. But I'm not a defeatist – not when I think I'm right – and the verdict sent tongues of fire licking through my bones. You've not finished with me yet, I thought. In fact you're going to have to try a lot harder to get rid of me.

What I did was deploy a particular type of legal argument known as a 'special reason' – that is, a mitigating or special circumstance relating to the facts of the case which the court should take into account when sentencing. (If successful it gives the bench discretionary powers not to award penalty points that are otherwise mandatory on a driving licence.) I reiterated how David had only been speeding to get away from the photographer because he feared there would be an accident.

Unfortunately the magistrates thought differently. They felt there were no 'special circumstances' in the case and that David's response was unreasonable. I sank back in my chair. Thanks to the 'totting up process' he would reach twelve penalty points and would be off the road for six months. Or so I thought. In a final flourish the magistrates slapped an eight-month ban on him.

It was outrageous. But I learnt long ago to keep my surface reactions in check. Having spent all those years in public school and suffered the kind of provocation that could make your hair curl, I never let the mask slip. But inside I was burning. The thing about a eureka moment is that it's often an epiphany too. If I can't convince the magistrates, I thought to myself, I want, with the agreement of my client, to take the case to the Crown Court.

We left the court so that I could go back to my office, get my car and then return that afternoon to make a request to get the disqualification suspended, as who could say how long it would take to get the case heard again?

However, my plans nearly came to an abrupt halt as I forced my way through the thronging press and stepped in front of Ned's car ready to dive in. Never do that when an SAS man is at the wheel. Ned was on the point of pulling away and nearly mowed me down, because of my own stupidity. I'd been thumped on the way in and almost flattened on the way out. This really was turning into a unique case. And not for the right reasons.

After grabbing a quick sandwich and discussing my strategy with colleagues at the office, I drove back to court that afternoon to make the application. Ordinarily this would have been a formality. Yet once again the magistrates rejected my request. This was getting beyond a joke.

I looked at my watch. It was already 3.30pm. But I was far from ready to throw in the towel. After some frantic phone calls I managed – and I still don't know how – to have the application to suspend the disqualification listed before the Crown Court the following morning. Usually this takes at least twenty-four hours, if not longer.

Thankfully, the next day the judge agreed to let my client hang onto his licence pending a retrial. For the moment Beckham was back on the road. At least I'd achieved something.

I should point out here that most unsuccessful defendants who have their cases heard in the magistrates' courts usually have the right to appeal to a higher court (usually the Crown Court). This appeal has to be lodged within twenty-one days of the sentence, and it can be an appeal against the conviction and/or the sentence. However, contrary to popular belief, an appeal isn't something that should be undertaken lightly. Just as a sentence can be reduced, this review of proceedings can also lead to a sentence being made even harsher. What's more, the defendant has to weather the costs of the appeal, and can only recover these if they win.

In Beckham's case, though, I was convinced that we could win. So, with such housekeeping out of the way, it was time to prepare to have the whole case re-tried in front of the Crown Court. Usually it takes several months before you get a date for a trial. We got one in a week. When a case is shifted up the legal food chain, it gives the opportunity for the whole thing to be heard again, as if it were for the first time. This time, however, I planned to let a barrister do the advocacy. I'd prepare the brief, but the Crown Court wasn't my playground. I like to pick my battles.

That was the plan anyway. It seemed my client and his agent saw things differently. It appeared that I was expected to defend the case in court myself. Fantastic, my ego shrieked. How many people can say they were David Beckham's defender in a Crown Court case? I wrestled with the dilemma. My conservative side argued, how the hell can I do this? However, the opportunist in me swept the thought aside. Was I mad? Why was I even hesitating? This was the highest-profile footballer in the land, the case had merit, and my client had faith in me to do it. Go ahead, face your fears! Before I let reflection trample over my words, I bit the bullet and agreed to do it.

That left me just seven days to make sure that this time the defence didn't fail me. I was utterly consumed by the case. It filled my every waking moment – and plenty of dreams too. I trotted off to Whippets in Manchester to get myself a court shirt, collar and gown. After all, this was going to be heard in the Crown Court and I had to fulfil the dress code. Like a child preparing to go to a new school, I couldn't help trying on my new costume at home, at least a couple of times.

As part of my preparations I spent even more hours familiarising myself with the scene of the incident. I knew every kerbstone and lamppost, every twist and turn of that bloody road. I knew the minutiae of the case so well, I even became nervous about how well prepared I was.

Despite all this effort there was a possibility that David would be unable to attend the hearing, which would have made the appeal against conviction a little more problematic. But I was still confident I could reduce the disqualification in his absence from eight months to six months.

For the first time in a week, I allowed myself the luxury of relaxing a little and that night I slept like a baby. I got up at my habitual time of 6.30am to do my 500 or so press-ups and tummy tucks before taking my dogs for their two-mile morning walk. I believe that when you're facing a difficult situation you have to clear your head of everything else that is cluttering your mind. That way you're ready for the mental challenge. Then my mobile rang. David was coming up from London.

After hassling the dogs round our circuit, I hurried home, showered, dug out my best suit and tried my gown on again. I was ready – though as I drove into Manchester I suddenly realised I'd forgotten to put on any antiperspirant. In a panic I rang my secretary, Denise, who dashed out to Boots to buy a bottle.

Despite enjoying the dressing-up, I've never actually wanted to be a barrister. Mainly because my father's best friend and study mate at school, Brian Appleby QC, a senior judge and a very accomplished fellow, had advised that it was much better to be a solicitor. (At the time of my case Brian was also the chairman of Nottingham Forest when Brian Clough led the team to two European cup finals – which seemed rather appropriate.) I still remember Brian's views on solicitors: 'They make more money than barristers and have an easier life.' Well, it was the right advice – in part.

I've never regretted not becoming a barrister. But as I stood in court, my new gown rustling around me as I outlined the case, I felt strangely at home.

Once again the place was packed. Curious members of the public and panting members of the media crammed into every spare seat. I blocked the pageantry out of my viewfinder.

It also helped that I knew of the presiding judge, Barry Woodward, through his reputation for fairness. OK, I thought, let the games begin.

The prosecutor immediately interjected, 'Your Honour, Mr Beckham has not identified himself.'

'Oh, I think we can assume who Mr Beckham is,' the judge responded dryly.

When called to the witness box, David, once again, delivered his part beautifully, explaining to the court that a white car, which he thought was a Ford Fiesta, had followed him for ten miles from his home and along the A34 towards Manchester. He also put his anxiety into a very real context, telling the court of two other occasions when he feared for his safety and that of his family. He referred to an incident outside Harrods in London the previous day when a fan had tried to grab his baby son, Brooklyn. The story was splashed across the tabloids – a terrible experience for the Beckhams, but, from a legal perspective, fantastic timing for me. What better illustration could there be of the problematic world of Posh and Becks? (Amazingly, some people thought I had orchestrated this situation myself.)

David described how he and Victoria had been given a police escort the previous June when they were pursued by paparazzi. Even though I'd heard this before, I was still shocked by the insight into the baleful cult of celebrity hunting.

In my closing argument, I returned to the fact that, astonishingly, within ninety seconds of this offence David had made three 999 calls. Here I tried to be a bit cute. 'So either my client has had the foresight to lay down the foundations for a defence of duress of circumstance, which is, as Your Honour will know, a rarely used defence. Or he is just telling the truth. In other words, who would go to these lengths of dialling 999 unless it was true?'

After retiring for about an hour, the court rose and the judge reappeared. Personally I felt it couldn't have gone any better. There was even a video identifying the paparazzo's car. And the judge even reiterated a shopping list of all the things he accepted David had said in evidence.

Fantastic, I thought. We've done it.

But what I heard next left me dumbfounded. For the judge added that he didn't, however, believe there had been a threat of death or serious injury. My defence, it seemed, was once again evaporating. I couldn't let it slip away and was on my feet immediately, ready with my next move: to ask, as I had in the magistrates court, if the same facts could constitute special reasons – namely, why the circumstances surrounding the offence should lighten the sentence. The judge was amenable to this and, after hearing my submission, retired again. The waiting was agonising. But it was worth it.

Overturning the driving ban, Judge Woodward said, 'We must consider this case for its own particular merits rather than on the person of Mr Beckham himself.' Oh, those sweet words! He found there were indeed special reasons – which meant no disqualification and no penalty points. I'd done it: my client had won.

Hearing the judge's words, David gave me a hug. (Good job Denise had bought me that antiperspirant.) I grinned like a Cheshire Cat in spite of myself. I felt justice had been served, and the victory tasted even sweeter because I'd proved my detractor, the magistrate at the previous trial, wrong. I should be bigger than that, I know. But who can resist an 'I told you so' moment – even if it's in the privacy of your own thoughts?

While David was keen to get away from court as quickly

as possible, I took my time, gathering my things together. Perhaps I was savouring the moment in my gown. Tomorrow it would be back to the suit.

As I left the courtroom I felt really special. With head up and shoulders square, I walked with a wise and lawyerly gait down the corridors and towards the main entrance. I was the man of the hour, the hero of the day. I'd saved one of our national treasures from a driving ban. Practising my best expression of restrained, dignified pleasure, I came out of court ready for the microphones and cameras. Ready for my profile. Except, er, no one was there. The media had gone home. The press, it seemed, weren't interested in talking to or grabbing a snap of the short guy in the gown who'd just won back Becks's car keys. I didn't mind (well, not that much). For me, the taste of following the hunch, grabbing the eureka moment and then going for the kill, more than made up for it.

It was back to business. I had a trial on the Wirral the following day, and having found myself locked out of the office (I didn't have my keys with me) I sat in the car, preparing the case before setting off to watch my daughter's school play. Life felt good. And then my mobile phone rang. It was my wife, Steph, who'd been in court, watching my case from the public gallery with her dad. 'You're not going to believe this, but they're saying on the BBC that you've lost,' she exclaimed down the line.

I couldn't believe it. Clearly the station's court reporter had misunderstood the intricacies of the appeal court. What could I do? This was no time for polite letters or demands for an apology. The record needed to be set straight there and then. Otherwise this celebrated victory would mutate into a crushing defeat.

So I did something I'd never done before. I simply rang

the BBC and spoke to the relevant editor to explain the
facts – only to find myself being invited onto the news programme that evening to discuss the case. I could have taken
the safe option and said no. But the publicity was priceless,
so I readily accepted.

It's worth mentioning at this point just how powerful
arguing a 'special reason' can be. Remember, this is not a
defence in law. It can only be applied when there has been
a guilty plea or – as in Beckham's case – the client has been
found guilty. But it gives the court discretion to waive mandatory points (which in Beckham's case would have led to
a minimum six-month ban because of the existing points
on his licence). The trick is to recognise the potential to use
a special reason, to know the law so that when you read the
facts of the case you can pull out the relevant part of the law
to assist your client.

And to make sure that special reasons are used properly,
they can be applied to a case only if the following criteria
are fulfilled:

There is a mitigating or extenuating circumstance.

It does not amount in law to a defence of the charge.

It is directly connected to the commission of the offence.

It is one which the court ought properly to take into con-
sideration when imposing sentence.

One of my favourite examples of using a special reason
involved a chap who went out on a stag night, got drunk
and then, on the spur of the moment, decided to pinch a
dustbin van. Having enjoyed a night of boozy carousing,
my client was stumbling through the streets in the early
hours of the morning just as the bin men were starting
their rounds. Seeing one of their empty lorries dawdling
by the roadside, and still in celebratory mood, my client
leapt in and drove it about 100 yards, before being stopped

by the police. He was charged with drink-driving and taking a vehicle without the owner's consent, pleading guilty to both charges. What immediately struck me about the drink-driving charge was that my client had travelled such a short distance – and it was a prank. In my view, therefore, the minimum mandatory ban – twelve months, though more likely to be twenty-four months because the alcohol reading was so high – would seem a very heavy penalty. For every ten yards he'd driven, he'd be penalised for up to two months off the road.

As it happens, what's termed 'shortness of distance' is something which, in law, is capable of being a special reason. Again it's not just a random state of affairs. There are seven factors that are relevant to the 'shortness of distance' argument, such as how far the vehicle had driven, the state of the car, whether the driver intended to go farther, the road and traffic conditions, whether there was a possibility of danger by coming into contact with other road users and the reason for the car being driven. In this instance my client hadn't had an accident, driven erratically or come into contact with other road users, as there hadn't been anyone about.

The court accepted my argument and my client was given a discharge with no disqualification, though he had to pay a small fine for taking the vehicle.

In a situation like this, the law is there to actually provide assistance – to allow a punishment to reflect what a defendant has done and the circumstances surrounding this. Special reasons aim to balance justice with an appropriate sentence which takes into account the specific details of the case.

But one thing to bear in mind about arguing special reasons is that it must be supported by evidence, usually but not necessarily from the defendant. They can't be argued in absentia. That's why I couldn't deploy this legal tactic when defending footballer John Terry, even though the circumstances surrounding his offence would have warranted it.

My client had been charged with speeding as he drove to a Chelsea game from his Surrey home, having been caught doing 77mph on a 50mph stretch of the A3. En route the Chelsea and England captain became aware of two paparazzi on motorcycles driving extremely close to his Range Rover and trying to peer in. Concerned at their behaviour, he accelerated to put some distance between himself and them.

John Terry accepted that he was a legitimate target for the press. But he didn't believe it was right for his privacy to be invaded every time he got into his car. What's more, there had been innumerable incidents where the 'paps' had been turning up at events which only a small number of people knew about. How was it that they seemed to know his every move?

Here was the bombshell. As I told the court, when Essex Police swept Terry's car, they found a tracking device had been planted underneath it. Little wonder he'd been discovered in such obscure locations as the local Christmas fair.

All of this presented powerful mitigation. And this was particularly helpful since my client already had seven points on his licence. Another six and he would be off the road.

The magistrates agreed and instead gave Terry a twenty-eight-day ban, instead of a minimum six-month ban or penalty points.

So special reasons and mitigation are there to help focus the court on the bones of the case and to take into account matters which could influence sentencing. As such they remain among the fairer aspects of our legal system.

★ ★ ★

Eureka moments are unpredictable. That's what gives them their unique sheen. But what is it that makes them unique? The shapes and forms are endless. In Beckham's case it was about grabbing a fairly unusual set of circumstances to mount a rare defence.

Sometimes, though, a eureka moment stems from nothing more than watching how the strolling players in the courtroom react to the facts of the case and then trusting your instinct when it picks up the scent of a possible defence. Take the time I defended a woman who'd been accused of assaulting two police officers when she had tried to force her way into her boyfriend's house. Now, we aren't talking about some butch mud wrestler. The lady in question was fairly slight, and at the time she was wearing a long dress and high heels. Not your average combat gear. Yet she was supposed to have kicked one officer in the, ahem, testicles, laying him out, and then assaulted the other one. Real Bond girl stuff.

It was one of those cases which hinged on a factual denial. The officer said one thing. My client said another. And my client was right. So how could I find a way to destroy the policeman's credibility before the court?

Watching him intently, resting my chin on steepled fingers as he gave evidence for the prosecution, I felt the hairs prickle at the back of my neck. It's the feeling I have when I get what amounts to no more than a hunch. There was something about him that got my mind turning. His manner was brusque, clipped. Was he ex-Army? No, that wasn't it, even though he stood ramrod straight. There was a control in his body language, yet a sense of alertness in his expression. A long-forgotten childhood memory flashed across my mind, taking me back to a time when, as a ten-year-old boy, I'd gone to jujitsu lessons. That was it! He was a martial arts expert. He had to be. With nothing left in my toolbox but pure instinct, I drew a deep breath and rose to begin my cross-examination.

'Tell me, Officer, how long have you done martial arts for?' I began calmly, while thinking, Christ, what on earth am I going to do if he hasn't?

His answer momentarily blinded me: 'How on earth do you know that?'

I couldn't believe it. I was right. With supreme will power I stopped myself punching the air and shouting, 'Ye-es.' It wouldn't have been a helpful move. Instead I paused, just to let the court digest the response, and then got on with hunting down my prey.

'You're quite accomplished as well, aren't you, Officer?'

The copper looked gobsmacked. 'Yes,' he conceded, clearing his throat to conceal his embarrassment at being flushed out this way.

'What dan are you?' I carried on, biting my lip to stop myself from breaking into a stupid grin.

It transpired that he was indeed highly accomplished. My shot in the dark was hurtling towards its target. I suppose having that killer instinct means looking at everyone and thinking, who are you, what are you about, what could you be, and how will that help my case?

Now to discredit him. 'So, Officer, you're a martial arts expert. Yet you're telling me that a woman with a slight build, who is quite tipsy and dressed in an evening gown and high heels, managed to kick you in the testicles?' I wanted to add, 'Perhaps your karate teacher should start looking for a new job', but I held my tongue.

What could he say? His credibility was shattering before the eyes of the court. At the end of my cross-examination, the court retired for lunch.

I nipped off to get a sandwich but returned quickly to the empty courtroom, reading over my papers in preparation for the rest of the case.

Suddenly I heard the door of the courtroom creak open. Turning round slowly I saw the officer I'd just demolished marching towards me. Oh hell, I thought, he's going to karate-kick my arse to kingdom come. Yet instead he put out his hand to shake mine. As he crushed my fingers in his weighty grip he said, 'I have to hand it to you. You did a fantastic job in there. How on earth did you know about the martial arts?'

I muttered something about it just coming to me. He seemed genuinely impressed.

'You know what?' he said. 'Your client is actually quite a lovely lady. I don't think she should really be here.'

This was incredible. Two gift horses in the space of half an hour. They were like buses! I put up my hand and said, 'Whoa, stop right there. I'm going to write down exactly what you've said, so you'd better leave now.'

For a moment he looked baffled and then the penny dropped. Here was a man who'd alleged in evidence that my client had kicked him where it hurt and laid him out flat. Now he was telling me, her lawyer, that she was 'lovely'. Talk about two clashing opinions. It completely destroyed his credibility. I wanted to take immediate advantage of the situation to get the case dropped.

When the prosecutor came back from lunch, I immediately told both he and the court clerk what had happened. But the prosecution still wouldn't drop the case. So I had no choice but to call the policeman back to give evidence.

When the trial resumed, I cross-examined the officer, asking him to repeat to the court what he'd told me during the break. With his eyes boring into me, he vaguely recounted what he'd said, fudging the issue as much as he could. It was my word against his.

In the event, the magistrates decided to convict my client of assaulting one officer – the one who had described her as 'a lovely lady' – but not the other. Talk about bizarre judgement.

I was absolutely furious. Despite the compelling evidence of a David and Goliath battle, and a tacit admission by my martial arts man, my client was convicted of one assault charge and acquitted of the other. But when I'm sure that I'm right, I can't let it drop. So we took the case to the Crown Court, where the trial was repeated all over again. This time I gave evidence as a witness in front of a judge, telling him word for word what had happened. Thankfully he threw the case out, acquitting my client of the charge.

I suppose being so determined is born of what might be termed a killer instinct. But there are times when harnessing a hunch with a softly, softly approach can be equally successful. I remember once going down south to do a speeding trial which was listed to start at 2pm. Ever the punctual clock watcher, I arrived with my client at 1.30pm and went over to have a tactical schmooze with the usher.

To my surprise she said, 'Sorry, Mr Freeman, we're still doing the first trial from this morning, and there are two other morning trials after that before we start the afternoon list. There's no way you're going to get on today.'

What can you do? Say, 'All right, I understand, these things happen', then get in the car and drive 200 miles home? Not a chance. I'd come all that way, I'd prepared the case and the issues were fresh in my memory. There was no way I was going to let this one slip – particularly since I knew the prosecution were under pressure. Time to take advantage and capitalise on the situation. The question was, how?

I was hoping to win my own case by showing that my client's summons had been received outside the six-month expiry date. And I had the post-marked envelope to prove there had been a delay. But I couldn't go charging in shouting, 'Everybody out of the way. Mr Loophole is in the house.'

However, I was desperate to get my case heard; I'd driven 200 miles, I was fully prepared for my trial and had been paid an agreed fee. Instead I was staring at a completely wasted day – and I'd have to foot the bill.

The question was, what should I do. I had to find a way to try and stall the existing trial. So I slipped into court to listen to the case as it proceeded.

After establishing eye contact with all the important players to remind them they had other cases listed, I took a seat next to the defence lawyer. Within a few minutes the chink of an opportunity began to crack open.

Why? The lawyer was fumbling over a piece of evidence that he had previously been unaware of. Surprisingly, he appeared to be unfamiliar with the Attorney General's disclosure guidelines: in short the Crown had failed to disclose something that they should have done. It was one of those nuggets I'd gleaned from my 'holiday reading', though, in truth, many lawyers may well have known the point too. But it was an absolute belter for this particular case. Immediately I jotted down the reference on a bit of paper, copying it from the original source material which I always carry with me. I then slid it over to the defence lawyer.

I whispered: 'This piece of evidence should have been disclosed.'

He turned to me, perplexed, but as he read the note his face broke into a grateful smile

Now for the killer opportunity.

Smiling back, I added: 'I happen to have the reference with me. Ask the court for a few minutes and I'll show it to you.'

He nodded gratefully and the call was made for the court to briefly retire. This was my cue. As the magistrates were about to leave the court I leapt to my feet and said, 'Good afternoon, Your Worships. I know you have an extremely busy list and hopefully I can lighten your load slightly. I have got a 2pm trial but if you would allow me a couple of minutes with my friend the prosecutor it would be of enormous assistance.'

They agreed, I gave the reference to the other defence lawyer, which left me free to speak to the prosecutor. I then explained about my own case and showed her the envelope. Clearly harassed, she agreed the Crown's case was flawed. So we got the clerk to call the magistrates back immediately. On their return the prosecutor told them she offered no evidence. I then invited the court to dismiss the case, which they did, I successfully applied for costs and made my exit. My client turned to me, his expression a mixture of shock and elation.

'Mr Freeman, that was the best *** grand I've ever spent in my life.'

One of the reasons I was able to win this case was, as I've mentioned, that I offered the defence lawyer on the previous trial a nugget of information he wasn't familiar with. (And no, I didn't bill his client.) That's what comes from reading thoroughly around your subject. From looking at the burrs under the microscope. You discover these fantastically obscure points of law. When I do, I file them away in my head. I've no idea when, or even if, they'll be of any use to me, but I have them there all the same. In this case the idea popped up and I then seized the opportunity to make myself heard.

Sometimes eureka moments rely on little more than phraseology. On countless occasions wording on legal forms has subsequently been changed because the way they've been drafted has opened the door to a defence.

I remember one constabulary unwittingly providing scope for a defence because of the way they had worded their Section 172 forms. This is the form which is sent out to the registered keeper of a vehicle after it has been zapped by a speed camera. The registered keeper is then legally obliged to fill in the form and state whether they were driving the vehicle at the time of the offence or, if not, to name who was or give any information as to who the might be the driver.

Now, each constabulary produces their own Section 172 form (though I believe it would make so much more sense to have one centrally prepared form), and consequently the wording may differ slightly from force to force. But in the case of one particular police authority, it struck me that the form had been worded in a way that seemed to exaggerate the penalty for those who failed to fill it in. The form stated – and please excuse the legalese – that the penalty for failing to provide information about who was driving was similar to the 'substantive offence' itself (that is, being found guilty of speeding).

At that time most people knew that speeding could bag the culprit between three and six points on their licence. However, failing to fill in the form would net three (actually it has since gone up to six). But the wording on this particular form suggested that failure to fill in a form could get you six points, since it implied that the penalty would be equivalent to that for speeding. Three points versus between three and six points? Who wouldn't feel it would be better just to fill the damned thing in? To my mind, this could be interpreted as the constabulary leaning on the registered keeper to dish up the information.

Because of this cases were dropped time and time again until the wording was eventually changed.

Similarly, some of the forms sent out requiring motorists to nominate who was driving did not specify that they were sent by or on behalf of 'the Chief Officer of the Police' – which they should have done. I spotted this and time and time again cases were dropped until the forms were eventually changed.

What this kind of situation illustrates to me is that finding a legal argument is as much about inspiration and instinct as it is about what is set down in statutes. Law might appear to be dry, dusty, inflexible. But actually the art of the loophole relies as much on the interpretation as it does on the legislation. In essence it's a marriage of the two. See what the law says, then let the imagination take flight with its possible interpretation.

This is what happened when I managed to get the comedian Jimmy Carr acquitted after he had been charged with using his iPhone while driving. Legislation on this subject is still quite new. It certainly hasn't kept pace with the frightening know-it-all pieces of computerised kit that now pass for a mobile telephone (and neither have I).

The TV star faced a £60 fine and three points on his licence after police saw him allegedly using his mobile while behind the wheel of his Bentley. But, as would be revealed at Harrow Magistrates Court, Jimmy explained to me that he hadn't been making a call. He'd picked up his phone while dawdling at a temporary red light, in order to dictate a joke. Essentially a great gag had sprung to mind and he wanted to make sure he didn't forget it. Of course, he wasn't disputing the fact he was holding the iPhone in his hand. And the Crown had agreed the evidence I presented about him using it as a Dictaphone – a tactically important move since we weren't disputing the facts, only the law concerning those facts.

But this was, to my mind, a unique situation, and certainly not one that I'd ever come across before. As I often say, unique situations require unique defences, so I went off and ploughed through the law books. After just ten minutes it hit me. The law regarding mobile phones always refers to their being used as an interactive device. But a Dictaphone is a one-way device. There was nothing interactive about it.

Any form of hand contact with a mobile was a breach of legislation, argued the Crown. Not at all, I countered. What my client did was no different from picking up a bar of chocolate or a banana or even checking the time on the phone as far as this particular legislation was concerned. If the device was not being used interactively, then he hadn't been doing anything unlawful.

Now, I'd never used this sort of argument before. That is why it's always fascinating to look at the law. The magical word was 'interaction'. It doesn't take Einstein to understand that a person can't interact with themselves – as much as they might want to. What Parliament intended was to prohibit mobile phones being used by a person who was driving at the time, and for good reason: it's dangerous. But they did it in quite a specific way. They referred only to 'interaction'.

I was feeling quite pleased with myself when the magistrates retired to consider their verdict. As I loitered in the courtroom, the clerk said to me, 'Will you take it to the High Court if you lose?' Oh no, I thought, it's going to go against me. So while I was waiting for the bench to return I wrote out a full notice of appeal so that I could submit it immediately. This offence carried three points and I wanted that suspended pending an appeal.

Feeling a bit glum, I watched the clock. The magistrates were taking their time. Finally, after an hour, they returned and recorded a not-guilty verdict! I was elated. Then, after shaking Jimmy's hand, I immediately tore up my notice of appeal, chuckling at my paranoia. Though they never did ask what the joke was.

I had a particularly special person in the courtroom with me that day. My teenage son, Ben, had been toying with a career in law and was also a huge fan of Jimmy Carr. So, for the first time ever, I took my boy along, and we had lunch with Jimmy before the proceedings began. After the case ended, I went over to Ben to get his verdict too – naturally, I wanted him to be impressed by his old dad. But, at the peak of my victory, all I got was a crushing shrug. 'That was simple, Dad. Dead easy. Anyone could argue that.' That was one argument I couldn't win. He was right: anyone could. But they'd have to bother to look at the law first.

I suppose to have a killer instinct you have to be prepared not to let things drop. I can't let things drop if I feel I'm right – and that goes for all areas of life. I once had a really big trial involving a soap star in Hull and I booked into a nice hotel near the court. I'd been preparing this case for months and what I needed more than anything was a decent night's sleep. I did get one – until 3am, when the fire alarm went off intermittently for no apparent reason. That ruined the rest of the night for me.

When I came to check out I said to the manager, 'You don't really expect me to pay, do you? I came here with an expectation of getting a decent night's rest before an important work day and I didn't get it.' He began to explain about discount or banking a free night for a return visit. I said that I was sorry, but if they wanted me to go away quietly they wouldn't charge me. I got it on the house.

On another occasion, I checked into a hotel before a big trial and discovered that the quiet room I had requested was actually next to the lifts. The last thing I needed was to have to listen to people spilling out of the elevators all night. So I asked for another room – and was given one above the air-conditioning unit. There's nothing like the sweet lullaby of a grating, churning piece of machinery to lull a hotel guest to sleep. Back I went to the reception desk, and the woman there burst into tears. She said, 'The hotel is full. I don't really know what to say.' I felt sorry for her but I needed a good night's sleep. I called the manager and told him quite firmly that I expected to have quiet at night and had requested a quiet room when booking. Miraculously they 'magicked' up a beautiful suite. I slept like a baby and won my case for an international rugby player the following day.

When it comes to my cases, I really push hard and find it impossible to take convictions – like noisy hotel rooms – lying down.

Of course, refusing to retreat takes energy and focus – essential tools for the loophole hunter. But if my instinct tells me that I could be right, I find neither is ever in short supply. Let me tell you about a case involving a client who had collided with a roundabout. When officers tried to breathalyse him at the police station, he just couldn't deliver, explaining his inability to provide a sample with a shopping list of health reasons. So an officer then took a sample of blood instead. But this was only after the client had rattled out the same shopping list of medical reasons for not providing blood – though he did give a sample anyway. The results were analysed and the client was over the limit. Sure-fire conviction? Not in my view.

The police officer had committed a serious goof. Once my client had cited his health as an explanation for his not being able to do the breath test, the copper had a legal duty to consult a police surgeon. Only a medical expert could decide whether what my client had said was valid or not. But the copper didn't do it. Maybe he thought my client was messing around. Maybe he thought it wouldn't matter so long as he got some form of sample. Maybe the guy was so drunk he began stripping to his own rendition of 'Big Spender' and the officer just wanted to prove his inebriation. Whatever the reason, taking a blood sample from my client as an alternative to a breath test was the wrong thing to do without seeking a medical opinion first.

This seemed a pretty watertight case and so I was astonished when magistrates went on to convict my client. I immediately ask for a Crown Court retrial, sure the judge would see the value of my argument. But no, once again I lost.

I couldn't let it drop. I was like a dog with a very tasty bone. Even my client held up his hands and was ready to walk away. But I was burning with indignation. I knew my law. In fact I was so adamant about this case that I wanted to take it to the High Court and was even prepared to do it *pro bono publico* ('for the public good'). It's not often I have those Father Christmas moments.

This all might sound a bit glib, like a petulant lawyer dragging his case from court to court until he gets the answer he wants. But it wasn't like that. I was just damned sure I had the law on my side. Anyway, it's always risky going to the High Court. You have to be very, very sure that you're right. At the High Court they are very keen to ensure that people don't get acquitted of offences on the basis of legal loopholes and if they get the opportunity to close one they do so. I was taking a risk (and potentially doing it for the princely sum of nought pence). But I was convinced I was right.

Maybe the magistrates and Crown Court thought that because my client was over the limit his case hadn't been prejudiced since he had provided a specimen of blood instead. What difference would it therefore make if a doctor hadn't been informed? I hold up my hands. Factually, if a man is proven to be over the limit, then what more should you need? But that's not what the law says. The High Court agreed and overturned the conviction.

I wouldn't care, except that this sort of thing happens frequently. That's why it's vital for a defence lawyer to know his law and trust his instinct.

In another drink-driving case a different client had given blood rather than a sample of breath. According to his statement, he'd told police at the station that he was suffering from various ailments, including asthma, and also had some difficulty providing blood. Now had this been the case, the officer would have been required to call a police surgeon to offer his expert medical opinion. But he hadn't. What's more, when I got the officer's statement I saw that he hadn't even mentioned that my client had health issues.

Immediately I could see a loophole opening up. So in court I cross-examined the police officer.

'Why didn't you record my client's ailments either in your pocket notebook or statement?' I began.

'I didn't record any ailments because the defendant didn't mention any,' the officer countered a little sniffily.

'I see you also make no mention of the fact my client had had problems providing blood,' I continued smoothly.

'There were no difficulties because we got a sample. If there had been a problem we wouldn't have been able to get one.' Smart.

After he gave his evidence, the officer stood down. Now it was my client's word against his. My chap delivered a different version of events. 'The police officer is talking rubbish,' he spat in frustration. 'I'd told him what was wrong with me.'

A difference of opinion then. But I really believed my client – my instinct trusted that his account was the truthful version. So, with a hunch on my side, I asked the prosecutor if there was a CCTV recording of what had happened in the custody suite that night. (This isn't automatically the case in all police stations.) And if so, could we have a copy – now, please?

The CCTV was duly produced within the hour and, hey presto, there's my guy, standing at the desk, disclosing all sorts of medical problems. Dear me. Treat that officer for a case of amnesia. If I hadn't had a hunch to ask for the video, my client would have been potted.

What I find astonishing is that officers are professional witnesses. They are supposed to be impartial, to make contemporaneous and accurate note of what has actually happened. What justification is there for this kind of spectacular forgetfulness on such a crucial point in a case?

What happens to knowledge of procedure when police officers are at the station? Maybe they prejudge the issue, maybe they like to win, maybe they think the guy is drunk and that's all they should be concerned with. Maybe they have a cavalier disregard for the law. Or maybe, just maybe, their memory fails them and they think they can get away with guessing in court.

When I took the calculated decision not to ask for the CCTV until the end of the prosecution case, I wanted them to give their evidence, tie them down so that there was no wriggle room. If you ask for a video at the start of a trial and one exists, the officer knows about it and it may affect the way he gives his evidence. He might not be quite

so assertive about something he has hitherto been so definite about.

Practising law like this is second nature to me – and, in
fact, in everything I do. I drive myself very hard from the
moment I wake up in the morning to the moment I go to
bed. My friends joke that even when I go walking on my
own, I'm racing against myself. If I do morning press-ups I
try to do more than I managed the day before. If I'm going
to eat dinner I have to earn the calories through exercise.
It's a reward system. On the squash court I'll chase and
chase to the point of collapse. I was the same at school, particularly in cross-country running. (I did say, after leaving
school, that I'd never do it again. You run so hard you actually throw up, it's so painful.)

The problem is I constantly feel that I have to earn my
relaxation time, though even if I do get time to walk on the
beach, I walk very quickly. Only at the end of a busy working day do I relax: in a hot tub for twenty minutes and then
ten minutes in the steam room, after which I usually end up
going in the cold shower.

Perhaps, then, it's that desire to win that sharpens the
instinct and give you the edge over people who are better
than you and more naturally talented.

Maybe it goes back to that times table test. Looking at the
kids in my class who were cleverer than me and wondering
how I could achieve the marks they did. Then pushing myself
till I got all the answers right. Living like this (or with this!)
may not be everyone's cup of tea. But I do it because it gets
me results – even if I nearly kill myself in the process.

One time I had a case involving a lap dancer (which is of
no relevance other than I like to recall her occupation) who
was charged with drink-driving. What was particularly
interesting about this case was that even though the young

woman was over the limit, the custody sergeant described her as sober. When a drink-driving suspect arrives at a police station one of the roles of the custody sergeant is assessment of the state they're in: a fairly sophisticated process involving ticking boxes marked either 'sober', 'had drink' or 'drunk'.

Having indeed ticked my client off as 'sober', the officer went on to confirm it in cross-examination.

Now, my client had been out drinking. That wasn't in dispute. Yet, according to her account of the amount she'd drunk, there hadn't been enough alcohol to push her over the limit. So why on earth was she?

My client explained, as would come out in court, that her drink must have been laced by someone without her knowledge. I knew immediately that this was a unique case as we weren't able to call any evidence to corroborate the lacing. It was the first time this had happened to me. But my hunch told me to press on, with the defence case hinging on the court accepting my client's evidence. It was all about her credibility.

I won the case. But that wasn't the end of it. The prosecution appealed the magistrates' decision to the High Court. Irritated as I was by this, I had complete faith that my defence would ensure an acquittal. I was right. The High Court said the magistrates were perfectly entitled to accept as evidence that my client had only knowingly drunk alcohol within the legal limit. Anything more meant that her drinks must have been laced. The prosecution were sure my client needed the lacer in order to win. The High Court said we didn't.

The beauty of acting on your instinct, of going with your gut, of seizing on these eureka moments is that they test the mettle of the defence lawyer. They keep the wits sharp and the antennae on red alert. It makes practising law all the more exciting and rewarding.

It's only afterwards, when the case is won and the client has shaken your hand, that you also realise you may well have set a precedent. Simply by thinking off the page.

So if there's an art to the loophole instinct it's simply this: go into court with four defences, but be ready to win with the fifth – the one that arises without warning, in a eureka moment; the one that tramples everything in its path.

4

Loophole: in sickness and in health

Around six months after setting up my own law firm, Freeman & Co, I was working away at my desk one chilly afternoon when I received a call that would change my career for ever.

Work, thankfully, had been busy enough since I'd decided to go it alone. But the pleasantly gruff Glaswegian gentleman who dialled my number that day would help raise my game to a completely different level. Not only because the prospective client was Sir Alex Ferguson, one of the most famous football managers on the planet, but because, once his case reached court, it would showcase one of the most memorable defences of my career and become a blinding example of the medical loophole. When it comes to law, the state of our health and well-being can have enormous implications for the Crown's case – and the defence lawyer's argument.

But first to Sir Alex. The facts of the case, as the media would go on to hungrily devour, were simply this: the Manchester United boss had been summonsed for driving on the hard shoulder of the M602, somewhere near Eccles, Greater Manchester.

He'd left the United training ground in his BMW to drive home when he began to suffer with a severe stomach complaint. The motorway was choked with cars and as the Reds boss crawled along in the traffic the need to go to the loo became increasingly urgent. So he decided to return to Old Trafford to use the toilet.

The only free lane was the hard shoulder, which left the United manager with one of two choices: to use it to get ahead of the tailback, or to surrender to the unpalatable alternative. To make matters worse, he already had nine points on his licence. Another three and he would be off the road for six months. But the call of nature was thunderous and quashed any pragmatism. He opted for the hard shoulder and put his foot down. He was then stopped by the police.

Though I'd already represented a few minor celebrities, Sir Alex was my first 'big name'. And they don't come much bigger. One of the best known managers in the world, he had taken Manchester United to 'the double' and received a knighthood for his efforts. It was both an honour and an opportunity to represent this legendary figure. (Though when I shout, 'Come on, you Reds!', I'm actually referring to my home team, Nottingham Forest.)

So I was thrilled to be representing Sir Alex. But I was even more excited by the blinding legal argument I realised I could use to fight his corner. Put simply, this was a 'medical emergency': a solid legal defence but one rarely heard in court. Indeed I've used it in only a handful of cases over the years. It has to be a genuine emergency, one you can't argue without the prospect of success. That's why it's deployed so economically. But in this case it was absolutely the right thing to argue.

So how did I arrive at my defence? Well, the law says it's illegal to drive on the hard shoulder unless it's an emergency. In my opinion, this was an emergency – a medical emergency. That's why my client had resorted to doing it. Think about it. What would you have done in that situation?

Let's scroll back to how the whole situation came about. As would be relayed when the case came to court, Sir Alex had been suffering with stomach cramps at home the previous day and suffered bouts of diarrhoea during the night. The next morning, at Old Trafford, he saw United's club doctor, Mike Stone, who gave him some Imodium (anti-diarrhoea medication).

Sir Alex told the court, 'Around lunchtime I was feeling much better. I thought the Imodium had worked and there wasn't a problem after all.' But, after he left the training ground at about 3.45pm to return home, his condition deteriorated. On the M602 he started to feel the cramps again. This information is critical to a medical emergency loophole. In a case like this, if someone sets off on a journey knowing he's ill and chooses to use the hard shoulder, then the law would probably regard him as guilty for his actions. If, however, he starts the journey genuinely feeling fine, then the law offers a potential get-out clause. One minute you're dawdling in a standing jam feeling nothing more than minor irritation at the sluggish motorway traffic. Five minutes later cramps crunch through your stomach and you realise that if you don't hit the hard shoulder the unthinkable might happen. In my view, that situation provides a lawyer with every ingredient to argue a case based on a medical emergency. All it needs is the client's testimony, backed up by expert medical opinion.

Sir Alex's trial was due to take place at Bury Magistrates Court in Greater Manchester. In the run-up to the date I pored over all the relevant case law I could find regarding medical emergencies. When the day dawned I knew I was as ready as I ever could be.

On the morning of the trial we met at the Four Seasons Hotel in Hale, Cheshire, and then travelled to Bury together.

Lightening the atmosphere was our driver, Ned Kelly, United's larger – much larger – than life Head of Security. His astounding build aside, Ned is a great guy, and one I'd met before: indeed he was one of the people who'd recommended me to the United boss. As he manoeuvred the car through the morning traffic, Ned made us both laugh with a fine selection of jokes and observations. Highly entertaining but I couldn't possibly repeat them here.

Feeling a little carsick – resulting from a combination of being both an appalling passenger and Ned's inventive driving – I was relieved when we pulled up at the court.

When I got out of the car, I was momentarily startled by the phalanx of press waiting to greet us. I knew there'd be media interest in the case, but this was my first taste of the real limelight. To be fair, though, there was no pushing or shoving. In fact the reporters were very pleasant and restrained as we walked past, flashbulbs popping as we went.

The courtroom was packed, the reputation of my celebrity client making the atmosphere crackle with excitement and expectation. I allowed myself to briefly taste the mood. It gave me a surge of adrenalin, which is always useful for mopping up any nerves. Then I switched into focused mode. I wanted to win. Badly.

Before taking my place, I had a word with the prosecutor, a very nice and able man whom I knew well. We freely exchanged our game plans before we parted to our respective battle lines.

I sat down in front of Sir Alex, then listened intently as the prosecution outlined their case and called their witnesses. Then the ball was in my court, and all eyes were on my client as he stepped into the witness box.

After he'd sworn his oath, I asked Sir Alex to give his

version of events and was impressed by his composure and professionalism, given that we were steering to the nub of our case. When we got there I felt it needed to be repeated clearly.

'So, putting it bluntly,' I said, 'did you need to go to the toilet?'

He held my gaze. 'That was very much the case. I just needed to go somewhere quickly.'

Sir Alex then told the court that he went onto the hard shoulder in an attempt to avoid the traffic queuing along the M602 so that he could reach the M62 and return to Old Trafford.

'Yet, when you were stopped by the police, you didn't tell them why you were driving on the hard shoulder?'

He shook his head and flushed slightly. 'No, I didn't. I was really embarrassed and, to be honest, concerned about the publicity I'd be getting.'

I shot the magistrates a covert, sideways look, trying to read their faces. I watched them intently as a statement from Dr Stone confirmed that he had seen my client on the day in question and had diagnosed acute gastroenteritis.

In my closing argument I told the court that the Manchester United boss had had two options while in the traffic jam. 'One is unthinkable and one is to take action.'

I also reminded the court that Sir Alex could have pleaded guilty and avoided any publicity, adding, 'It's not easy for someone in his position to come into court and, with respect, explain his toilet difficulties on that day.'

The trial spanned the morning, after which the court retired for an hour to let the magistrates deliberate. I felt the case had gone well, that there hadn't been any hiccups. Sir Alex, relieved to have given his version of events, said very little during the recess, his expression unreadable. I think the embarrassment of admitting his problems that day had now been eclipsed by the possibility of losing his licence if things went against him.

When the magistrates returned to court, I held my breath. This was such a unique defence. Momentarily, some of my confidence began to drain away. What if the bench thought my argument far-fetched or even implausible?

It appeared they hadn't. On the charge of driving along the hard shoulder of the motorway, Sir Alex was found not guilty. I wanted to punch the air and shout 'Yes!', but managed to control myself. I thanked the court, and warmly shook Sir Alex by the hand. Ever the gentleman, he signed autographs for Reds fans who had gathered outside the court.

I was elated. It had been a massive opportunity that had gone exactly the way I'd wanted it to. I felt like a professional footballer – one of United's strikers, or more appropriately, their defenders – scoring the winning goal. On the way back to my office, after parting from Sir Alex, I couldn't stop grinning.

The press, as anticipated, leapt on the story. It had everything: drama, celebrity and a bit of naughty-postcard humour too. But, for a lawyer, it was also a master class in how the unpredictability of a person's health is ripe for the application of legal loopholes.

Following the success of the trial and press coverage of the Ferguson case, having the runs became quite a popular defence. A procession of potential clients came beating a path to my office door, all pleading the same storyline. Had some virulent gastric bug been rampaging through the stomachs of the nation's motorists? I don't think so. But I couldn't unilaterally dismiss every person who offered this story: as a lawyer you have to judge every individual on their credibility. And there were some who were completely genuine but who hadn't realised such a defence existed. I remember using the same argument a short time later for a speeding case at Chester Magistrates Court – and winning.

Equally, there were those who were clearly dreaming up tales of gastric problems. I soon developed a tactic for, pardon the pun, flushing out the fibbers. When prospective clients came to me with tales of stomach cramps I'd say, 'Did you tell the officer who stopped you about this? No? Why not? If you were so desperate that you couldn't wait to get to a service station down the road, then why didn't you tell the police officer this?' Cue silence, then swift exit by any potential Pinocchios. Any genuine sufferer would have blurted out their reason for racing down the motorway or been able to say why they had not done so. If I'm going to defend someone, it has to stand up to legal scrutiny.

As you can see, modern medicine and the state of our health can be a rich source of legal loopholes. But while law tends to be black and white, medicine comes in all shades of grey. It's ambiguous, irregular, unpredictable. After all, one man's indigestion is another's suspected heart attack. Often it's about mounting the right sort of defence and getting the right medical opinion.

Indeed, is there such a thing as a right medical opinion? Doctors often disagree. As patients we sometimes take our chances with the advice we get. Or we get a second opinion. The judiciary have to weigh up the medical evidence they're given and, like a patient, decide whether they want to go with it or not.

I'm particularly sensitive to this area of law because I know from personal experience how conflicting medical opinions can be. A few years ago, without warning, I suffered a blood clot in my right eye. It literally struck me, left of field. On the day in question I'd driven over 200 miles to do a case in Dartford, Kent, only to discover that a police witness hadn't appeared. Despite my strenuous efforts to push on with the case – after all it wasn't the fault of the defence – the magistrates granted an adjournment. And refused to grant costs as well!

Feeling pretty stressed, and with a case to do in Exeter the following day, I arranged to spend the afternoon playing golf. The game was going well, the stress started to lift, then I hit a wedge from 120 yards out, stiff. And just as my club struck the ball the vision in my right eye went murky.

One minute I was hitting a ball and the next I could barely see a thing out of my right eye. In an instant I'd lost all my peripheral vision. It was like looking through grey frosted glass. I couldn't make out shapes or colours. Or for that matter the lie of the land. It was bizarre. But, because I was so busy with work, I decided, in my naivety, that it would just clear up. I even finished my round of golf that day. Anyway, I was due to go on holiday to France after my Exeter trial and thought I might just be stressed. It was a classic example of me looking after my clients but not looking after myself.

However, by the time I got to France I'd lost about 80 per cent of my sight – I'd hold up a newspaper and be unable to read the headlines with my right eye. My bravado went out of the window and I was panic-stricken. I dashed to see a specialist in Cannes and tests revealed a huge clot behind the optic nerve, a condition called retinal vein occlusion.

The surgeon then lit a grenade. He told me that my condition could be fatal if the clot moved. The only solution was an urgent operation to remove pressure on the vein from the adjacent artery so that blood flow could be improved and the clot reabsorbed by the body. That was his medical opinion, and he added that I would still be left with speckles of permanent blindness.

I was in total shock. How could a game of golf cost me my life? It didn't make sense. The thought, however, of simply going ahead with this massive operation without a second opinion terrified me. So, with the help of a top Harley Street surgeon I'd recently (and successfully) defended for crashing his Aston Martin while allegedly drunk, I forwarded my scan results to an ophthalmic surgeon at Moorfields Eye Hospital in London to seek his verdict.

Talk about a difference of opinion! The specialist there confirmed the diagnosis, but warned me not to have the operation as the risks of lasting damage to my sight were high if it didn't succeed. I also learnt that many eye specialists on the Continent take a more experimental approach to the condition and that in the UK it wasn't standard practice to operate on retinal vein occlusion.

I didn't need telling twice. I packed my bags and dashed back to London to see the surgeon there in person. He organised a battery of blood tests which established that I had no pre-existing health issues such as high blood pressure or cardiac problems.

What was astonishing was that my specialist decided that, far from needing an operation, I should do nothing for a month, then take 75mg of aspirin every day for the rest of my life and be patient that the clot would be reabsorbed by cells in the retina. A regrowth of blood vessels and cells would, he assured me, repair the eye naturally. Which they did. Within a few months my sight was back to normal. I remain eternally grateful for relying on his opinion. To this day I still shudder at what might had happened had I listened to the French expert and undergone such risky surgery. But that's what happens when consultants collide. The patient has to be judge and jury. That's why, in law, if I'm going to use a medical defence and home in on a medical loophole, then I need to believe it, an expert needs to substantiate it and the courts need to be convinced of it. You can't just shop around hoping to find a doctor who'll say what you want him to. As such it isn't something any defence lawyer can undertake lightly.

So, medical opinions can conflict. I once had a case in which my client had failed to provide a specimen of breath. My medical expert prepared a report in which he opined that my client had been unable to do this because of poor lung efficiency. These reports were served to the prosecution. They in turn obtained their own expert report based not only on the defendant's medical records (without examining him) but, critically, on his criminal history. It emerged that he had been previously convicted for drink-driving and had successfully provided a specimen of breath. Therefore the prosecution, in my view, seemed to be suggesting that the defendant and indeed my expert were trying to pull wool over the court's eyes.

Ah, but they had goofed in a matter of law. The court weren't entitled to know my client's antecedent criminal history. Therefore, in doing this, the prosecution had contaminated the defendant's case so that he could not get a fair trial. He was being dealt with in a prejudicial way, as they had revealed details the court were not entitled to know.

It would be so much easier in cases which hinge on medical evidence if experts could prepare their reports together rather than in conflict with one another.

Sometimes having two reports can actually be to the detriment of the prosecution. In one drink-driving case the prosecution brought their expert to court but decided to delay calling him until the end of the defence case. I then called the defence's expert. After I'd finished, the prosecutor decided he did want to call his expert after all. I immediately objected to this. Their chap should have been called as part of their case. The court agreed and, on the basis of the defence expert, whose evidence was therefore not contradicted, the client was acquitted.

Why on earth we need to have two experts is beyond me. There should be one and he should be non-partisan. The expert should be appointed by the court. That's all that's needed. But it doesn't happen.

It's just another example of how drawn out and creaky the legal procedure is in this country. The law gobbles up an exorbitant amount of time and money.

Why, as another example, don't we have a system where a defendant enters a plea and is then given a trial date? Instead there are endless administrative hearings where countless details are discussed, such as which witnesses will be called. The phrase 'justice delayed is justice denied' beautifully sums up the administrative havoc that hampers so much court work.

So, with so many medical opinions flying around, what exactly is a medical defence? In simple terms, it's a health reason which justifies or excuses committing an unlawful act. So, driving on the hard shoulder is illegal – unless the driver has, for example, an unexpected case of the runs and desperately needs the bathroom.

But I should make it clear that it's not the medical problem itself but the effect of that problem on an offence that hands the lawyer the argument. That's why when a prospective client comes to see me, I'll often ask about their health. Have they been ill recently? Are they taking medication? Asking someone about their health is like throwing a fishing net into the sea. You've no idea what you might catch as you reel it back in. In an old boot or broken shopping trolley there could be a prize koi carp.

Of course, not all medical conditions are relevant to a case. Stubbing your toe a week before getting arrested for drink-driving doesn't offer an automatic get-out clause. What the lawyer has to do is be alive to the potential effect that illness – or stubbed toe – might have on a client's case. The Ferguson case taught me this and I learnt from it – fast.

There will always be prospective clients who – and I wish I had a tenner for every time I've heard this – literally beg their lawyer with the words, 'You have to get me off. Just find something, anything.' If there's a legal defence, I'll find it. If there isn't, then I can't help. There has to be a connection between the medical problem and the legal defence. Otherwise I suggest they go down to the NHS walk-in centre or swing by the local pharmacy.

That's not to say there aren't plenty of people who think they can outsmart the police by pretending that they've been ill or that they've got a medical problem. One classic ruse is to plead not being able to blow into a breathalyser. It sounds very cute, but it's as old as the hills. So when clients tell me this happened to them I'll start by digging into their health. I need to find out whether I've got a time-waster on my hands or if I'm dealing with someone who really does have a lung, breathing or even technique problem that they simply weren't aware of. When I'm taking instructions, a typical scenario might run like this:

'Well, Mr Smith, have you got any respiratory problems?'

Blank look. 'Er, no.'

'Are you a smoker?'

Equally blank look. 'No.'

'Well, have you ever had this kind of problem before?'

'Er, no.'

'Blowing up balloons, running up stairs, anything that makes you breathless perhaps?'

Contrite client puts on his coat. 'No.'

Anyone who has been asked to give a sample of breath can tell you that it's not that easy to use a breathalyser. You have to blow continuously for several seconds and there'll be some resistance as you do. Any pause will abort the reading. You can be fit and healthy and still struggle. And that's without considering the stress and anxiety of having to do it after being marched down to the police station. So you can see how difficult it is to prove that a problem with blowing is down to a suspect's state of health.

But I'm not a doctor, so I can't make the judgement call. What I can do is pull in an expert – usually a police surgeon – who will take a test to measure the suspect's forced expiratory volume (which means how much air they can force out of the lungs after taking a deep breath). Depending on the results, different options are open to my client, as I'll explain to them.

You may think that you're pretty familiar with your own state of health, but it's not always the case. A good lawyer should be open to a possible medical defence even if his client isn't. For example, I remember one client who'd tried and failed to blow into a breathalyser. Wondering why this was, I requested the custody record. This is a full account of everything that takes place at the police station relating to the defendant, yet, rather bizarrely, isn't part and parcel of disclosure (all the relevant information relating to the prosecution case). That's why so few defence lawyers ask for it. I always do.

overwhelming fear and anxiety. Is someone who's feeling like this really going to understand what is happening to them and what the law requires of them?

Think about this too. When you're asked to give a sample in the context of a possible charge of drink-driving, you're being asked to give evidence against yourself. 'Got that, Mr Jones?' says a copper. Well, no, not if Mr Jones is quivering and shaking after being arrested, his heart thundering in his chest as he sits, dazed and baffled, in a police station.

To make matters worse, the statutory warning which the officer trots out before carrying out a breathalyser test is bewildering. In fact it's hard enough to understand when you're of sound mind and stone-cold sober. But try understanding this when you've had a few pints:

'I require you to provide two specimens of breath for analysis by means of an approved device. The specimen with the lower proportion of alcohol in your breath may be used as evidence and the other will be disregarded. I warn you that failure to provide either of these specimens will render you liable to prosecution. Do you agree to provide two specimens of breath for analysis?'

Meanwhile, if our hapless driver doesn't agree to provide a sample, he's bombarded with more words:

'I warn you again that failure to provide either of these specimens will render you liable to prosecution. Do you now agree to provide two specimens of breath for analysis?'

How's that for a party game at a drunken get-together: reading this long-winded legalese when you can barely stand up. I'd love to meet the scholar who penned that statutory warning, though I imagine he wouldn't be a man of few words.

When the warnings are trotted out to a person who has all their wits about them, they can be difficult enough to grasp. Factor in a serious mental health issue plus the trauma of being held at a police station and these words might as well be double Dutch. The suspect may just about understand they need to be breathalysed. But would they understand the consequences of failing to do so?

So here's the loophole. Even if a person with depression does provide a specimen and they are over the limit, they can still be acquitted if a lawyer can prove the police haven't taken the trouble to find out if they understood what was going on.

What you have here then is an anomaly – a drink-driver who is over the limit but who walks free because the law provides them with the possibility of a legal escape route.

This happened to one client of mine, a young woman, who faced six months in prison and a two-year driving ban after being arrested for driving down the middle of the road and almost hitting a police car. She couldn't blow into the breathalyser, so the officer charged her with failing to provide a breath sample.

Pretty straightforward, you might think. But here's the loophole. The officer didn't bother to read her her rights because he thought she was too incoherent to understand. True, she had been drinking heavily. But this lady had also been taking sleeping pills and antidepressants after being diagnosed with agitated depression following her crumbling marriage.

Where drink-driving is concerned, failing to make sure a suspect understands what happens to them can be the gateway to a huge loophole. If you fail to provide a sample because you're too drunk to understand, then it makes no difference. You can't automatically rely on intoxication as your defence for everything. It's just tough. You have to face the consequences. But, if you don't understand as a result of depression and drink, then it's possible it was the depression and not the drink which clouded your understanding – whether you provided a specimen or not.

So, in this case I called in a medical expert, who confirmed in court that depression could have befuddled my client's understanding. Once that point was raised, the Crown needed to contradict it beyond all reasonable doubt. Which they couldn't. My client was acquitted.

By now you will be able to see that drink-driving laws are massively complex. They can coil round the facts and tie the Crown in knots. That's why so many lawyers lose their cases. They can't face wading through the nitty-gritty. But I'll say it again: set your mind to the admittedly epic task of sifting through the statutes, and keep your antennae pricked up, and the rewards are massive.

In another case I had a client who was said to be three times over the limit after she was found slumped over the wheel of her car in a motorway service station. (She had been there for two hours when the cops found her.) In fact she was so drunk that the officers claimed they couldn't rouse her when they found her, passed out, in the driver's seat with the door open and a stray vodka bottle lying on the ground outside.

But at the nearby police station – where she had to be propped up and was unable to answer most questions put to her – she wasn't cautioned. After taking two samples the officer called a police surgeon and my client was taken to hospital. To my mind, this was an utter disgrace. The lady should have been taken straight to hospital since she clearly needed medical attention (it also turned out that she had taken a number of blood pressure tablets). Yet the police took it upon themselves to argue that she was too drunk to understand anything. In court I argued that she couldn't have been that drunk because she was able to coordinate her faculties enough to provide a specimen of breath. I told the officer, 'You unlawfully deprived her of her rights. You are exaggerating her drunkenness.'

It's a fact that the more drunk you are, the less likely you are to be capable of providing a specimen of breath. But in this case the police had their specimen. So my client couldn't have been that drunk. Sure, she was guilty of driving over the limit. But the right legal procedures weren't followed. This lady was stripped of her rights. A loophole, some might say. No, just the law.

It's also worth pointing out that there are several other 'medical' situations that can affect a person's ability to understand what goes on when they are arrested. Being in pain, for example, or even just crying – yes, crying. If it's bad enough, then is raised by a lawyer as a medical reason and proven evidentially by an expert witness, it offers a perfectly legal way out for the drink-driving offender. It makes sense. Most people are pretty upset when they find themselves hauled into a police station. Who wouldn't be? That's why, when clients come to see me, I ask what state they were in at the time they were pulled in. 'Were you calm? Or were you crying your eyes out?'

If the person was sobbing, the police should note this down in the section of their station procedure form marked 'manner of accused'. Some officers don't. Perhaps because they're trying to be smart and think that if they write it on the form it might cause a problem. And it can. If you're crying really hard, not only can it be difficult to blow into the breathalyser, but it might also blur your understanding of what's going on. You're hardly going to pick up on the intricacies of the statutory warning I've mentioned above, or the consequences of failing to comply. Instead you function like a robot, doing as you're told.

But have you understood what's involved? Unlikely. That affords you a defence. Bring on an expert who says in court that when people cry they are emotionally distracted and you're on pretty strong ground. The issue has been raised. Now it's over to the Crown to prove beyond reasonable doubt that crying didn't make a difference to your level of understanding. Invariably they can't.

What all this shows is how important it is, particularly where medicine and health are concerned, for the lawyer to explore things that are not directly obvious. That's why I'm obsessive about foraging into every dark corner of the law.

I'm not looking at the facts of the crime when I'm searching for that killer medical argument – particularly in drink-driving. I'm looking at the mental and physical state of my client and whether it can impact on a defence.

It's the same issue when a client is in pain – which can be a huge distraction from understanding something as alien and complex as the statutory warning a police officer trots out at the station. (There doesn't seem to be a speed limit on how fast these things are read out!) The pain might be triggered by a headache, or a throbbing finger. It doesn't matter what the cause is. Pain is pain.

Unfortunately some drink-driving cases result in calamitous accidents. And calamitous accidents often cause equally calamitous injuries. But even at this level of pain – in fact even when a client is facing a life-or-death situation – procedures still have to be followed. As a lawyer, I was the first to leap on this seemingly callous anomaly, and it has generated numerous acquittals.

A case involving a millionaire businessman was a classic example of this. My man was hurtling along in his Mercedes ML320 when he lost control and was catapulted through the roof about fifty yards away from his car, before landing on the ground with a vicious thud. Time was of the essence. Emergency services raced his broken, unconscious body to hospital. As the trauma team battled to save him, a police surgeon was called to take a sample of my client's blood.

Pretty callous, as I've said. But that's the law. Regardless of his injuries, this man may have been guilty of a motoring crime. There was a protocol to follow.

Meanwhile my client had lapsed into a coma and was surrounded by a cluster of doctors struggling valiantly to save his life. Since the police surgeon couldn't get near him to get his sample, he asked one of the doctors to do it for him. Sample secured, the police surgeon left his medical colleagues to press on with the urgent job of saving my client.

All fairly straightforward. A few weeks later, after my client had regained consciousness and was beginning his slow journey to recovery, he was visited by the police: not with a bunch of grapes but with news that they wanted to analyse his blood. It's one thing taking blood from the suspect, but the law says that the suspect has to give permission for it to be analysed. Of course, my client was clinging to his life by a thread when the blood was taken and had no idea they'd even got a sample.

When I reviewed the facts a loophole immediately sprang to mind. If a client consents to his blood being analysed and the reading is very high, he is likely to be charged not only with drink-driving but also dangerous driving. If he is convicted, he faces the prospect of jail, a lengthy disqualification and a compulsory re-test. On the other hand, if he doesn't agree to having his blood analysed, he will probably only be charged with failing to provide a specimen of blood without a reasonable excuse. He is unlikely to be charged with any other offences and if convicted will simply receive a fine and a disqualification.

As always, it's not for me to tell defendants what to do or say. I just tell them the law and explain the legal ramifications of all the options open to them. As would be revealed in court, my client decided against having his blood analysed and was charged with failing to provide. So, what to do next?

I remember turning this case over and over in my mind while on holiday. I was sitting under an awning in the south of France wading through *Wilkinson's Road Traffic Offences* and combing through all the statements, searching for that killer loophole which would demolish the prosecution case. And then . . . the light bulb moment. Reading back over the law, I realised that, in cases like this, samples of blood can only be taken by someone who isn't involved with the direct medical care of the suspect.

Cue the police surgeon.

But he hadn't been able to do his job – he simply couldn't get near to my client at the time – so one of the NHS doctors had done it for him. Ah ha! This would leave the prosecution case with nowhere to go.

As I planned my defence, I couldn't help but be privately troubled by the incongruity of the statute. How could a police surgeon – a man who, first and foremost was a doctor, dedicated to saving life – try to muscle in when his colleagues were battling to treat a patient with potentially fatal injuries? How could he prioritise what the law obliged him to do, when to do so flew in the face of every syllable of the Hippocratic Oath? The main concern with my client was to save his life – and it would have been wrong to force the letter of the statute. The Hippocratic Oath aces the legal system every time. So it should. In fact, I think this police surgeon should be congratulated for prioritising his medical obligation over his legal one. As it says in the Talmud, 'He who saves one life saves the world entire.'

Yet, when the correct legal procedures aren't followed, the doors to an acquittal swing right open. Maybe the law needs to be changed. But that's how things stood in this particular case, that's the law I applied – and my client went free. The police missed out on a conviction but a doctor saved a life.

There are so many other cases where a person can be factually over the limit. Yet, because of flawed medical procedures – which I find by testing the system – they go free.

I hate drink-driving, but if the law hasn't been applied properly, then that is that.

Another client, a businessman, was four and half times over the limit when he jumped a red light. Two policemen immediately set off after him, but lost sight of the car. Seconds later they found it smashed into railings, with my client stumbling around in the road. But the police didn't stop in time, and the patrol car ran into my client, sending him catapulting into the air. All of which was captured on the coppers' in-car video. Clearly in a bad way, my client was rushed to hospital for treatment and a sample of blood was also taken. The reading was 359mg of alcohol per 100ml of blood – enough to possibly kill him, whether he was driving or not!

At the trial the officer who had been given the task of explaining the drink-driving procedure to my client at the hospital told the court that my man had been conscious at the time.

My mind flicked onto red alert. First off all, I'd seen the footage of the accident. My client had literally been jettisoned by the patrol car. How on earth could he have remained conscious after his body had taken such a thrashing?

What's more, as I would outline in court, when my client first spoke to me he told me that he couldn't remember whether he'd been conscious or not.

Fantastic. A difference of opinion. In court I set about exploring it – ruthlessly. It went something like this:

'Officer, do you have any definite recollection of my client being conscious when you were called to explain the procedures to him in hospital or are you being guided now by what is on the statement in front of you?'

'No, Mr Freeman, I definitely remember,' the policeman replied emphatically.

'So where were you when you went through the procedures with him?'

'In a booth at the hospital.'

'Was my client sitting up or lying down?'

'Lying down, sir.'

'How would you describe the state of the defendant while you were going through the procedure. Was he attentive, paying attention?'

'Not that attentive.'

I sensed a small chasm opening up. 'What do you mean, Officer?'

'He seemed to be drifting in and out of consciousness,' the witness told the court earnestly.

Dramatic pause.

'Oh, and yet, Officer, you completed the procedure and filled in the relevant forms on the basis that my client was conscious. Is that because there is no particular part of the forms that relates to drifting in and out of consciousness?'

In truth, the forms only dictate what a police officer should do if a) the suspect is conscious, or b) if he isn't.

'Yes. But I do remember him drifting in and out,' the policeman replied.

Wonderful. I had him.

At the time that the officer was going through this crucial wording, a time when it was essential that the defendant should understand what was happening, my client was drifting in and out of consciousness. Despite the high reading, the court had no alternative but to acquit him.

Now, I'd be the first to concede that my client was guilty of consuming a vast quantity of alcohol. In fact, it was the highest amount of alcohol in a drink-driving case that anyone has escaped from. But the procedures at the hospital were fatally flawed. Should a drinker be allowed to hide behind the fact that the police haven't acted properly? Of course not. It doesn't make sense. As a private individual I baulk at such incongruity.

But, as a lawyer, what else am I supposed to do? Having come across a flaw, do I give the judge a nod and a wink and say there's been a cock-up here which has ruined the case? That I don't know if that's down to sheer incompetence or some other reason? But, either way, that I'll withdraw my legal submission now so that the prosecuting authorities can go ahead and convict my client. As if!

My humanity doesn't let me rest easily with the way those who are factually guilty can be legally acquitted. Playing the devil's advocate rather than an officer of the court, I privately rail against this. But I chose to be a lawyer.

I touched earlier on how the kinds of pills or tablets a suspect is taking can potentially provide structure to a legal argument. After all, medication can do all sorts of things to your body. Look at any packet of drugs and you'll find leaflets warning of a whole string of potential side effects. Who's to know whether that pill you pop in all innocence will give you headaches and nausea as it works its magic. So, as soon as clients tell me they're taking any kind of drugs, my mind is alive to the impact that this could have on their defence.

It's a strategy which yielded what is perhaps one of my quirkiest defences to date. It involved world snooker champion Ronnie O'Sullivan, whom I defended on a drink-driving case – he was charged with failing to provide a specimen of urine without reasonable excuse.

As would be relayed in court, when the police arrested my client he wasn't asked to do a breath test at the station, though he had done one at the roadside, because there was a problem with the machine, and so they asked him to provide a sample of blood instead. My client told them he couldn't because he didn't like needles. The police surgeon accepted this as an excuse and asked him for a urine sample instead. Ronnie was given copious amounts of water to drink to help him do this, but nothing happened. He just couldn't pee to order. While I was preparing the case, this fact had sent my mind spiralling off at a tangent. Could it be possible that there was some kind of link between medication for depression and failure to provide a urine specimen? Off I went to do some loophole hunting.

I asked the chief police surgeon of Greater Manchester Police, a brilliant man called Dr Stephen Robinson, if he could confirm a possible connection. He did, preparing an expert report which was served to the prosecution. Medical opinion is, of course, subjective and the prosecution could have attempted to contradict this argument with their own medical report. But they didn't.

The hearing itself was initially burdened by the rather peculiar behaviour of the chairman of the magistrates' bench. From his very arrival in court it was clear how much he relished presiding over such a high-profile case.

He reminded me of Alf Garnett, playing to the gallery by rolling his eyes and sighing dramatically almost every time I spoke.

In fact when it came to the first adjournment of the day, he even extended his humour to my client. 'We're going to take a natural break now,' the magistrate told the court. 'No doubt, Mr O'Sullivan, you'll find that most useful.' Poleaxed by his crass comments, I made my feelings known to the court clerk. But it was early in the day. There wasn't much she could do.

When the magistrates returned I pressed on with my defence. Ronnie had initially been breathalysed at the road-side. So I started by asking the police officer who'd tested him whether he had changed the mouthpiece on the device between unsuccessful or bungled blows. In my view, in cases like this such action is critical because the handbook says the mouthpiece has to be changed every time the breathalyser is used. The High Court have since ruled that there is no necessity to change the mouthpiece between blows if used for more than one blow (provided the police are sure the mouthpiece is not defective).

Otherwise, according to the manufacturer's handbook, alcohol can easily build up in the mouthpiece and affect the reading. (I happened to know this because I obsessively read all the instruction manuals and general bumph that relate to the devices used in motoring cases. They're a gold mine for potential legal arguments.)

At the end of the prosecution case I made a submission that because the mouthpiece hadn't been changed, the roadside test was invalid. Therefore my client had been arrested as a consequence of flawed procedures. The magistrates retired to consider this, only for the court clerk to come running back in five minutes later.

'The magistrate has just blown into the mouthpiece!' she declared, white-faced.

The prosecutor and I looked at each other in disbelief. How could he do something so stupid? By blowing into the mouthpiece, the chairman of the magistrates was contaminating the evidence! The prosecutor and court clerk wanted him removed from the bench immediately. But, always alert to turning situations to my advantage, I thought differently.

I had many better points to argue – including the medication issue – that I didn't really need to rely on the mouthpiece defence. Perhaps if I offered the chairman an olive branch by telling him I was ditching the mouthpiece argument, then I could save his face and get him onside. I abandoned that particular submission and we carried on.

However, if I thought the man's gratitude was going to be forthcoming, then I was sorely mistaken. Instead, his behaviour became increasingly erratic. At the end of that day's hearing he practically inflated his chest and boomed at me, 'Mr Freeman, we are going to retire now until 10am tomorrow. And if you are late I shall kick you up the backside.'

I looked at him in astonishment. Where on earth was this guy coming from? Only that afternoon I'd saved him from acute embarrassment. And here he was, talking to me like some halfwit lawyer who couldn't even make it to court on time. A particularly stinging insult since I'm never late. In fact I'm always the first to arrive.

As the chairman swept out, I went back to complain mildly to the court clerk. This man was brimming with prejudice, a loose cannon rolling around the deck. I didn't have enough to get him thrown off the bench that day. But by registering my objection with the clerk – who agreed with my view – I was laying the foundation for an application to get him kicked out.

The next morning I decided to try to put it behind me. I had a case to win, and proceeded to outline my arguments. Again the magistrates retired for a short time, and this time when the chairman returned his face was arranged in a grotesque smirk, as if to say, 'I don't care what you tell me, Freeman, I'm having your guy.'

I was right. With a flamboyant sneer he declared, 'Mr Freeman, I don't uphold any of the reasons you have presented to defend your case.'

And as he did so, I saw him turn to the press bench and wink. Yes, wink.

I was astonished. I'd never seen anything like this in court before. It was the last straw. I had to get rid of this guy. His prejudice towards me was overwhelmingly obvious. There was no way my client was going to get a fair hearing.

So I challenged him. 'Sir, did I see you wink at the press bench?' Inside, I wasn't even sure where I was going with this.

'No,' he retorted defensively.

He was lying. And now I was going to put him on trial for it. I turned slowly to the journalists sitting on the press bench.

'Did he wink?'

'I saw him, Mr Freeman,' one reporter called out. Another guy echoed this. 'I saw him too.'

Tasting blood, I turned slowly back to the chairman. 'I'm sorry, sir, but I distinctly saw you wink at the press bench.'

The man's upper lip curled into a snarl and he looked at me with barely disguised hatred. 'Why would I do that, Mr Freeman? Do you think I'm gay or something?'

I had to bite my lip. Winking was bad enough. But then

throw in a dash of homophobia. Well, let's just say he'd already lassoed a noose around his own neck. Now he was pulling it even tighter. Before he could say any more, the clerk practically manhandled the chairman from his seat and ushered him out through the back door. Mission accomplished. He had behaved like some ridiculous court jester, and now had no choice but to be recused, that is removed from the case. I didn't even need to ask.

Unfortunately my triumph was short-lived. We'd been there for two days yet there was no way of recovering costs at that time. I could hardly bill my client because I had taken the case on an agreed fee. And we'd have to wait for a new trial date. In this situation I had to foot the bill – even though the blame lay at the chairman's door. (Though if you win, you do have the power to recover costs.) My only consolation was the certainty of knowing that I'd have had no chance of winning with that man on the bench. The press loved the story. The newspaper headlines the following day shouted, '£100,000 winker.' I don't know where they got the figure from – the implication being that was my fee. If only. But that magistrate was definitely a winker.

The hearing was eventually rescheduled and this time took place before a district judge. I was going to focus on my main argument – how depression had hampered my client's ability to provide a urine sample. As this had been raised already, it was on the record, so the judge didn't need to hear Ronnie's testimony. Instead it was straight to the medical evidence.

All I needed was what I had: Dr Robinson's expert opinion corroborating a connection between my client's inability to provide and the medication he was taking. That was quite a high bar for the Crown to overcome – to disprove the theory beyond reasonable doubt.

My expert duly gave evidence about the combined effect of antidepressants, the stress of being arrested and the pressure of having to wee to order. The Crown had no evidence to negate it.

Client not guilty.

Ronnie was delighted. He was about to play in the snooker world championships and he told the press, 'If I play half as well as my brief plays I will be world champion.' It was a lovely thing to say. And he did win.

So, as you can see, we never truly know how taking a tablet might affect the decisions we make and the actions we take. Especially when they involve situations we can't possibly anticipate. But it's this uncertainty that allows medicine to provide a receptive lawyer with revolutionary, quirky and watertight arguments.

Perhaps the most powerful example of this involves a man accused of drink-driving who came to me with a most unusual story. The chap had been on a night out in Manchester city centre when he was attacked by an unknown assailant. Deeply distressed, he got in his car and was later stopped by the police on the motorway. He had been driving erratically and, it transpired, in the opposite direction to his home. Officers would later describe him as 'dazed and confused'. He was also three times over the drink-driving limit.

The man – a chap of previous good character, I should add – was duly charged. As would be revealed in court, he could just about remember being attacked, but had no idea why he was driving the way he did. His only possible explanation was that his drink had been spiked in one of the bars he had visited.

As soon as he said this, my mind started buzzing. My way of practising law relies on more than a touch of the old Sherlock Holmes: an ability to put two and two together. If what my client was saying was true, it was likely his attacker had slipped something like the so-called date-rape drug Rohypnol into his drink. Colourless, odourless and tasteless – ideal for spiking drinks undetected – this type of medication has a sedative effect and has been associated with many cases of non-consensual sex. Afterwards the victim has absolutely no recollection of what they have been through.

It all made sense to me. Confused, highly distressed and clearly still under the influence of the drug, my client had clambered into his car. The next thing he remembered was waking up in a police cell.

I began researching Rohypnol and found that the hypnotic drug leaves those who take it in a compliant, subconscious state. They remember nothing nor have any recollection about what they do.

I then combed through every defence in the criminal calendar, hoping to find one that would tally with what had happened to my client. Most of the defences that exist in criminal law can be applied to motoring cases but sometimes lawyers don't stretch their minds to see how. I needed one that fitted perfectly. And then it came to me. A sparsely deployed criminal defence that I'd never used before – I just knew of it from my law-school days.

Its name? Automatism. A state of behaving robotically, without any understanding of what you have done. It was blindingly obvious. I didn't have to make a quantum leap between the facts as I knew them and my client's mental state. It was the perfect defence.

I searched but I couldn't find any drink-driving cases to support my argument. But when my instinct is kicking off, I've never been stalled by the absence of a precedent.

I immediately instructed an expert to see if my hunch was right.

One thing was clear. My client's symptoms didn't match those of someone who'd had the proverbial skinful of alcohol. Even the police acknowledged this at the station. He was bewildered and confused. The expert agreed that it was highly likely that my client had been given an unlawful substance and therefore would have been acting like an automaton. He hadn't intended to drive and so, from a legal perspective, he had a defence. This was raised and the Crown had the daunting task of negating it beyond reasonable doubt.

The way I saw it, my client hadn't been in control of his faculties on the night of the offence. And not just because of alcohol. So why should he be punished? Why should his life be turned upside down? He was actually a victim, and being victimised further for what he'd unknowingly done.

In court police officers on the case described how they'd found my client. Drunk, yes, but his confusion and bewilderment went beyond the recognisable effects of alcohol. And they told me so, not realising, as witnesses for the prosecution, how helpful they were being.

My own defence was based on a hunch because I couldn't prove it. (As I said earlier, trusting your gut instinct is vital for the loophole strategist.) But I could explain the probability. And the court were also left with the impression of a man whose account just didn't make sense – until you added the Rohypnol scenario. Then it made perfect sense. My hunch paid off and my client was cleared.

So far I've focused on how the health of a client and the procedures revolving around their health can help them win cases. But what about when ill health strikes any of the other players in a courtroom drama?

Personally, I'm one of those people who never seems to get ill when it matters. I think I've only ever had one day off work in all my career. (That's why I soldiered on when the sight in my right eye gave way!)

Not everyone is like that, though. Take the time *EastEnders* actor Dean Gaffney was accused of doing 131mph in his Audi on the M40 in Warwickshire. I trekked down from Manchester to Leamington Spa to defend his case, only to discover that a police officer who was a vital witness for the Crown had called in sick. The prosecution, of course, wanted an adjournment.

Now, no one can help being ill – always sad news – but we'd travelled a long way. What's more, the last thing I ever want is an adjournment. You've prepared your case, you've crystallised that knowledge, it's all up there in your head and suddenly someone fails to show up. An adjournment means you have to hold onto that knowledge for six months. It clogs your brain as it languishes there, waiting to be revisited.

And so to tactics. The first thing I had to establish was how important this officer was to the Crown's case. That way I could decide very quickly what approach I needed to take. If his testimony wasn't going to make much difference, then I was ready to push ahead. However, if the prosecution felt his evidence was vital, well, that was an opportunity. And I'm always ready to capitalise on an opportunity.

It turned out the officer was crucial to the Crown's case and the prosecutor pressed for an adjournment. Not so fast, I thought. If he's that important, let's try and get this case on.

So I began firing questions at my opposite number. I wanted to know the nature of his missing police officer's sickness, how long he'd been ill for, when the Crown were first notified, why we hadn't been notified and, above all, why we'd been asked to come all the way down from Manchester when the Crown knew it would be an abortive hearing.

Unfortunately for the prosecution, their witness had been off sick for some time. Excellent, I thought. Time to bring out a bit of case law to give my argument a boost. From my briefcase I pulled out transcripts of various High Court rulings which had shown that allowing an adjournment on the basis of an administrative failure is as good as encouraging it. (Having spotted this potential loophole a few times before, I made sure I always had this case law to hand.)

With such a weighty argument, beefed up by a walk-on part from the High Court, the magistrates found in my favour. The Crown were told they had to proceed. Their problem was that, without their police officer, they knew they couldn't prove the case and reluctantly offered no evidence. The case was thrown out.

It's remarkable really. If someone integral to my case falls ill, I make sure I have my back covered. I ask them to get a sick note from their doctor explaining that they are unfit to attend court. (The note needs to spell this out: some courts won't accept sick notes that simply refer to being unfit for work.) I then serve it to the prosecution and the court. I make sure all the relevant parties know. Unfortunately the Crown and police aren't always diligent enough.

So I was able to use the same medical loophole again when I was called to defend soccer star Paul Ince. The then Wolves player had been accused of speeding at up to 110mph on the M25 near Leatherhead, Surrey, and his case was due to be heard by Guildford Magistrates Court.

At the time I was making a documentary about my work for ITV's *Tonight with Trevor McDonald* and had cameras following my every move. Fine when you're winning cases. But on this particular morning I wasn't too thrilled by their company. It was one of those rare moments when I wasn't confident about winning my case, because the prosecution had produced relevant documents at the eleventh hour to counter my defence about defective speed devices. And it was going to happen in front of a television crew. My brain was spinning over all the law I'd ever absorbed. And I still couldn't find an argument.

On arriving at court I met the ITV team and told them that I needed to have a quick word with the prosecutor. As I made my way across the car park, deep in thought, I whispered a prayer to my late father, who'd died from a brain tumour just a few months earlier. I've never done anything like this before, but I was desperate. 'Dad, I need a lift here,' I muttered under my breath. I just couldn't see a way out.

As I walked into the courtroom I was greeted by the prosecutor, his face creased with concern. Then came the immortal words, 'Looks like we have a slight problem.'

I couldn't believe it. Had I heard him properly? But, like a half-decent poker player, I kept a straight face. 'What's wrong?' I asked.

It appeared that a vital witness, one of the arresting officers, hadn't appeared.

'He's sick,' the prosecutor said glumly. 'I'll need to ask for an adjournment.'

Thank you, Dad, I thought, overwhelmed with gratitude for whatever silent force had pulled me out of this fix.

And so to business.

'Well, I'd like to make some enquiries first before I agree to postponing the case,' I said crisply, preparing to dig a little to see what I could find.

And so I started asking the vital questions. What is the

nature of this officer's illness? How long has he been ill for? When were you notified? What steps were taken to notify us? Why should my client and my case have to suffer because nobody bothered to tell us this before we arrived?

Further enquiries revealed that the officer had been suffering from flu for over a week. The problem was that no one had taken the trouble to notify the Crown or the defence. The system had broken down. With gloves off, the prosecution and I tussled over the proposed adjournment. We argued all morning, after which the magistrates retired for an hour to make a decision. As the clock ticked by I wondered if my prayer had made any difference. It seemed it had. When court resumed, the bench agreed the prosecution had not notified us in sufficient time about the absent witness. The court ordered the Crown to proceed. But they couldn't because the sick witness was crucial.

Out went the case. Client not guilty.

It seems that in sickness, in health – and even after death, I strongly believe – mental and physical well-being can have a huge impact on fighting cases.

Thanks, Dad.

5

Loophole: identification

Identity. It's the buzzword *du jour*. Barely a day goes by without some breaking story about terrorists, fraudsters or illegal immigrants pilfering personal information to fuel their criminal activity. And with identity fraud so rife, it's not surprising we're constantly being hammered with requests to prove who we are.

Only recently I had to see a solicitor who was doing some conveyancing work on a property I was selling. The guy has known me since I was thirteen. OK, I'm a little taller now (well, not much) but there was no question of mistaking who I was. And yet he still had to request proof of ID! Such is the climate we live in.

Actually, confirming my own identity isn't too much of a problem. It's not unusual for me to be buying underwear in M&S when a hapless shopper meanders over and says, 'Er, excuse me, but aren't you that bloke who gets all the footballers off?' Since I'm also the bloke who's trying to find a three-pack of boxer shorts, I tend to nod affably and retreat behind the thermal vests. It seems that thanks to my alter ego, Mr Loophole, and his frequent appearance in the papers, I'm a dead giveaway.

It's one thing, however, thinking you've spotted a *Coronation Street* actor buying a few litres of Four Star and a BLT sandwich at the local filling station. It's another being absolutely sure. And in criminal law you have to be. If a conviction is to be upheld, there's no room for mistaken identity. That's why the one central question for every criminal investigator, from Inspector Morse to Agatha Christie, is simply this: whodunit? It's the one the loophole hunter asks too.

Of course, it's quite different at the movies. When you look at the way gumshoe investigators try to nail their suspect on the big screen, the process usually follows a typical pattern. Driven by the knowledge that every crime needs a criminal, the hangdog detective snares his suspect and marches him off to court.

Then it's over to a spitfire prosecutor to point the finger and thunder that the State has got its man. Ah, but then, enter stage left, the hero of the hour: the criminal defence lawyer. They will storm at the jury that they can only return a guilty verdict if they're satisfied beyond reasonable doubt (actually, out here in real life, this phrase has been junked in favour of the far less sexy 'so that they are sure of the guilt of the accused', though Hollywood has taken no notice). If there's any question mark over identity, then the defendant walks, closing credits roll and it's time to grab a takeaway on the way home.

That's what happens in the land of John Grisham. And it's not that different here on planet earth. For when you fillet away the glamour, the legal process is applied in much the same way for someone who has been flashed belting down the M62. The question the Crown have to prove is who was behind the wheel of the car when the offence took place. As I say, put simply, whodunit? That's because a fundamental principle underpinning every area of criminal law – even the most unglamorous of road-traffic cases – is that the Crown must prove the suspect/defendant's ID in order to make a watertight connection between the crime and the accused.

I've lost count of the number of cases I've done that have caved in because of a question mark over the true identity of the suspect. Not that this is any great surprise. Every day people get names wrong, spell them incorrectly or match them to the wrong faces. Have you ever walked up to someone in the street, convinced you know who they are, only to find they're a complete stranger?

I'll never forget an unusual episode that happened in my own office shortly after I'd successfully defended Premiership footballer Ashley Ward. Ashley had been found not guilty of speeding and the case snagged plenty of press attention: indeed one newspaper splashed with 'Mr Loophole Strikes Again' and printed underneath the headline a fairly unmistakable picture of Ashley Ward.

A few days later I received a call from a lady who'd received a speeding ticket and who wanted me to represent her. I told her to send in the papers and I made an appointment to see her a short time later. On the day of our meeting she arrived at the office and she was stunningly beautiful, a breathtakingly tight-fitting dress snaked around her slim frame. Ever the professional, I stood up to introduce myself, trying not to do that alpha male thing of flashing a toothpaste-white smile in a bid to look dazzlingly impressive. Rather perplexingly, she refused my proffered hand and instead looked me up and down with barely concealed disdain.

Then, in a tone drenched with disappointment, she complained, 'You don't look much like your photograph from the newspaper the other day.'

For a moment I was confused, then the light bulb went on, 'Oh, that wasn't me, that was my client, Ashley Ward,' I said, smiling. She had to be joking, hadn't she?

To my absolute astonishment she walked over to my desk, swept up her papers and marched towards the door. 'Well,

I think I'm going to get him to represent me instead,' she said sourly, before making a swift exit.

I still chuckle about this incident (though I'll admit my ego was a bit bruised at the time). But this lady's visit to my office remains a judicious and funny example of how we can all slip up when it comes to identifying people.

However, when it comes to criminal law the issue of identity is no laughing matter. In everyday life the ramifications of mistaken identity can be embarrassing, inconvenient or annoying. In court, the ripple effect can be dynamite.

What was ironic was that I'd won Ashley's case itself by hinging my defence on the issue of identification. I'd successfully argued that the police couldn't prove the footballer had been the driver of his Aston Martin DB7 sports car when it was recorded at 110mph on the M56 in Cheshire. More of which later.

The gorgeous would-be client who came to see me afterwards perhaps hadn't appreciated the finer points of law and instead concentrated on the finer points of Ashley's picture. Clearly, when she saw the guy behind the desk, two and two hadn't added up to four.

So much for my disappointing pretty soccer-star fans. But, in law, the question of identification is a minefield in the statue books. It's riddled with dark corners, anomalies and, yes, loopholes. What I've tried to do over the years is sift through this complex area and use the law – in the face of what often seems to be overwhelming evidence – to secure acquittals.

You might think that in our over-scrutinised, flash-happy age of the speed camera, proving the identity of the driver in a motoring case is fairly easy. Not so. Never assume, when that notification drops onto your doormat, that the situation is an open-and-shut case. Nor is it so even when you're having your collar felt at the roadside. It's a matter of knowing where those landmines are and then detonating them in court.

As I've already said, it was never my game plan to be Mr Loophole. Nor was it my intention to develop a strategy that would suggest I was trying to 'dodge' the law. Instead, from very early on, I used my free time to plough through my law books on the hunt for defences that wouldn't be obvious to the naked legal eye. It became clear to me that ID – that is, whodunit – was one of them.

However, a couple of events early in my career really brought home to me the loopholes surrounding identity. The first involved a client who'd received several speeding notices but who denied being the driver or even having been anywhere near where the offences were said to have taken place.

As I later said to him in court, 'Are you sure it wasn't you?'

After all, even at that stage in my career I'd heard just about every excuse in the book for trying to dodge a speeding ticket. And believe me, there are hundreds. But this chap was quite adamant.

I thought to myself, OK, we'll ask the officer who pulled this guy over if he still recognises him. Let's see if the face fits.

Now, you have to bear in mind that trial dates are often set months after an alleged offence has taken place. So when the prosecutor and I asked the affable copper before we went into court if he could describe my client, he told us, sorry, he just couldn't. There was no way he could remember his face. I then introduced him to my client and asked if this could jog his memory. The officer shook his head. 'I can't remember if it was him or not,' he replied apologetically. With no confirmation of identity, the case was thrown out.

Until then, like so many lawyers, I'd made a rather lazy assumption that if a person is named on a summons for speeding, then he must be the driver. Back then I was still fairly young and green.

About a week after this case, while still reflecting on what had happened, another incident occurred that, for me, really blew open the crazy complications of proving identity. I was in Leeds Magistrates Court doing a speeding trial when, minutes before the case, I was approached by a smartly dressed, rather nervous looking young man.

'Mr Freeman,' he began hesitantly, 'I'm a trainee barrister and I've been following your work. Do you mind if I come and watch your case?'

Did I mind? Hell, I was flattered. Though I also thought to myself, this'll be so embarrassing if I don't win!

'Of course not,' I said with a smile. 'Come and sit behind me.'

As it happened, I'd told my client that I wasn't planning to call him as a witness. So he decided not to come to court as it saved him having to take a day off work. This left a space behind my seat, and I motioned to the young barrister to sit there.

The proceedings began and the prosecution opened their case by calling their first and only witness, the copper who had stopped my client for speeding. As always, I was scrutinising every element of the proceedings, particularly the witness's behaviour, and when the police officer reached the point where he mentioned my client's name, I noticed that he gave a very slight inclination of his head towards the young barrister behind me. It was as if to say,

'I stopped your chap driving the car.' I couldn't believe it! He was pointing the finger at the wrong man. With supreme control I leant over to the young barrister and whispered something irrelevant into his ear such as, 'I hope this is all proving useful for you.' I then turned to the prosecutor and asked if he could ask the police officer to clarify who was driving.

'Of course,' said the copper. 'It was the man behind Mr Freeman.'

This was priceless. I immediately invited the court to retire in order to talk to my learned friend the prosecutor. With great relish I sidled up to my opposite number and said with poker-faced gravity, 'The person who has just been identified by your witness is actually a trainee barrister observing the case. Would you like to take a view?'

I won't repeat his expletive here, other than to say the case was abandoned, costs came from central funds, and it was good day for everybody. I then shook the hand of my observer, the young barrister, as he rose to leave.

'That was really useful, Mr Freeman, thanks a lot. I've learnt so much.'

Not as much as I've learnt from having you there, I thought to myself, as I wished him well with his career.

It's clear then that a great many loophole identification defences take root in human error. And it seems to me that establishing that you've got the right man, that you're feeling the right collar, is an especially grey area.

Mind you, the law doesn't help either. That's why defence lawyers have to test the system and make sure things are done properly. When a driver gets stopped by the police many officers assume that taking the person's name, address and date of birth is enough to enable them to finger the suspect. But prosecuting a motorist on the basis of such scant information seems to me absolute madness. If a copper hasn't ever seen his suspect before, how on earth could he possibly know the driver is who he says he is?

What this means is that a defence lawyer can then conduct a cross-examination in court in the following way:

'Officer, did you know the person who said he was Gary Smith when you pulled him over?'

'No, sir.'

'Have you ever met him before?'

'No, sir.'

'So did you ask for any other ID?'

'Erm, no, sir.'

'So, Officer, can you really be sure the person who said he was Gary Smith is in fact Gary Smith?'

This probably reads back like the kind of cross examination Basil Fawlty might dish up to a hapless hotel guest. But, believe it or not – and at times it is unbelievable – this is how the Crown can lose their case. If a policeman doesn't ask for some kind of concrete ID such as a driving licence with a photo, he leaves himself wide open to being unable to confirm identity.

Can you blame me then for becoming increasingly fired up about ways to find out as much as I could about undiscovered ID defences? Not an exciting prospect to many lawyers. There are probably more diverting ways to spend a Sunday afternoon. But by now I was on a quest and spent hours reading, thinking or chewing over the law. I was deep into this one weekend when my parents came to stay with me, and I jumped up in the middle of a family dinner because something had just occurred to me about a case I was working on and I had to get it down on paper. That's how it was, and still is – not always the best party manners. But my mission was unstoppable.

So it was that, while browsing through my law books one rainy afternoon, a rabbit sprang out of the hat. In fact I had to re-read it a few times to make sure I wasn't imagining it. In dry terms my textbook pointed out that, according to Section 122 of the Magistrates Court Act 1980, a client is not considered absent if their lawyer is present. Sex this up and what this little-known clause means is that a defence lawyer could fly solo, get on with the job of defending the case, without taking his client into court with him.

At first I thought, no, this can't be right. But there it was in print. And it was the law.

I was almost shaking with excitement (that's what loophole hunting does to me, and that's why I say that sometimes it's even better than sex – well, sometimes). I'd never heard of this before: batting for your client when they aren't even there. And yet what an incredible advantage this could be for the defence lawyer.

As I saw it, if the client wasn't there, then how could they be identified? Who could a witness point the finger at? It took only a short leap of the imagination to realise how difficult it would be for the Crown to have to prove the issue of ID. In principle it sounded like a perfect legal loophole. But could it work? The only way to find out was to cautiously test the theory.

So when I was asked to defend a rather striking-looking businessman for speeding it seemed the perfect opportunity. How can I describe this particular client? Well, he was swarthy, scrawny to the point of looking under-nourished, with a mop of curly chestnut hair and very 'strong' facial features. Not exactly film-star looks; more, shall we say, an acquired taste. But few people could forget a face like that, it was so distinctive.

The other thing to bear in mind, however, is that my

client's summons related to an offence alleged to have taken place almost three years before. Astonishingly, various administrative hiccups had delayed the case for what seemed like an eternity. With so much time having elapsed, could the officer who'd pulled him over really be expected to remember what my client looked like? That was even less likely if my client wasn't sitting in the courtroom with me. Not that I was doing this deliberately. I just wasn't intending to call him to give evidence, so why should he come to court?

Anyway, my client had business commitments which meant he couldn't be in court before 11am. But this had no bearing on the trial.

The case began and the prosecution called to the stand the police officer who had stopped my client. After the officer had given his account of the events of that night, I was on my feet with what I hoped would be white-hot ammunition.

'So, Officer, describe, if you could, my client's appearance,' I began.

An innocuous enough question, and one which the copper good-naturedly answered.

'Well, sir, he was six foot two, big muscles, blond hair, blue eyes. Extremely good-looking,' he explained.

I nodded amiably, pausing for a moment to check that this description had planted itself in the magistrates' collective imagination as they scribbled down his response.

Then, almost on cue, the doors at the back of the courtroom whispered open and my client slipped in. His meeting had finished. The timing was magnificent.

'Oh, Officer,' I continued, 'it seems my client has just arrived in court now. Do you think you could identify him for me?'

The witness looked bewildered. Well, of course he couldn't. There was no sign of some towering blond beefcake. The police officer shook his head.

So when it came to making my closing speech, I said, 'You've heard the officer's description of the suspect and he has also appeared before this court. He is five foot ten inches, has curly hair and a slim build. Not six foot two with blond hair, blue eyes and, with respect to my client, a powerful physique. Can you be sure, based on the evidence and beyond reasonable doubt, that he was driving? Of course you can't.'

My client walked, followed by one red-faced boy in blue.

In this case, what really juiced up my defence was the extremely lengthy delay between the date of the alleged offence and date of the trial. That's not something as a lawyer you can legislate for. It's a flaw in the system. The wheels of justice sometimes crank along at a snail's pace. But that in itself makes the ID loophole even more powerful. As I say, unless a police officer gets some pictorial or secure ID when he stops a suspect, he has to dredge his memory for the face behind the wheel – and be sure of his recollection. Otherwise how can he connect the suspect with the name on the charge sheet?

It's all about the police gathering, and the Crown producing, sufficient evidence for the court to be sure who was driving.

In the case of Ashley Ward, the police officer who pulled the driver over took his name, date of birth, address and occupation. Now, Ashley wasn't in court with me, and I asked the police officer giving evidence whether he could be sure that the man who provided Ashley Ward's details was in fact Ashley Ward.

'Could it have been someone else giving his details?' I queried.

The officer conceded that this was a possibility since he didn't recognise the driver and had no means of knowing it was Ashley Ward. Of course, had the officer got him to produce documentation that could confirm his identity at the roadside and had this been produced in court, then he wouldn't have had a problem. But he hadn't done so.

Despite video evidence which showed the car as it sped down the motorway, the district judge said that ID had not been proved and so threw the case out.

That said, I do wonder sometimes if cases that fold over the issue of identity owe as much to the misplaced eagerness of a police officer enthusiastically volunteering information about a defendant's appearance. Take the time I had to defend a well-known Premiership footballer down south for an alleged speeding offence. Actually my client was on international duty at the time it came to court, and since I didn't need him to be there, the case went ahead without him.

However, what I did need were certain documents relating to the case, and so my client's brother kindly brought them to court for me on the day of the trial, very courteously wearing a suit to do so, even though he wouldn't be coming into the courtroom itself. I was waiting in the corridor outside the courtroom, along with the police officer who had stopped my client on the night of the alleged offence, when my client's brother appeared with the relevant papers. I was glad to see him and we chatted pleasantly until the case began.

The Crown called as its first witness the police officer who had been waiting outside the court with me. Before long it was my turn to cross-examine him.

'Officer, how can you be sure the person you stopped that night was my client,' I began good-naturedly. The issue of identification – as in so many speeding cases – was to be central to my defence.

The officer allowed himself a thin smile. 'It was definitely him. Even though it was months ago. I'd still recognise him today.'

I looked at him, perplexed. He was almost suggesting he'd just seen him. Yes, my client was a famous sportsman, but even so . . .

And then the penny dropped. Of course! The policeman had seen me talking to my client's brother outside the court, drawn his own conclusions and assumed this was the man himself. I realised immediately that the officer had just handed me the lever to the trapdoor on which he had placed himself.

'What do you mean, Officer?' I said, bewildered.

'I saw you talking to him outside, Mr Freeman.'

At my side, my learned friend the Crown prosecutor drew an audible gust of breath, his expression one of abject horror. I was right. The policeman had got the wrong man, and, from left field, was about to drop an acquittal right in my lap.

'Are you saying the man you saw talking to me outside was the man who was driving?' I persisted.

My obliging witness confirmed it was, handing me a bat with which to smash the Crown's case to pieces. The prosecution had no choice but to throw out the case.

So, yes, defending my clients in their absence has been a very successful tactic. But it didn't exactly make me Mr Popular with other officers of the court. They thought I was at best taking the proverbial and at worst making a mockery of the courts. I'd constantly face prosecutors, magistrates and judges who thought they could stop me from proceeding without my client in tow.

I'll never forget one particular judge going ballistic when I turned up to defend a speeding case – alone.

No time for niceties with this particular member of the judiciary since we'd sparred before on many previous cases.

'Where's your client?' he barked on seeing that I was alone.

'Sorry, sir, he isn't here,' I responded calmly.

'Well, where is he, Mr Freeman?' he bit back, his tone going up a notch.

'I'm sorry, sir, does that have anything to do with the case? We can still go ahead.'

He looked at me with thinly veiled disgust. 'Where is your client?' he fumed.

'Sir,' I responded in a measured and polite tone, 'he's deemed not to be absent, as you surely must know, thanks to Section 122 of the Magistrates Court Act. Could we now please proceed?'

The judge clenched his fists as his face contorted with rage and frustration.

'Mr Freeman,' he almost screeched, 'I want to know where he is.'

'Sir, with the greatest of respect, my client's whereabouts are an irrelevance to these proceedings. I am ready to proceed.'

It seemed this was the final straw, because the judge went berserk and started shouting, 'I'm not doing this case until you bring your client in. How dare you. You tell me where he is right now!'

Oh dear. Quite clearly the man had momentarily lost all sense of reason. I wanted him off my case.

'Would you like to retire for a few minutes while I speak to your learned legal adviser?' I said, suggesting that this was in order to sort out the misunderstanding.

The judge didn't need telling twice and went steaming out of the court.

I went over to the court clerk, who had been watching what had happened with a mixture of bemusement and horror. I said, 'That judge isn't doing my trial. Based on his behaviour, he would be totally prejudicial. He is not entitled to know where my client is. I don't want him doing my case and I hope you agree.'

The clerk said she did. After all, she had just witnessed a spectacular tantrum by a member of the judiciary – and she'd also checked the law.

A few administrative changes having been made, my case went ahead in another court with another bench. My client was acquitted because the Crown couldn't prove ID. I was elated and went to the court canteen, where he'd been sitting all along nursing a cup of tea – waiting to hear if I needed him to give evidence or not.

What I found remarkable is that even though I repeatedly deployed this tactic, it took an eternity for the police to get into the habit of gathering sufficient evidence at the roadside so that they would be able to secure identification in court. As I said earlier, it simply boils down to this: have they got enough to say we know whodunit?

Sometimes there'd be the occasional rumble in the press after I'd won a case this way. This is what happened after Darren Ferguson, son of the legendary Manchester United boss Sir Alex, was cleared of travelling in his BMW at 98mph. Darren's no-show at Wrexham Magistrates Court meant that a traffic policeman was unable to identify him. Afterwards North Wales Police declared they were in high-level talks with the Crown Prosecution Service (CPS) about how to close this so-called loophole. They feared, in particular, that thanks to

the publicity surrounding the case, my strategy would be
aped and used again and again. As far as I'm aware, their
consultations never came to anything. Because I did go
on to use this loophole again and again.

It's one thing using the law to checkmate the constabulary.
But what about the robotic world of the speed camera?
These devices have taken away the frailty of human error
because they don't rely on a copper standing up in court
and giving the defence lawyer a chance to discredit him. Yet
in the battle of man versus machine, the law can still clobber the camera with a foolproof defence.

Actually the part of the law which relates to the identity
of drivers zapped by speed cameras is fairly clear-cut. As I
mentioned earlier, when you get flashed, the keeper will
receive a Section 172 form asking the recipient to either
confirm they were the driver or, if not, to name who was.
Failing to do this can net a fine and six penalty points or a
discretionary disqualification, as well as a fine. If, as the
keeper, you can't be sure whether it was you or your husband or wife who was driving last Thursday night, then
think hard. The law clearly states that the registered keeper
of the vehicle must have exercised 'reasonable diligence' or,
in simple terms, done his absolute best to discover the identity of the driver.

All pretty watertight? No scope for loopholes? Well, there
shouldn't be. But splice together an intricate knowledge of
the law with some errors in the prosecution case and you'd
be amazed how it's possible to ace a speed-camera case.

For example, if you are the registered keeper, and you get
a speeding notice, then you're the one who has to fill it in.
However, when I receive the paperwork on a case after
being instructed by a client, I go through it, as always, in

minute detail. And sometimes I'll discover that the wrong person has filled the form in.

This happened with my client Dwight York. The Manchester United star won an appeal against a fine and penalty points because he hadn't personally filled in the form declaring that he was behind the wheel of his Porsche 911 Turbo when he was caught doing 61mph in a 40mph zone in south Manchester. His agent had hurriedly filled in the form – the fact that it wasn't Dwight's signature was confirmed by handwriting analysis – because the player hadn't been around to do it himself. The prosecution failed to pick this up. To me, this meant the Crown couldn't prove, beyond reasonable doubt, who the driver was, since the confession had not come from the player himself.

Initially magistrates ignored my argument and fined Dwight £350, as well as ordering him to pay £1000 and endorsing his licence with four penalty points. I took the appeal to Manchester Crown Court, where the argument was also rejected. But ever since I was a small child I've refused to roll over if I think I'm right, and I wouldn't give up. So I took my case to the High Court. The judge there overturned the guilty verdict, accepting that the claim on the form, that Dwight York had been driving, could not be considered to be his own confession, without his signature.

It was an especially sweet victory for me, after being knocked back by both the magistrates and the Crown Court. The High Court ruling also made a very important point. It is not for a client – in this case a Premiership footballer – to come to court to be asked whether he was the driver after being flashed for speeding. It is for the prosecution to prove beyond reasonable doubt that he was, by producing the form with the driver's signature on. In this case they had not. In cases like this the Crown could instead slap a driver with a charge of failing to furnish – that is, not providing information. Then the driver would have no choice but to plead guilty. He hadn't provided the information, someone else did. That's a matter for prosecutors to consider. But in not doing so, they leave the way open for the ID loophole to get a speeding conviction overturned.

So identity is not just about who you are in the flesh but about the client confirming who he says he is. It's a subtlety, a loophole, that many lawyers overlook. But I think it's also vital to point out that you should never try it on with the courts by maintaining someone else was driving. Motorists often think that if they fudge the issue of who was behind the wheel when a speed camera flashes them, then they can avoid getting a fine and points on their licence. But providing false information is a very serious crime – one that almost inevitably leads to a custodial sentence.

Look no further than the allegations involving Liberal Democrate politician Chris Huhne, who is alleged to have asked his wife, economist Vicky Pryce to take the three points he faced after being caught speeding so he could avoid a driving ban. Miss Pryce's driving licence is clean apart from the 2003 offence at the centre of the furore.

So, if you get a speeding ticket and are genuinely unsure whether or not you were driving at the time, apply to the central ticket office for a photograph of the car from the speed camera involved. It may not always help, because sometimes, rather bizarrely, these cameras only take a rear view, which makes absolutely no sense as there's no way the driver can be identified. But it may be useful.

Remember, if you're the registered keeper, it's your legal duty to nominate who the driver was at the time of the alleged offence or provide such information as you are able that will lead to his or her identification. It might seem tempting for motorists to think they can duck a speeding charge by simply pleading they weren't behind the wheel. But in doing so they face a far greater penalty. Either take your medicine or get a decent lawyer.

Identity loopholes might sound complex – the form filling, the naming of drivers, the cameras, the photographs – but sometimes cases collapse because of the simplest failings. What astonishes me is that the Crown don't bank their errors to try to prevent them recurring.

This happened most notably when I was defending one of my golfing heroes, Colin Montgomerie, on a speeding charge. Now, a year before Monty's case, I had been in Staines Magistrates Court, south-west London, defending a client on a similar charge. The prosecutor went through all the evidence, but didn't produce any proof of who was driving – which has to be established by halfway through court proceedings. We got to half-time and I stood up and said, 'Your Worships, wouldn't you like to know who was driving?' as I raised a quizzical eyebrow at my opposite number. The prosecutor shrank a little in her seat. She hadn't asked her witnesses any questions that could pinpoint the identity of my client, such as their full name, address and date of birth. (In fact she had not even referred to my client's surname.) Instead she had assumed identity. Her doing so meant there was no evidence to prove who had been driving. The case was thrown out. She was a very nice woman actually, and I felt a little sorry for her, because she clearly felt humiliated.

A year later I was back in the same court, this time to defend Monty. When I arrived for the trial that morning, I did a double take. Prosecuting the case was the same lawyer I'd embarrassed twelve months before. I already knew there was no way I could argue identification as the officer who stopped Monty had recognised him. And when I saw this same prosecutor it really confirmed that I couldn't put the prosecution to proof on identification. After she'd been so badly burned by me last time, surely she must have done her homework and been ready to settle that score.

I went to introduce myself to the prosecutor and she instantly remembered me. We exchanged pleasantries and she then advised me that she had a problem: one of her police officers would not be attending as he was due to give evidence at the Crown Court. Fifty per cent down. Excellent, I thought, more than happy to proceed with just one officer, and I confirmed her view that she didn't need him as he wasn't the officer who had conducted the check. She agreed and we proceeded. There was certainly no need for an adjournment.

I did have a clutch of other defences. (I'd been tempted, though, to say to his agent several weeks before the case that the best thing Monty could do was sink the winning putt in the Ryder Cup. Surely no one would have the heart to convict a national hero?) As we prepared to start I pondered which defence might give me the best shot at winning.

Once we got started I listened intently to the prosecutor call her only witness, the copper who had pulled Monty over. As she began to question him the most astonishing thing happened. The police officer simply identified the golf ace as 'Mr Montgomerie'. No full name, address or date of birth. Just 'Mr Montgomerie', plain and simple. My learned friend didn't even ask for his first name. In other words the prosecutor was slipping up in a way that was similar to what she had done a year before when she hadn't proved the identity of the driver.

I opted to move to my closing speech and got straight to the point.

'Well, Your Worships, you've heard Mr Montgomerie was driving, and that's fascinating. But I'm sure there are lots of Mr Montgomeries in this country. So which one are we talking about? We don't have his full name. What about his address? Or date of birth?'

No one had made reference to these details. Out of the corner of my eye I could see the prosecutor slumping in her bench. But this was no time for chivalry. I continued apace: 'In my mind there is insufficient evidence for the court to be satisfied beyond reasonable doubt that Mr Colin Montgomerie, the defendant before you today, was driving.' That was it: case not proved. Deathly silence from the prosecutor, a quick 'Good day, madam' to my mortified opponent, and off we went. Oh, and we were awarded costs too.

Identity defences are opportunities to really test the system. And I've always been an opportunist. In a court of law that translates as being alive to the paucity of evidence, to every remark or gesture made by one of the courtroom players.

As I digested the events afterwards on my long drive home, I thought about the prosecutor. How could she have let that happen again? Since she'd lost a case on this point a year before, you'd think that when the same issue arose, if she was a lawyer who was taking her job seriously, she wouldn't make the same mistake twice. I know we're all human (though sometimes I'm accused of not being!). But I take the reverse view. When I net an acquittal that has been triggered by an unforeseen opportunity, I bank the tactic, ready to use it again when I can.

As for making mistakes myself, the only way I get over them is by learning from them – after no small amount of self-flagellation – making damn sure they don't happen again.

Yet, in fairness, the prosecutor in Monty's case wasn't the only one throwing away a case by not using a defendant's full name. It happened frequently. And I always pounced. As I did in a case involving a businessman doing 175mph in a souped-up motor. Now, in this instance the stakes were particularly high as my client faced prison if convicted: as well as being summonsed with speeding he also faced a dangerous-driving rap and had several previous convictions.

What's more, I worked out that the officer who'd stopped him had done all the necessary checks to prove his identity. When a speeding offence happens on a motorway, the law states that all you need for a conviction is for a police officer to express an opinion that the driver was going too quickly – there doesn't need to be any corroboration.

As usual I had various defences at my fingertips: perhaps the speeding device was faulty or there'd been a failure to follow some kind of procedure at the roadside?

But as the officer entered the witness box to give his evidence, it happened again. He made the critical mistake of simply referring to my client as 'Mr X', just using his surname without referring to his full name, address or date of birth, or to any ID checks he'd done. Maybe the prosecution should have guided him better. But they didn't, leaving the officer to skim over the facts.

When the magistrates adjourned after the Crown rested, the script was almost a repeat of the Colin Montgomerie case. Again I approached the clerk. 'Am I missing something? Did the prosecutor refer only to a "Mr X"? And if so, couldn't this be any "Mr X"?'

The clerk agreed he had and it could. I parked all my other defences and opted to go straight to a quick closing speech. It didn't matter how fast the guy was going: the Crown need to establish who was driving. They didn't.

They could have done, but they didn't. No checks? Checkmate.

What's even more ridiculous is that I'd actually seen the officer's notes detailing the incident and the information he'd taken at the roadside. But because these details hadn't been read out during the hearing, the court hadn't heard sufficient evidence to convict my client.

Identity isn't just about drivers or passengers – real people. It can relate to cars too, and herein lies another loophole. Let me take you back to a dark night on the M6 when a couple of traffic cops were alerted to the roar of an engine before seeing someone tearing off at what seemed to be great speed in an Audi RS6 – a fairly rare car – which displayed an equally rare Guernsey number plate. The officers temporarily lost sight of the car before they eventually snagged my client. It was then that they were able to read the vehicle's number plate for the first time and my client was reported for speeding.

In court everything seemed to motor along fairly uneventfully until I lobbed my hand grenade. I asked one of the traffic cops, 'Do you know for a fact that there was only one Audi RS6 with a Guernsey plate on the M6 at that time of day?'

He looked at me blankly and said he didn't. In all likelihood there probably was just the one. But could the Crown prove that beyond reasonable doubt? Not a chance. My client was acquitted.

So, knowing that a case refers to the right car can be as vital as pinpointing the right person. Cars can present difficulties, though, since they may well roar past before they can be properly identified.

Thankfully, British motorways aren't often the scene of dangerous high-speed car chases. But when the police do high-tail it after a speeder, it's possible that they lose their prey – and, more significantly, sight of their number plate – for a few seconds. If they haven't had a chance to jot down the registration but eventually catch up with the speeder, who's to say they've got the right car? One black Porsche looks very much like the next.

This is where the law offers yet another choice identity loophole. Without a registration number to identify a car, all an officer can say in court is something like, 'I lost sight of the speeding car for a few seconds. I didn't see another car on the road that looked in any way similar. So I assumed this was the defendant when I finally pulled him over.' Not only is this kind of evidence far from watertight: it leaks with doubt. And the client could walk.

I remember one speeding case where the traffic cop in the dock said he'd been following the driver at a constant speed of 90mph on the M55 and that he had been approximately 100 yards behind the car when he had actually logged his speed (what's known as a speed check). To me, this was nonsensical. If the police had been that close to the car, my client would have spotted the police car and stopped. During further cross-examination the officer actually admitted that my client's car had revved up and sped away after the speed check. I could feel a loophole opening up.

I asked the officer, 'If you were concerned you might lose him, did you radio ahead with all the identification marks?'

'Yes, Mr Freeman,' he affirmed enthusiastically. Misplaced enthusiasm, as it would turn out.

I began to close the net. 'So there'll be a tape somewhere, Officer, of your conversation with HQ relaying this.'

The witness looked slightly uncomfortable, shifted on the spot and said, 'Yes, there is.'

So I invited the prosecution to produce this tape, which they did. When it was played the officer could be heard saying, 'I'm driving along the M55 and in the distance I can see a Porsche speeding. I can't tell you the colour or reg. I'm losing it and I'm doing 120mph.'

So much for being 100 yards behind my client. That was the end of the case.

So far I've talked about identifying the right driver or the right car. But there's another rather juicy loophole that the law hands out – and that's connecting the right driver *and* the right car. This isn't about forms or administration. It's about establishing whether the physical proximity of a car to a client in any way establishes guilt. Often it doesn't.

I once defended a police officer who turned up for work reeking of booze. He was immediately asked to hand over his car keys, and a breath test at the station confirmed that he was more than twice the legal limit.

However, in court I argued that no one could prove my client had actually driven to work, since not one of his colleagues had seen the car arrive. I also told the court that the police had never proved the keys my client had handed over were the ones to his car. The magistrates not only agreed with me, but my client was even awarded costs. On every level a result, simply by using the law.

Though I'm sorry to say this, even after all these years of defending road-traffic cases, I'm still flabbergasted at how the police trip themselves up over such basic identity issues. In fact there's a whole world of ways in which the prosecuting authorities make unnecessary mistakes and we'll come to these later in the book. But, for now, let me give you just another example of how a case can fold because the police failed on something as simple as establishing identity.

I had a client, a top-flight business executive, who had been charged with speeding in a 30mph zone. He already had penalty points on his licence and if things went badly he was in jeopardy of losing his licence. As I began my cross-examination I asked the officer on the case if he was familiar with the details of my client.

'Yes, Mr Freeman, I was because I checked when he was stopped.'

'How did you check?'

'Well, sir, I looked at his licence.'

A chink immediately opened up. 'So, you looked at the photo on his driving licence and then at the man who was driving and satisfied yourself that they were one and the same person?'

'Yes, sir.'

As any advocate will admit – though some under duress – we're none of us immune to the theatrical possibilities of the courtroom. In fact I like to use them to full advantage. So, displaying all the panache of a B-list movie star (or rather a seasoned turn with the local amateur dramatics club), I reached into my briefcase and with a flourish produced my client's licence. I saw a pulse leap in the officer's neck as he swallowed hard.

'Officer,' I continued smoothly as the licence was passed to the ashen-faced copper. 'Look at this document and tell Your Worships what you can see before you.'

'It's a driving licence,' he stammered.

'Ye-es,' I continued with Oscar-winning patience. 'Now then, would it be one of the new-style licences with a photograph of its owner, or one of the original licences that don't carry a picture?'

'The old style,' he replied hoarsely.

I'm not a sadist – even though it can be tempting to make

the constabulary squirm when they are being so manifestly untruthful. Instead I simply asked the officer if he accepted that he'd been mistaken. That he'd thought my client's licence had a picture on it.

He nodded dumbly, at which point the prosecutor stood up and offered no evidence. And we all went home – in my case to prepare for the next trial the following day.

As I said at the beginning of this chapter, identity is the downfall of so many cases, be it accidents, drink-driving or any other number of crimes. Many times I pounce on these loopholes, string them up to show that the Crown can't prove their case and trudge off to my next port of call.

However, there have been times when identification can make it almost impossible to defend or prosecute success-fully. It's times like this when I'm grateful that, though I can only operate within the law, it is for others to use their wisdom to reach a judgment based on the legal arguments I bring to the table.

One case that has long stayed with me concerned a teen-age client who'd been involved in a car accident which had killed his best friend. When the police arrived at the scene and discovered my client's vehicle in a ditch, they found both boys had been thrown from the car. One, tragically, had been killed. The other – my client – was unconscious and would remain in a coma for several weeks.

In court the judge heard that there were no seatbelt inju-ries to suggest who the driver had been. My client owned the car and was the registered keeper but sometimes let his friend drive it.

In the fog of post-accident amnesia, my client nudged slowly from his coma, genuinely unable to remember who had been driving on that terrible day. It was more likely to have been him – it was his car – but he couldn't be sure. His memory loss placed him in an excruciating position, and he was distraught. My young client had just lost his lifelong best friend. What's more, what had caused the accident was a mystery. It had happened on a straight, remote, rural road. Yet the car, for some reason, had somehow hit a tree and ended up in a ditch, throwing the two occupants clear.

As you can imagine, the families of both of these young men were overcome with grief, anger and bitterness. From being old friends, they were now at war. I could sympathise with the other side. They were reeling from their bereavement.

But as a lawyer I had to focus on the issue of identification to defend my client. And so I pressed ahead with my argument. To put it simply, my client probably had been the driver but there was no evidence to prove, beyond reasonable doubt, that this was the case. However, even if he was the driver, there was a second prong to my legal argument (my client was charged with driving without due care and attention). Had he taken some kind of evasive action? Was that why the car had skidded?

With this case I struggled to set aside the immense human tragedy so that I could take a broader view, focusing instead on what on earth could have caused such a catastrophic accident.

I've always been a great lover of the countryside, and go walking in Wales or the Lake District whenever I can. Also I live in quite a rural area and am used to having to anticipate pheasants and other wildlife scooting across the road. And that's what set me thinking. Could the driver have swerved to avoid a bird or an animal?

I know from personal experience that it's not always possible to avoid hitting these creatures. I remember once driving towards Calais late one evening, at the end of a holiday in France, when a pair of cat's eyes suddenly glowered out of the gloom as a dark and tiny animal went scampering across the central reservation. I had seen it ahead of me, but I knew that I had to hold the car steady because if I swerved there could be a disastrous accident. It went against my every animal-loving instinct, but I had no choice. Though I was travelling at speed, those critical seconds stretched before me in eerie slow motion and I hit the cat.

Knowing what I'd done, I didn't stop until I reached the Channel Tunnel, where a station guard pointed to the blood, gore and fur spattered on the car's grille. It was the remains of a cat. I couldn't bear to look and when I got home I took the car straight to a garage and asked them to valet it from the inside out.

I think it was a combination of these thoughts and experiences that led me to ponder which way to approach this difficult, tragic case.

The scene of the crash may have been an isolated country lane, but there would have been an abundance of wildlife lurking around its margins. Maybe the driver – whoever he was – had swerved to avoid a rabbit or a bird? It was possible. And, though it sounds brutally clinical, in legal terms it was a powerful hypothesis. By raising the possibility of a cause of the accident, the Crown would have no choice but to try to negate it beyond reasonable doubt.

And so, as the day of the trial dawned, I had two defences to fight my case: a) there was no evidence to say who the driver was, and b) even if my client had been driving it was possible that something external had triggered the crash.

As I explored my legal arguments during cross-examination, the family of the dead boy glowered at me with undisguised disgust. Of course, I could understand their anger and pain. The tension between the two families was stretched to breaking point. But I had to be a lawyer to my client. All I could hope for was that the judge – in this case an experienced and thoughtful member of the judiciary – would make the right call. It's all very well looking for loopholes within the law, but it's down to the court to decide whether they're of value or not.

In this case the judge, to my mind, displayed the wisdom of Solomon. In declaring his verdict he began by saying that he found as a fact that there was an injury to my client's shoulder which, despite expert evidence to the contrary, was consistent with a seatbelt. That would point the finger at my client as being the driver. However, the judge then added, 'I also find it possible that this accident happened as a consequence of no fault of the defendant and that he may well have swerved to avoid an animal. So I find him not guilty.'

The judge's words floated through the still air of the courtroom and settled slowly on all of us. I think we all needed a moment to digest his analysis. Of course, as a lawyer I was glad I had successfully defended my client. But I was deeply impressed by the way the judge had framed his decision. My client was driving but the accident was quite literally a freak of nature. In arriving at this conclusion, the judge therefore gave both families closure and at least a starting point from which to move on.

And so, as this and many of my cases have shown, the issue of whodunit remains the gateway to so many legal loopholes. Things are changing. Police officers, by and large, are starting to remember to ask for photographic ID when they pull a motorist over. They can also do a Police National Computer (PNC) check on the car and establish if the defendant is the registered keeper, which is potentially another piece of evidence.

But even if the Crown is starting to fortify itself against identity loopholes, it's possible an eagle-eyed lawyer, with sleuth-like tenacity, may still be able to find a way to conduct an investigation and capitalise on the mistakes of others.

Fighting a case on the basis of identification, or pointing the finger and establishing whodunit, says as much about the skill or knowledge of the lawyer as it does about the weakness of other players in the courtroom drama. If your lawyer knows his law and the prosecution or constabulary don't, it's an explosive combination. As I wrote at the beginning of this chapter, throw in human error – the fact that we're all vulnerable to making mistakes about people's names and faces – and there's every opportunity to ambush the Crown simply by using the law.

I'll never forget defending a dog owner who was being prosecuted for not keeping his pet under control: the German Shepherd had been accused of killing sheep on a farm in the Derbyshire countryside. The farmer making the accusation claimed he'd discovered the bloodied, lifeless lambs in a field and a German Shepherd scampering away from the scene. He immediately raced after it, keeping the dog, he claimed, in constant view, until it came to a halt at the doorway of a large county cottage. Assuming this was its owner's home, the irate farmer rapped on the door to level his accusation.

Now, setting aside the fact that I am a huge dog lover, I realised after visiting the 'scene' of the crime and following the route the farmer maintained he'd taken, that he could have got the wrong dog. After all, the area in which he gave chase embraced a skyline of bruise-coloured hills. Even if the farmer had spotted the dog running off, he couldn't keep it in his vision the entire time. So by the time he caught up with *a dog*, how could he be sure it was the same dog he'd seen galloping away from the sheep? What's more another German Shepherd was also said to live in the area.

Having done a 'recce' and reached this conclusion, I invited the bench to don their wellies and wax jackets and join me on a field trip – literally – to understand for themselves that an element of doubt lingered over the credibility of the farmer's testimony. Off we trooped into the countryside where the magistrates assessed the crime scene. They agreed the undulating terrain would make it impossible to positively ID the right German Shepherd. So the dog – and its owner – walked.

So you see, ID is essentially about deconstructing a case and looking at its component parts – whatever those parts may be and however they may or may not lead to cases of mistaken identity.

And speaking of parts, let me finish this chapter with one case I had which hinged on another form of ID – identifying body parts. It's not gruesome, though the more genteel among you may choose to look away.

The case involved a university student who faced an allegation of indecently displaying his person with intent to assault a female (quite a mouthful, so colloquially known as indecent exposure). He was from a well-to-do family and they felt the outcome of his case looked rather bleak. Not the view of a defence lawyer who takes a case apart.

Here's what happened at the time of the alleged offence. One evening a member of the university staff had been using a payphone reserved for the disabled. The phone was situated at 'wheelchair height', so she had to crouch down to make her call. This woman claimed my client had approached her, revealed his person (the legal term for penis) and then used it to make indecent gestures over her head. He was duly charged with what's commonly known as indecent exposure.

My client's version was quite different. He had been terribly drunk, paid a trip to the Gents and then afterwards failed to zip up his trousers properly, leaving his testicles partially, ahem, exposed. The reason he was waving his hands around his 'person' was that in his inebriation he was fighting a losing battle to locate his zip and pull it up.

The defence I prepared hinged on three specific points, all of which had to be proved beyond reasonable doubt.

The first point was an ID issue, and a fairly delicate one at that. The court papers referred to my client as exposing his penis. He claimed that it was his testes. Could the Crown be sure beyond reasonable doubt that they could ID his anatomy?

The second point was that this crime requires specific intent. My argument was that my client was so drunk he couldn't possibly have been able to have had that intent.

The third point was that not only did my client not intend to insult the woman, but he had immediately said sorry and went on to send her a fulsome letter of apology. Hardly the actions of a sexual maverick.

In court that day there were three lady magistrates, and both the prosecutor and court clerk were also women. Not the easiest audience when it came to discussing such delicate anatomical matters! In my head, it seemed at times like some kind of surreal *Carry On* film, or a naughty seaside postcard. But we were all very professional about it. The Crown couldn't prove their case. My client was acquitted. I'd love to know on what grounds.

* * *

I'm particularly satisfied with the cases I've won using identification. But before my ego gets a little over-inflated, it's worth acknowledging that since making a name for myself in the public eye, I tussle with identification almost daily. As I said earlier, I get stopped in all sorts of places, and at times I've even been confused with *X Factor* judge Simon Cowell!

But perhaps my most embarrassing reminder of the uncertainty of identification happened when I represented the *EastEnders* actor Dean Gaffney in Leamington Spa. On the day of the trial he brought a friend with him whom he introduced to me as Omar. I couldn't help but notice that Omar was wearing a pair of very tight jeans which show-cased a not so easily hidden talent.

At lunch we popped out for a sandwich and Omar and I were standing outside the shop while Dean went inside. Despite having defended so many well-known faces, I still couldn't believe how many people recognised me. Motorists drove past tooting their horns and waving, while people across the road were pointing me out to their friends. I had no idea I was so well known in Leamington Spa and I was smiling and waving back until eventually I realised that it wasn't me they were waving at. It was Omar.

It transpired that he was a very famous international porn star. Suddenly a very attractive young lady ran over and said to Omar, 'Can I have your autograph?' After he'd signed one for her she turned to me and said, 'You look familiar, I'm sure I've seen you somewhere before.'

'You may well have done,' I beamed. 'My name's Nick Freeman.'

'Are you a porn star as well?' she asked doubtfully.

'No, he's not,' Omar quickly intervened. 'He's Mr Loophole, the celebrity lawyer.'

'Oh right,' she said, with evidence of disinterest, before turning to walk away.

A bit crushing really as it would have been my first autograph. The one time when my ego would really have liked to have offered proof of ID. Clearly we lawyers just can't compete with porn stars . . . .

6

Loophole: don't talk unless you can improve the silence – or the defence

Most people love to talk. Especially about their favourite subject: themselves. So the simplest way to make conversation with a stranger (or even spin a chat-up line) is to ask about their life, their work, their family. That way they're on home turf and it's easier for them to open up.

Most human beings – even the strong, silent types – are hard-wired to offer chapter and verse whenever the opportunity arises. Everywhere you go, there's an overwhelming urge for people to talk, talk and then talk some more.

Yet despite all this chattiness, many people seem unable to reply to a simple question with a direct answer. Maybe I'm turning into a grumpy old man, but it drives me crackers. Especially since I'm always being cornered and asked for on-the-spot legal advice – regardless of where I am. Only the other week I was playing golf with a chap who mentioned in conversation that he'd been done for speeding.

'How fast were you going?' I replied absent-mindedly, as I really wanted to focus on my next shot.

'Well,' he began, 'I used to drive a Ferrari, but I sold that because what I really wanted was a Porsche. Though, to be honest, I'll probably change it for an Aston Martin . . .'

And on he went. It was like a verbal version of the BBC's *Top Gear* – but without Clarkson's biting wit. The torrent of words seemed unstoppable. Why can't you get to the bloody point, I thought to myself, as he rambled on and on about his motoring history.

I'm not blessed with a lot of patience and in the end I cut across him mid-flow and – since I knew him well enough to do this – rasped, 'Sorry if it was a difficult question. All I asked was how fast you were going, not for a list of every car you've ever owned.' He sheepishly apologised and never said another word. At least I was able to play my round in peace. Irony was, had he got to the point I might have been able to help him!

It seems that for some people getting to the point is harder than getting to the North Pole. The programming is set on 'waffle'. So, if you get accused of doing something wrong, anything wrong, is it any wonder that instinct urges you to speak out, address the claims, tell your side of the story? Instead of just saying, 'So sorry for not phoning you, darling' or 'I didn't mean to be late for dinner with your parents', there's an inclination to go into meticulous detail in order to mitigate your misdemeanour.

It's no different when the offence involved is a criminal one rather than the lesser transgression of keeping the in-laws waiting. When a person stands accused of committing a crime, their natural reaction is to race to a solicitor and pour out every last syllable. And if TV courtroom dramas are anything to go by, the wise and sober lawyer will listen carefully, chewing thoughtfully on the end of a pencil or scribbling notes on his legal pad while his client gives his version of the alleged offence. And in general this is what tends to happen. Most clients want to tell their solicitor the whole story. And most solicitors feel it's their duty to listen. After all, isn't that what they're paid to do?

So when the lawyer calls the client into his office and begins by asking, 'Why did you get in the car when you'd been drinking?', he's likely to be in for a long, meandering narrative. It'll be something along the lines of, 'Well, it all started last Thursday when I realised I'd run out of milk.' No wonder office furniture companies do brisk business supplying law firms with comfy chairs.

However, unlike many other lawyers, the starting point for me does not lie with my client's account of the events in question. I don't want to spend hours listening to their version of what they did or didn't do. I just want to look at the prosecution papers and be left alone to see if the Crown have done their job properly. Only when I have trawled through the Crown evidence and when it seems to me that everything is procedurally in order will I dial the client's number.

Now, your natural reaction might understandably be that this sounds an absurd way to practise law. And unapologetically arrogant to boot.

If you've just been stopped for drink-driving and are about to dig into your pockets to pay a lawyer to fight your case, you want to be in their office, unburdening yourself of every detail. But, trust me, it doesn't help. In fact it can be a case of putting the cart before the horse. It isn't the right approach. And solicitors who think otherwise are missing something. When a client rings up and says they have a problem, what I do is politely interject with something like, 'Do you mind if I stop you there? I know you want to tell me all about it, but just hold your fire. Send me your papers, let me get hold of all the Crown evidence [everything the prosecution rely on to prove their case]. Once I've gone through it I'll give you my opinion and then take your instructions.'

The advantage of working this way is that you may never need the client's instructions because the Crown have to prove their case. A client could spend two hours giving me their version of events (including all those riveting narrative extras such as why they were going to Tesco on a Tuesday instead of a Wednesday). But if, say, the prosecution paperwork is defective – something which, as we'll see in chapter eight, happens frequently – then I don't need instructions from my client. There may be mistakes which range from the insignificant to the significant and even to those that are fatal. At that stage, that's all I want to focus on.

By not talking to your client first, they save a lot of time and money. When I take a case, I want to focus on the real issues. If they're already lurking in the court papers, why would I want to spend hours talking to my client about things I don't need to? It's not doing the client any favour. I only want to speak to him if it will help him and me. Remember, the foundation principle of justice in this country is the presumption of innocence – the fabled innocence until proven guilty. The Crown have to prove their case. And there could be a whole assortment of defects in the paperwork alone that might stop them from doing that.

There's also another very good reason for avoiding the client. It stops you being compromised. How so? Well, best really to explain by example. So here's a typical scenario. A young lad turns up at his lawyer's office charged with driving while disqualified. He's madly agitated and clutching fistfuls of court papers. It's obvious he's itching to tell his story. However, what I would do in that kind of situation is head off his long and winding account as I want to tell him how I operate. In other words, no story-telling yet, thank you very much.

Clearly crestfallen, the young lad blurts out, 'But the

thing is, I've been banned, so I need you to say I wasn't driving even though I was.'

Thanks very much, I think. Inordinately helpful of you to compromise me by your admission. For in doing this I am now severely limited in how I conduct the case. I can't call the lad to give evidence – even if I was thinking of doing so – as it could lead to a criminal offence being committed by both of us. If he were to take the stand, inevitably he'd be asked whether he was driving the car. And inevitably he would deny it in an attempt to exculpate himself. Not only would this be perjury – since he'd be lying on oath – it would also be perverting the course of justice. Furthermore, it limits my scope in cross-examining police officers because I can't suggest something that I know, as a consequence of my client's instructions, to be untrue.

So I give this lad a choice. 'Either go and see another solicitor or let me put the Crown to proof on the basis of their evidence. But you cannot give evidence and I can't suggest that you weren't driving. It's up to you.'

The lad frowns at me for a nanosecond, then says, 'I want you to defend me.'

'But do you understand what I'm saying? I cannot call you to give evidence.'

With a shrug of disappointment, the lad says, 'Whatever. Can you just defend me?'

As it happens, it's quite hard for the Crown to prove the defendant is a disqualified driver. In much the same way as I explained with identity issues earlier, the prosecution have to prove that the man who stands before the court is in fact the man who was disqualified on the last occasion. Is it a Gary Smith or *the* Gary Smith? So it may well be that in this kind of scenario, despite the client's over-enthusiastic ideas about how I should defend him, I may well still win the case. It's not my job to prove he wasn't disqualified – it's the Crown's to prove he was. But that aside, the scenario illustrates how any legal foreplay with your client may well be a burden rather than a bonus.

Naturally, not every client would be quite so forgiving about being told that I wouldn't go near their attempts to pervert the course of justice.

I once had a drink-driving case and about two weeks before the trial the client came to see me, handing over a list of prescription drugs he claimed he'd been taking at the time of the offence. He hadn't mentioned any of this in his statement but pleaded forgetfulness. Well, I wasn't terribly impressed by his credibility, so I told him I'd like to get an expert to corroborate this. He then told me that he'd like to remove two of the drugs he had just mentioned from his account. 'Let's just say I never took those.' Well, I simply cannot represent someone who chops and changes their evidence. So I told the man that I was no longer prepared to act for him. 'Why the hell not?' he barked.

'Because I have been professionally compromised,' I replied smoothly.

His face contorted with rage. 'What do you mean? I can tell you whatever I want. You're my lawyer.'

That old chestnut: my tab, my version of the story.

'No you can't,' I retorted firmly. 'In my view, you are changing your instructions at the outset. I am accepting your explanation late on and have been generous. However, having given me a list in writing of the medication you are taking, you have then told me to forget the last two items on there. I am not happy at all. You'll have to go and see someone else, thank you.'

The guy's voice cranked up a few decibels, fury bleeding

into his words. 'I'm going to report you,' he threatened as he jumped up to leave.

'Feel free – here's the address of the Solicitors Regulation Authority.' I paused. 'Of course, I will have to explain to them why I couldn't continue to act. Now, if you wouldn't mind closing the door on your way out, thank you.'

I stopped myself asking him not to bang the door, but he gave it a good slam anyway.

Though such delightful exchanges are rare, you can understand why I don't get involved with clients unless I absolutely have to. I rely on an old Vermont proverb: 'Don't talk unless you can improve the silence.'

In fact, on many occasions I've defended cases where I've never even met the client. This particularly happens with minor road-traffic cases such as speeding. I tell them rather pleasantly that I don't need them but, if they don't have to be at work that day, could they try to be somewhere nearby? That way, if something unexpected comes up and I need them to give evidence or perhaps if I'm going to argue exceptional hardship in the face of a disqualification, they're only a gnat's whisker away from the court.

Happily, though, on many occasions the case goes my way and I ring the client to say we've won. And even though they're nursing a cappuccino round the corner sometimes I don't even get to see them because I have another case. What then often happens is that, delighted by the acquittal, they'll say something like, 'Thanks, Mr Freeman, we'd love to meet you, just to shake your hand.' But, inevitably, I've already got another case lined up and I have to apologise as I'm off to another court to do the same thing all over again. It's not arrogance, just the occupational hazard of having a lot of miles and cases to cover. Instead I tell them, 'I'm pleased you've won, enjoy yourself and drive carefully. I hope – and I mean this in the nicest possible way – that our paths don't cross again. I'll drop you a line when I receive a cheque from the court.'

Most lawyers will tell you that the moment you put your client in the dock, the case starts to go downhill.

Why?

Well, however much you try to warn a client about how nerve-racking giving evidence can be – and I'll come back to this later – the fact is that standing in that dock can be terrifying. There's usually a lot at stake and it can affect the way the client speaks or gives their account. Their throat goes dry, words tumble out in a tangle, facts may get mistakenly jumbled up. By not calling your client to give evidence, you rob the prosecution of the chance to enjoy open season with a nervous defendant.

On the other hand, if a defence lawyer takes the view that the prosecution have failed to mount a decent case, they may make a submission that there is 'no case to answer' – that is where there is a duty to stop the case at that stage, where the evidence taken at its highest is such that a reasonable judge or bench, properly directed could not properly convict of the offence. This takes place at the halfway point in a trial, between the prosecution case and the defence case.

Well, most defence lawyers would do this. My tactics are slightly different. After the close of the prosecution case, I generally elect not to make a submission of 'no case to answer'. Instead I make a closing speech, which severely limits the power of the prosecution to repair the damage I cause by revealing holes in their case. This ratchets up the burden of proof which the Prosecution has to discharge as in order to convict, then, in simple terms, the court must be sure of guilt.

Let me explain why I love closing speeches. It's that beautiful moment in a case when it boils down to pure advocacy. You can throw away your notes, stand on your feet and just speak (and this is one situation where it is good to talk!). It's an opportunity to give your case the hard sell, homing in on all those wonderful technicalities and anomalies that may demolish the Crown case.

What's more, from a tactical perspective the burden of proof is much higher at the end of a closing speech. By recapitulating the facts, evidence and testimony presented during the trial, you can deal a fatal blow while limiting how the Crown can respond.

I suppose in some respects clients are part of the troops and I'm the general. I'll have thought of my strategy from every angle and argued with myself over the likely response to my every move. You need to see it from start to finish before you put your troops into action. I think to myself, should I talk to the prosecutor or legal adviser beforehand – is it worth it? I may have something that could cause this case to collapse, and if the prosecutor is someone I can talk to, better to get him onside from the start before the trial begins. This may also, again, negate any need for the client to testify.

I remember going down to Epping Magistrates Court to defend film director Matthew Vaughn after he was alleged to have done 95mph on the M11. The first time I met him was at the case. Actually, since he is a director and spends so much time behind the camera, I only recognised him because he'd been photographed in the papers with his supermodel wife, Claudia Schiffer.

Before the trial began I went to have a chat with the prosecutor. I could see immediately that he was a decent chap, one I could talk to. He had a firm handshake, a warm smile and a very obliging manner. So I told him that my argument hinged on a breach of police guidelines and asked whether he wanted to go through it before we went into court. He was quite amenable to this and realised, as I outlined my defence, that I had enough to demolish the Crown's case. So he agreed to bin it. Matthew, by all accounts, went off a very happy man. He told reporters afterwards, 'I'm over the moon. I've been cleared by one of the best lawyers in England.' Most kind, since we'd only met for the first time that morning.

So there are many advantages to not getting embroiled in long conversations with the client. Sometimes, though, it's not so easy to stay so far removed. I remember once defending a rabbi who had been charged with doing a u-turn on a motorway slip road. We were pleading guilty to what was an unusual offence with serious potential consequences.

Now, being Jewish myself, though admittedly not much of a practitioner, I did feel a great deal of respect for this good man (though obviously not for his driving skills). I wanted to give him my personal attention. I've always been proud of my Jewish heritage and, believe it or not, around the time of my bar mitzvah even thought fleetingly of becoming a rabbi myself – though this probably had more to do with my teenage crush on the rabbi's daughter

Anyway, I looked at the papers and there was no way round it. He was facing an almost certain disqualification. In that situation I couldn't find a breach in the Crown's case, so it was then that I turned my attention to the client instead. As would later come out in court, my client explained that he'd done the u-turn because he was preoccupied and had gone down the slip road by mistake.

Though the rabbi was entering a guilty plea, my job was to try to prevent a ban being slapped on him. My intention was to tell magistrates when the case came to court why the rabbi needed to drive: his work involved visiting the sick, the bereaved or indeed anyone who needed him. He had to conduct wedding services and funerals and attend circumcisions. This was a spiritual life on the road. I wanted the court to appreciate that this was a man of good character.

With a head crammed with all these arguments I met my client a few weeks later at Bury Magistrates Court in Greater Manchester. In fact he was waiting for me when I got there. Now magistrates courts aren't exactly the most salubrious of places to hang around, for obvious reasons. I felt bad that a rabbi should be left to wait outside the court with the pick and mix of characters lurking around the grim corridors. So I managed to secure him an interview room where he could wait for his case to be called.

As I guided him in, he suddenly grasped my arm and began pouring out why he'd done what he'd done and how it had affected him. All of which he'd already told me. I wanted to be respectful but I had to think about the case. In a few moments I was going to be standing before the court. I needed my wits about me. Yet all I could hear was this continuous, angst-ridden stream of sorrow. I just couldn't stem the flow of the rabbi's narrative. He talked about how he'd been unable to sleep, suffered sickness and diarrhoea and . . . I won't go on. But *he* did.

This verbal tsunami was of absolutely no benefit to the case and, as his lawyer, I didn't need to hear it two minutes before I was due to be on my feet in the courtroom. So I turned to him and, seizing on the most appropriate words I could think of, said, 'Look, Rabbi, you're talking like this. Well, it's not helping me. In fact it's stressing me. I've got all the information I need. You don't need to say anything else. Now, I would never dream of telling you how to do a sermon, so please don't tell me how to conduct a plea of mitigation. Please just sit and listen.'

I felt a small twist of guilt at having to address him this way. But I knew it was for the greater good. Anyway, the words hit their target, and I didn't get another peep out of him. He remained as quiet as a lamb while we waited to go into court.

I did the case and explained all the mitigation I had prepared to justify the rabbi's need to continue driving. The magistrates retired and, to our joint delight, returned and agreed to penalty points on my client's licence rather than a ban. I'll never forget what this holy man said to me afterwards. 'The Lord has given you a gift, Mr Freeman. Use it well.' He has since passed away, but I hope I have continued to do so.

The rabbi was not the only one I've had to stop in mid flow. I remember one drink-drive client whom I only met the night before the trial, which was taking place in London. Time was of the essence. So we sat down in her hotel suite with a friend of hers and I said, 'How much alcohol did you have in each of the bars you visited on the night you were charged?'

She gave me a sad smile, batted her incredibly blue eyes at me and tilted her delicate face so that strands of golden hair fell across her flawless skin. And then she embarked on what amounted to absolutely irrelevant drivel. She told me why she was going out, what she had chosen to wear, why she'd chosen to wear it, where she'd bought the outfit.

I listened to this deluge for a couple of minutes and then abruptly held up my hand. 'Please stop,' I said firmly. 'I asked you a very simple question and we've got very limited time. So can we just focus on your case? Just please get to the point.'

What I really wanted to say was that I didn't have the time, patience or need to listen to all this waffle. And in fact when she looked a little crestfallen I had to smoothly remind her that I was on her side. 'But please,' I repeated, 'do get to the bloody point.' Which, surprisingly, she then did.

Just as a client's over-active narrative can hamper a case, it's equally frustrating when the opposite happens. There are certain cases when I really need the client's help. Take the case of Katie Price – who was charged with talking on her mobile while driving her £115,000 pink horse transporter.

The day of the trial hadn't started well. I always want to be in a hotel within walking distance of the court, which in this case was in Crawley, West Sussex. That way I don't have to fret about traffic or my car breaking down. So my office always make sure I'm staying close by. On this occasion they'd booked me into a gorgeous hotel. Once there, I went through my usual routine of checking that I had a quiet room: not one by a lift, staircase, door or flagpoles (they flap at night!). If you don't get a decent night's sleep, you won't perform your best.

I was told it was a short drive to the court, so the following morning I left at about 9.10am for a 10am start, thinking a two-minute drive lay ahead of me. Punching the address into the Sat Nav, I was horrified to see that the court was twenty-nine miles away and that it would take forty-two minutes to get there. I drove (within the speed limit) to arrive just before proceedings started at 10am but then couldn't find a parking space. Already slightly flustered, when I entered the court I learnt that my client hadn't arrived yet.

I was confident I had a sound legal argument, that Katie had been told at the roadside by the officers who had pulled her over that she would be reported for driving without due care and for using a mobile phone.

However, she was actually being prosecuted for a different offence: not being in control of a vehicle. Katie, the prosecution claimed, had veered across the motorway in her 7.5-tonne horse transporter.

That was the legal argument – and it was a good one. What I also needed, to beef up the case even further, was the factual argument – that is, why and how Katie disputed that she had ever been using a mobile phone.

Katie turned up at 10.10am amid a flurry of paparazzi flashbulbs, dressed for the occasion in mandatory celebrity uniform of sunglasses and fur-cuffed jacket (I've no idea if it was real or faux fur).

When you represent such a celebrity, you know it's going to be in the glare of the media spotlight. Of course, you want to be good every time you do a case. But with a celebrity client you're under more pressure.

I was confident with my defence. I said that the proceedings were 'defective' as Ms Price had been told she would be prosecuted for using a mobile phone and for driving without due care and attention. Unfortunately my legal submission was rejected and she was convicted of not being in such a position as to be in control of her pink horsebox. She was fined £1000 and received three penalty points on her licence. It just shows that even when you have the law at your fingertips and your client giving evidence, it isn't always the recipe for success.

At times like this I get incredibly frustrated but I draw on my reserves as a golfer. When I was a young lad I dreamt of being a professional golfer and I read the life story of South African golf supreme Bobby Locke over and over again. In the book he recalls a time when, as a fourteen-year-old, he played golf with his father and a famous golf champion. He was playing well and after he hit an amazing four iron at a short hole to within five feet, holing it should have been a formality. But he missed the putt and in temper winged his putter into the undergrowth. His dad and the South African champion motioned to their caddies and left the course, leaving Bobby to complete the round on his own. When he met up with them later back at the clubhouse, his father said, 'If I ever see you do that again I'll make sure you never go near a golf club again. If you feel annoyed count to ten. By the time you get to three you'll be in control.'

It's the same with clients. When you are in court you are there with a responsibility not only to represent your client but to demonstrate who you are and what you are. For me to show any anger, frustration or upset would be extremely unprofessional – and make me vulnerable to the opposition.

I have seen it happen from the other side. Like the time I was defending Carlton Palmer in Sheffield for drink-driving. In this case my client had provided a specimen which was [allegedly] over the limit and so he was arrested at the roadside, taken to the police station, processed by the custody sergeant and taken eventually to a room which housed the breathalyser machine.

The officers went through the appropriate warnings and explained that Palmer would be liable for prosecution if he didn't provide a specimen. He duly obliged and provided two specimens of breath.

But there was a problem with the machine – a disparity between the two readings suggested that either the machine wasn't working or that the readings were unreliable. The police then had three options: a) restart the machine and give my client another opportunity; b) give him the blood or urine procedure as a requirement, or c) take him to another police station and start the process all over again.

This was the first case in my career when the police decided to take the last option and they drove to another station about seven miles away. Twenty-five minutes later Palmer was whizzed through the custody area and to the machine. He provided two readings, the lower of which showed that he was over the limit. End of. Or so you might think.

What the police hadn't done was read my client the statutory warning again when he took the test at the second police station. In court I argued that the proceedings were therefore fatally flawed because he should have been given a warning again and, if he hadn't, then the Crown would have to prove that the initial warning he'd been given at the station had remained imprinted upon his mind.

The prosecutor became so annoyed that he slammed his papers down. Hardly a discreet way to excise frustration and anger. The magistrates threw him a disapproving glare and then went on to acquit.

Perhaps as a sign of further frustration, the Crown appealed the acquittal to the High Court. However, they lost and Carlton Palmer remained acquitted. The prosecutor's fit of temper, in my view, sealed the deal for my defence.

But I also felt disappointed that this guy had let himself and the whole profession down. You like to see people with decorum, behaving properly. As Bobby Locke had to learn too, it's all about counting to ten. I was still counting when I read the headlines about Katie Price.

So there are situations where it doesn't matter whether the client is involved. Sometimes their presence can even be a hindrance. You might have a legal argument that is already a little fragile. A defence lawyer has to judge whether the client will be someone that the court could have empathy with or feel hostile to. If you think there will be hostility it's better to use legal argument and if that fails, then as a last resort call the client.

I think judging the value of a client to the case is almost like being some kind of armchair psychologist. You're weighing them up, working out their potential contribution, seeing if they can be of use to you. And I also feel that to be a decent defence lawyer you have to have a real understanding of human nature.

I'll never forget the case involving a woman who had been stopped and breathalysed after an evening out with her husband. My client had been three times over the limit, and when I looked through the papers it seemed to me that the prosecution had done everything correctly. It looked as if it was going to be a straightforward guilty plea.

For some reason, I phoned the lady myself to explain the position. But when I called I noticed that she sounded slightly emotional and that when she spoke there was an almost unnatural hesitancy in her voice. I felt there was something she wanted to tell me. My antennae pricked up. There was something more here, something beneath the surface of this seemingly unexceptional case of drink-driving. Gently I urged her to come to my office to see me.

It seemed my hunch was right. As would later come out in court, I discovered exactly what had happened the night she was stopped. I did this by first asking why she had driven when she had drunk too much. After all, she knew the law, so was it just a momentary error of judgement? No, there was more to it than that. A bombshell admission by my client seemed to suggest that she had driven because she'd had no choice. Her husband had forced her to.

The couple had been out for a meal at a restaurant.

Afterwards, unable to get a taxi, the defendant said her husband grabbed her arm and made her go to their car and get into the driver's seat. She would go on in court to describe the incident as 'terrifying and horrific', telling the magistrates, 'My husband saw some people he didn't want to be associated with and decided we had to get away. But we couldn't get a taxi, and he started panicking and getting worked up.'

The car was then seen 'weaving' through the streets of the city centre. My client would tell the court she knew she had drunk too much but said she felt she had no alternative but to drive the car.

Once I'd digested this information I remember thinking to myself, you couldn't make this up. This woman had been made to drive, because if she hadn't she'd have been in line for a bloody good hiding. Of course, I felt terribly sorry for her. Believe me, this was not about being some kind of hero (anyway, I'm too short for that kind of role). And yes, I hate bullying and abhor violence, particularly guys who threaten to hit women – even more so if they do it to try to avoid a criminal offence. But from a legal point of view it was a situation I'd never confronted before. Let me get my head in the books, I thought. It can't be right. Let me do some digging.

What I found was the 'coercion clause' of the Criminal Justice Act 1925 – a defence available to any wife who has been forced to commit a crime by her husband. It would go on to be the first time the law would be used successfully in a driving case.

The 'coercion clause' was introduced to replace the old common law presumption that a wife formed part of her husband's chattels.

What was fascinating was that there hadn't been the

slightest clue in any of the papers that this had been the reason the defendant decided to drive. Nothing in police statements to suggest there was some kind of emotional subtext. That's why, in cases where there really seems nothing to argue, I then speak to the client. Just to be sure nothing has been missed.

There's a guiding principle in law that you don't ask a question unless you know the answer. You can have a case that is going quite well and you can undo a lot of the good by getting the wrong answer. It's a moving game. I always endeavour to agree as many of the facts with the prosecution as I can. But in this case I'd reached the point and had to ask a question to which I didn't really know the answer. It's that hunch I mentioned earlier in this book: a feeling in the pit of your stomach that you're onto something. As I did indeed feel in cross-examination when the arresting officer was called to the dock.

'Officer, would you make a note of someone's demeanour when you arrest them for drink-driving?' I began.

'Yes, I would,' the policeman replied.

'Well, in this instance the details are scant. You simply describe her as a lady with a high reading who smelt of intoxicants. Can you remember any other details that might assist the court?'

'Yes I do. She was very upset.'

Fantastic. 'How did that upset manifest itself? How did you know she was upset?'

'She was crying, she clearly had been crying. The conversation was emotionally charged.'

'Very helpful, thank you, Officer. So do you accept that you haven't made a full note of everything that took place at the roadside?'

'Sorry, it's very difficult to do that . . .'

'Did she give any explanation as to why she was driving the car?' Here goes, I thought, fingers crossed. After a pause which seemed to span a lifetime, the officer said, 'Yes, yes, actually. She said her husband made her do it.'

It was like manna from heaven. Thank goodness I had an officer who was telling the truth. Some just can't remember. In moments like this you have to maximise that evidence. You look at the magistrates, exchange glances as if to say, wow, did you hear that?, and check it has registered. I'm not going to move on until I know you've really got this point, I thought. You want the full impact of the evidence to be digested.

Of course, the prosecution weren't too thrilled with this turn of events. And so my opposing counsel cross-examined my client on the basis that she had concocted the whole story. Fantastic, I thought. I can now do my closing argument and put this chap in his place. Tactically, his had been a bad move. In my view, what he should have said was that despite the formidable mitigating circumstances, which everyone accepts is a truly sorry state of affairs, it nonetheless did not excuse the offence. That might have swung it for the Crown.

But he didn't.

Which left me the glorious option of presenting to the court how a lady of good character, one who had given her evidence in a compelling and truthful way, had been forced to drive by her husband. The Crown needed to negate the case beyond reasonable doubt and they didn't have a cat in hell's chance. It was a hunch, sheer instinct, a feeling that something was bubbling beneath the surface. Someone else might have been less sympathetic, perhaps not picked up on the clues. Call it instinct, or just fate, but it nailed the case.

The magistrates acquitted my client, finding her not guilty of driving with excess alcohol and awarded her costs.

Sometimes, then, it is good to talk. Just as I pick up smoke signals from the clients, I'm also ready to listen if they can steer me. I once defended a chap charged with burglary who had been accused of stealing a TV and video from a woman with whom he'd had a casual relationship. He was currently serving a sentence for another burglary and had been on home leave at the time of the alleged crime. Anyway, I went to see my client in the bowels of the central detention. It's a grim, windowless place, the magnolia paint peeling from the walls, harsh fluorescent light glaring from above, hard benches angled round the room, and prowling security officers. But my client looked pretty at home. One doesn't like to stereotype but he had tattoos scatter-gunned over his head, neck and arms and, well, looked like the type of guy who might commit a burglary.

I'd already seen the complainant and the lady was my client's polar opposite: immaculately groomed with flawless make-up, an elegant suit and beautifully styled hair. Her glacial expression suggested butter wouldn't melt . . . Contrasting her appearance with my client's, I reckoned that my chap was going to have to hold his hands up. You've clearly done this, I thought, so you're better pleading guilty, as you will receive a lesser sentence. After all, who were the court going to believe: him or her? Yet my client wouldn't have it, and looked at me as if to say, 'Go ahead, cross-examine her, see what happens. Just you wait.' But all he said was, 'Thanks for the advice, but I'm pleading not guilty.'

The prosecution opened their case and the lady gave what seemed to be a truthful and credible account of the burglary. Oh, heck, I thought, what am I going to do with this one? I stood up to start my cross-examination. I had a client in the dock who looked like he'd steal the steam from your tea if given half the chance and I had Mother Teresa in the witness box. No choice, then, but to press on, and I opened with a relatively innocuous question.

'How long have you known the defendant?'

It was like watching a volcano erupt. Her dark eyes flashed and her face twisted into a menacing snarl as she hollered at me, 'You think you're a f***ing film star, don't you, or that you've just stepped out of *Dallas*?' Not, then, the answer I had expected. In fact, I was stunned; everyone in the courtroom was. Yet she didn't seem to care. On and on she ranted with a toxic tirade of abuse, all of it stemming from this innocuous question. It was just unbelievable. The court couldn't control themselves. It was hilarious. But that was the end of the case and it was thrown out at half-time.

I've no idea why the woman reacted like that. Though I suspect since she'd edited her involvement with my client out of her angelic testimony she wasn't too thrilled that I'd brought it up. But the client clearly knew what she was like and he led me to victory!

So the decision as to whether to involve the client or not is all about the defence's lawyer's judgement. But if I am involving the client I want them to feel they can talk to me, that we can communicate. I think I am someone that they can be comfortable talking to. And it frustrates me that I'm thought of as the rich man's lawyer. It's a misconception. I'm comfortable talking to anyone. The darker the more fascinating. That's why I enjoy defending alleged gangsters or bank robbers. I find them intriguing. And I love the stories they have to tell.

My favourite tale relates to one of the many serial criminals I've met over the years. He told me a great story of how the police were once called to his house after neighbours

said he was hanging his dog. He opened the door to a duo
of officers, and said, 'Fine, do you want to have a look?' In
the back garden his Stafford was swinging on a rope from a
tyre. He said to the coppers, 'You try and get that tyre out
of his mouth if you can.' When I hear stories like that I feel
it justifies my decision to become a criminal lawyer. I wanted
to work with people, not just paper. People, that is, from all
walks of life including criminals with broken noses, rogues
and villains. People who inhabited a world light years away
from my own upbringing and code of ethics.

I suppose wanting to be with people, find out about
their world, draw out their innermost thoughts, was initially a reaction to being holed up in public school. I
remember, just after I'd finished my A levels, sitting in the
kitchen at home in Nottingham and saying to my mum, 'I
haven't got a clue about this world. I barely even know
what a woman looks like.' I had a craving to learn about
life. I felt incredibly frustrated. I then hot-footed it off to
Paris on a year off after my dad got me a job packing jeans
in a Wrangler factory. The first night there I sat in my grim
little room in the Hôtel de la Gare in Louvres, the walls
rattling from passing trains, and played some Leonard
Cohen on my cassette recorder. Then I started to cry, I felt
so incredibly isolated and lonely. But after the tears had
dried I said to myself, 'This is what you wanted, get off
your backside and go and do it.' I went on to get a job as a
driver for UTA, working my socks off – by choice – up to
80 hours a week transporting people and aircraft parts to
different airports and helping to keep the fleet of cars and
lorries immaculate. A few months into the job a senior
executive said he had been impressed by my work ethic
and offered me a chance to join the company's training
scheme. 'A boy like you could go all ze way to ze top,' he

intoned. And I was tempted, though it would have been au revoir to Monsieur Loophole.

It was certainly a colourful time, meeting people from all walks of life. I knew then I wanted to know about people, about what makes them tick. I think having a grounding like that is a massive advantage to a defence lawyer. It means you are tuned into what your clients say – and the loopholes this might yield.

Of course, when you do speak to clients it doesn't automatically guarantee that they'll supply you with a defence. That's why I listen to every word, pick up every inference. There might be a throwaway comment that you latch onto. When I represented *EastEnders* actor Steve McFadden in a drink-drinking case, it appeared, as would be revealed in court, that he was a man who could take his booze. That's why he didn't realise he was over the limit when he drove his Rolls-Royce home from a party at 3am having drunk, as a breath test subsequently showed, the equivalent of nine double vodkas.

I got an expert to verify this by plying my client with equivalent amounts of alcohol and then producing a report on the effect. As the judge would hear, despite downing so much booze, my client barely seemed affected. Meanwhile I looked at the police statements, which didn't once mention that my client had been staggering or slurring his speech. Some people can consume vast amounts of alcohol yet not display any symptoms. Others can have a glass of wine and be on their back. I told the judge at Horseferry Road Magistrates Court in London that the actor's 'remarkable capacity' for alcohol meant he would not feel drunk, despite being two and a half times over the limit.

I also explained that he travelled widely for charities and was particularly involved with terminally ill children.

My client was disqualified for eighteen months rather than at least two years or more. The judge explained that the ban would have been longer but for McFadden's special plea of mitigation.

In another case, a lady approached me after she was spotted doing 90mph on the M56. I looked at the prosecution papers and their case seemed in order. So, as usual, with no apparent legal argument to hand, I spoke to the client to see if I might excavate something from her version of the events. When I did, she had a very good reason for driving so fast, as would later come out in court. In fact it was a unique medical situation. In 1975 this lady had undergone what she'd thought was a complete hysterectomy after a growth on her womb had burst and caused septicaemia. However, it seemed – as scans would later show – that her entire womb had not been removed, and medication she had been taking for another complaint had caused a haemorrhage in her uterus. This had triggered bleeding, which was why she was racing down the motorway: she needed to get to a hospital.

Now, it's not the kind of information a woman might readily volunteer, and the phrase 'women's problems' is often muttered by a blushing client. I'll ask the usual questions when taking instructions, such as, 'Do you accept you were going this fast?' and 'Anything that can help us?' In this case, my client responded to the latter with, 'A lady's problem?'

In these situations there's no time for niceties and anyway I've heard it all before, so I really don't blush myself. But my client's testimony, together with the relevant medical experts and records, provided concrete mitigating circumstances for her speeding.

As this was a situation where the court have a compulsory obligation to endorse the licence, I decided to argue a 'special reason'. Just to remind you, this means that the defence lawyer advises the defendant to make a guilty plea but then offers a set of circumstances in an effort to avoid disqualification and/or penalty points. My idea was that if we could establish a special reason on the balance of probability, then the court might give her an absolute discharge. (This is pretty much the lowest sentence a defendant can receive. They are convicted but not punished, but instead discharged without conditions, although they may still have to pay compensation.) After all, my client had responded to a medical emergency. And an absolute discharge is exactly what the court gave her.

So you see, it's very easy for a case to superficially appear unsinkable. That's why so many defence lawyers rush to enter a guilty plea. But, in situations where you can't turn the Crown's case upside down, continue loophole hunting by talking to the client and see what they have to say.

I remember when Lee Ryan, the singer of boy band Blue, was accused of throwing punches at photographers after leaving the London nightclub 10 Room. On the surface it looked like another pop star spitting out his dummy and having a tantrum. But Lee felt he was justified in doing what he did. First of all, as I would tell the court, the mob of photographers acted like 'a pack of wolves', the worst Lee had seen thus far in his four years in the public eye.

But I also explained that the girl who was with Lee as he left the club was profoundly deaf and dumb, and as such was frightened by the aggression they met. In her silent world, the blizzard of flashing lights and thrusting cameras must have seemed terrifying. Lee maintained he asked photographers politely to back off but, after they persisted, he resorted to throwing punches, smashing a camera. He did what he did because he was trying to protect the girl.

The judge accepted that Lee Ryan had acted in defence of another and so dismissed the assault charges – for which my client could have gone to prison. He was found guilty of criminal damage and was ordered to pay £500 compensation for the damage to the camera. There was no other fine or punishment. Lee was so relieved that he invited me and my wife to his twenty-first birthday party.

I've always taken the view that celebrities are not looking for a new best friend. They're looking for a lawyer who is going to deliver. So I've always kept a dividing line between the professional and the personal (much to the chagrin of my wife, who felt I missed out on numerous opportunities to go to celebrity bashes). But I got on so well with Lee that when he invited me to a ritzy club in London, I thought, why not? Steph went out and bought me a swanky black and white shirt for the occasion. And it was great fun: the drink flowed, the food was tasty and so were the pretty models. I also enjoyed chatting to Lee's family.

Several years later I was at Wimbledon when a uniformed security guard jumped out and said, 'Right, I've got you.' I nearly leapt out of my skin. 'Only joking,' the guy grinned. It was Lee's dad, whom I'd met at his son's twenty-first.

I'm often asked if I find it thrilling to meet so many celebrities. Hand on heart? Not when I'm working. I'm so fixed on winning the case.

But I'll admit I do get a thrill when someone from *Coronation Street* approaches me. It's simply because I love the programme. Obviously I love the Manchester connection, but Corrie has everything: humour, pathos and tragedy, while the script is often so wise that it can hold a light up to human nature. And those characters! A journalist once said to me that they couldn't imagine me with my feet up watching Corrie. But that's exactly what I do. In fact I've got a circle of friends in fairly high-profile jobs who do the same. It makes for great discussion on the golf course and is better than being asked for advice on a speeding charge.

However, once I actually embark on the case, I forget about my favourite soap and concentrate on defending the person behind the character. Ever the professional, I don't call them in for client meetings: the protocol remains the same. I look at the prosecution papers and if there's nothing I can use, then I'll see what the client has to say.

So, when I represented *Coronation Street* star Ryan Thomas, I had to forget I was such a Corrie fan and concentrate solely on the evidence. The facts of the matter were simple. Ryan had been out in his car with two friends when, shortly after 4am one autumn morning, he hit crash barriers at the junction of Cambridge Street and the Mancunian Way in Manchester city centre. He was then seen leaving the scene in a taxi without reporting the accident.

But there was more to it than this. Ryan had been behind the wheel of his Chrysler car when he skidded on a pool of water, 'aquaplaned' and hit the crash barriers. As he got out of the car, a group of people started taking pictures of him with their phones, perhaps realising he was a Corrie star. Feeling uncomfortable, Ryan jumped into a taxi and left.

Now, failing to stop and failing to report an accident are two fairly serious charges. The penalty for failing to stop alone is between five and ten penalty points. Or disqualification and/or a fine, or, in the worst-case scenario, a prison sentence.

My client pleaded guilty but what I had to do was

mitigate the potential severity of the sentence by homing in on the facts of the case that could minimise this. So I argued that Ryan was guilty of a 'technical' offence because he did not know that the law required a driver to report an accident as soon as possible. I also pointed out that he was driving perfectly properly before he hit a pool of water and aquaplaned. Thankfully, the court accepted that he was not at fault for the accident. He was fined £2020, given five penalty points (the minimum) on his licence and ordered to pay £35 court costs and a £15 victim surcharge by JPs. In the light of the circumstances and the offences, this was a good result.

So, there's no hard-and-fast rule about involving clients. My tactic is to see how they can contribute to the case, if they can at all. But if I do involve a client, then I think they can never be over-prepared for their court appearance. You're taking them into an adversarial environment. They'll be nervous, and I want to do everything I can to offset their anxieties. I have been a prosecutor and a defence lawyer. So when a client gives me instructions I question everything they say because I want the truth so that I can deal with it. I test the evidence and their instructions all the time, because you've got to be credible in court. Otherwise it's a waste of the client's time and money and my credibility.

When taking instructions I try to explain as much as possible about what is likely to happen in court. Many times clients have suggested that the experience of going through the case in my office was far more scary than going through it in court. It's more spontaneous, and it enables me to evaluate the quality of the evidence and how this witness will cope in a courtroom environment. If the evidence is truthful, it should stack up.

I don't just stop with cross-examination. I'll answer

questions – and I'm asked this a lot – about how my client should dress. In my view, what's best for a man is a dark suit, white shirt, plain tie and clean shoes, and for a woman a similarly sober and smart outfit. No flesh. And, in both cases, no flash jewellery. When clients ask how they should stand when giving evidence, I suggest trying to establish eye contact, not to fidget, chew gum or swear, and to watch the magistrates as they will be taking notes. If I'm asked for any other advice, I suggest watching the magistrate's body language.

As Dale Carnegie says, 'The best argument is that which merely seems an explanation.' In terms of legal argument, what the defendant says should seem to the court over-whelmingly obvious, making the defence appear effortless. Much the same way as professional golfer Fred Couples fluently and fluidly unleashes his drive.

So the client–lawyer relationship is all about strategy, tactics, when to speak and when to stay silent. It's not always easy. Often both of you think you know best. A client may know about himself. But I know about the law, and we have to agree on that.

However, though I may sound like I've got a PhD in understanding people, I'm the first to admit I don't always get it right. One instance I've never forgotten was when, as a young prosecutor, I was having lunch in the officers' mess at a local police station. About a dozen of us were sitting around a large table, and I was chatting away, brimming with youthful self-confidence and holding forth on how people behave. At full throttle I said that it always amazed me to see someone respectable and then discover they have a tattoo. I felt it said something totally different about them. Why would they mutilate themselves in this way?

The chief superintendent who'd been listening to my

monologue leaned forward, rolled up his sleeve, revealed a tattoo of Jessica Rabbit and said, 'Well, what does that tell you about me, Nick?'

This was a chap who knew the art of the ambush. Ego deflated, I retreated into my lunch. What it told me was that you should always expect the unexpected, particularly where people are concerned. And also that even lawyers have to know when to speak and when to remain silent.

7

Loophole: crown cock-ups

I've made lots of good friends over the course of my career. None more so than the officers I met when working as a young prosecutor for Greater Manchester Police nearly thirty years ago. These men and women were smart, friendly, resilient and often in good cheer. I used to really love eating with them in the officers' canteen each morning. The air was thick with the smell of buttery toast and as blue as the uniforms worn by those demolishing a full English breakfast. But the buoyancy of the banter could really set you up for the day.

My fellow prosecutors were an equally fine bunch, the hard grind of the job offset by their relentless sense of humour. We were all target practice for someone's rapier wit. In my case, I was nicknamed Lionel Blair because of my apparently 'dandified' walk. It wouldn't be uncommon for me to be waiting to get one of my cases on at a magistrates court when 'Mr Lionel Blair to Court Three' would boom over the public address system. I got so used to it, when I heard the announcement I'd leap to my feet without a second thought. Though I resisted doing the soft-shoe shuffle into court.

I enjoyed the work so much that when, three months into the job, a large criminal law practice tried to headhunt me, I turned them down. Anyway I'd promised the police prosecuting authorities that I'd stay in the job for at least two years. And that's what I did, until ultimately I was drawn away by my own restless ambition. But my spell as a prosecutor remains one of the most enjoyable periods of my working life.

So, having been out there on the shop floor, batting for the Crown, I really do understand the challenges facing police and prosecutors. The stress can be enormous, the tasks thankless and the pressure sometimes overwhelming. The workload is as massive as it is unrelenting. I still shudder at the memory of the leaning tower of road-traffic files heaped on my desk each day.

However, when you switch sides, there's no room for sentiment. Your colleagues become the opposition. You square up to them to see who'll blink first. Or rather who'll find a hole in the other's argument. And one so-called loophole that I've used again and again to do this is exposing Crown cock-ups.

If I find a procedural mistake with the potential to win my case, then I grab it. It's nothing personal. It's purely professional: the business of being a defence lawyer. But I suppose it's no surprise that plenty of police officers, prosecutors and even judges have crossed me off their Christmas-card list. They don't like what I do and they don't like how I do it.

To be honest, I don't blame them. They're only human, and none of us like our mistakes to be paraded in front of our peers. But that's how it has to be. If the prosecuting authorities make a legal error that's relevant and significant to my defence, I'm going to optimise its impact to win my case. Just as any prosecutor would. If they get it wrong, then I'm going to milk that loophole and hopefully net an acquittal for my client. I'm not in any way suggesting that the police or Crown Prosecution Service are especially incompetent. Mistakes happen in every area of professional life. We're all vulnerable to human frailty. Though, I didn't feel terribly confident after reading about a Government review of British police pay and conditions last September (IE 2011). The review's author, lawyer Tom Winsor, suggested that some officers are 'barely literate' because the educational standards required to join the force are so low. Mr Winsor also claimed he was told by a former Met Commissioner and serving national Police Federation officer that standards were lowered to attract more diverse applicants.

It's a shocking admission and, if true, this ethos of being PC to attract a PC could well explain some of the howling errors I've encountered by the constabulary over the years. And if educational standards and requirements continue to nose dive, the situation may only get worse.

That aside – though it's a big aside – we all have bad days, or can be a little slapdash at times. But, in a court of law, the ripple effect of a mistake can be devastating.

In fairness I would say that, where the Crown is concerned, there's formidable scope for error, simply because of the complex procedures police and prosecutors have to follow. That's why even the most brilliant of lawyers or most dedicated members of the constabulary can mess up.

The police have a particularly difficult task because they're not qualified lawyers and, in my view, don't get a great deal of legal training relating to drink-driving cases. Not when you think of the acres of statutes, procedures and forms relating to motoring law. So what happens? Well, they've no choice but to get their training on the job instead. Inevitably this can lead to mess-ups.

Then again, it's not easy, down at the station on a busy Saturday night, trying to follow intricate procedures while your detainee is some roaring drunk who can barely stand up and is hollering at you as if his life depended on it. In all the hullabaloo, things may not be done the way they should. Months later, when the case comes to court and the client has sobered up, these mistakes erupt in the cold light of cross-examination.

My cross-examination. But I can only do this because as soon as I get the prosecution papers, I look at every aspect microscopically, combing through the small print and sifting through case law to an almost painful degree. I need to know what I'm going to argue, how I'm going to argue it, and what all the possible ramifications may be.

So when I get a police officer in the witness box, I make him jump through hoops about his legal knowledge. It's a bit like *Mastermind*, I suppose. But unfortunately not all of these coppers are up to speed on specialist subject. So perhaps that's why, on some occasions, I've come across police officers who have actually tried to cover their tracks rather than face having their mistakes paraded in front of the bench.

One instance that sticks in my memory is a drink-driving case I did at Macclesfield Magistrates Court in Cheshire. My client had been driving his Bentley erratically on his way back from Oxford and, not surprisingly, was pulled over by the police. As the officers opened the door of the car, he actually fell out! A roadside breath test confirmed that the driver was substantially over the drink-drive limit.

However, when I received the paperwork for the case, I noticed a blank space on the statement of the officer who had breathalysed my client. He had omitted to fill in the serial number of the breath-test device that had been used that night. I should add that the blank space was of no legal significance or consequence to the case. Yet little details like this do tend to lodge themselves in my mind. They make my antennae twitch. What we have here, I thought to myself, is a police officer who hasn't been as thorough as he should have been. He hadn't broken the law, of course. But my instinct prickled anyway.

Several months later the case came to court. And when I cross-examined the officer about the device he'd used to breathalyse my client, he reeled off the machine's name and serial number without missing a beat. Like a neon light, the blank space on the statement form suddenly flashed in my head, and a warning bell rang. Hang about, I thought. Where on earth has he got this information from? What do we have here?

It was a totally unexpected development. But, clichéd though it sounds, I always expect the unexpected. Time to start digging. Calmly, I asked the officer if I could look at his statement. There it was, in bold blue ink: the name and number of the breathalyser. Yet the last time I'd seen this form this space had been blank. Surely he hadn't tampered with the form?

'Officer,' I began carefully, 'have you added any supplementary information to your statement?'

The witness bristled, his body tensing. 'No,' he replied.

I paused for a moment – always useful to boost the tension – then showed him my copy of the statement.

'Is this a copy of the original? With your signature?' I continued.

The officer nodded in agreement but I could see the flicker of alarm in his eyes.

I cleared my throat and shot a sly glance at the bench.

'Can you explain, then, why the imprint of the serial number is on your statement but not on my copy of it?'

The witness floundered helplessly.

'I d–don't know, sir.'

I did. He had added the serial number to his form at a later date. Case thrown out.

Unfortunately this was by no means my only experience of police officers tampering with their statements. On another occasion I represented a man who was allegedly involved in an incident while driving his BMW in London. When I received the officer's statement it declared that when he stopped my client he'd warned him at the roadside that he might be prosecuted for driving without due care and attention. However, when my client was formally summonsed, it was also for dangerous driving – a far more serious offence, since it can carry a prison sentence together with a minimum twelve-month ban and a compulsory re-test. Yet when I took instructions from my client he assured me that the officer had never mentioned the possibility of a dangerous driving charge to him.

Now, you have to bear in mind that an officer prepares his statement on the basis of notes he makes at the roadside. So to clarify the position, I immediately requested the officer's pocket notebook so that I could read for myself his record of the events. I raked through it carefully and there, in neat, bold strokes of the pen, it was clearly written that he was reporting my client for both offences.

I felt a prickle of uncertainty. Something was wrong. I drew the page closer to my face, suspicion sparking in me. What was it? I squinted at it over and over again. Of course! The words 'and dangerous driving' appeared to have been written in a slightly different shade of blue and the letters were squashed together as if the words had been squeezed in as an afterthought. This simple little notebook had suddenly turned into a hand grenade. And I had the pin. But I needed my hunch to be corroborated. So I called in a handwriting expert. He confirmed that the words 'and dangerous driving' had been added at a later date – and in a different pen!

It was clear that the officer must have gone back to the station after stopping my client, mulled over the incident, decided he'd been a little too lax and that my client should face prosecution for dangerous driving too. But how could he pull this one off? The only way to do this was to squeeze the charge into his account in his notebook as an afterthought, thinking that he could hoodwink the court into believing that he had warned my client of this possible charge at the time of the incident. Oh dear. Out went the case.

So why would a police officer do this? Well, in any sphere of life – be it lifting a few quid from the office till or sleeping with the neighbour's wife – those who don't play by the book do so on the assumption that they won't get caught. In the case of the police, I think they need to remember that they are there to help prosecute, not persecute. It is not their job to act as judge and jury. An officer may believe, myopically, that he has his guy and may want to nail him. But that is the wrong approach. It is a matter for the courts. This isn't about 'them and us', the police versus the public.

And the police need to be truthful. I remember once representing a landlord accused of using his pub for unlawful purposes.

Prior to my client being charged, two undercover officers had gone to his premises in order to pursue their investigations. Considering they were in attendance at what amounted to a racy stag-type party, I decided to question them about whether and how much they had been drinking. I was aware as part of disclosure that the coppers both had approximately two pounds on them when they left the pub. Yet, during cross examination, I discovered that they had been given £20 each to cover their expenses for the night. And that no food had been served. Both officers maintained they had only had a couple of pints each. And therefore were not only sober, but their evidence was reliable and truthful.

However, in my head, I immediately did the maths. Two pints, twenty quid and only a couple of pounds left. Where on earth had the other eighteen smackers gone?

In my mind, with no food on offer to buy, that was worth of booze each. And that's a lot of booze. Enough to take them into the realms of inebriation. Could it be that these members of the constabulary had partied more enthusiastically than they should? And more significantly, had they lied on oath?

They both took a moment to 'reflect' before accepting they had slightly underestimated their alcohol intake.

Case thrown out. Costs awarded. Client happy. Coppers reprimanded . . . ? I won't drink to that one.

In fact the constabulary have been known to be equally overenthusiastic with their own peers. I once had a case involving a detective inspector who was arrested when he turned up for work apparently drunk. His eyes were glazed, his speech slurred and his face flushed. He gave a positive breath test and admitted when questioned that he had driven to work. He was therefore charged with drink-driving. However, the case was thrown out because the conversation in which my client made the admission that he'd driven was in fact an interview. Therefore he should have been told that he was under caution before the conversation had taken place and also that he was entitled to legal advice.

A whole host of other codes had been breached too, including not giving my client the opportunity to read and sign the notes that were taken by the two officers following the interview. I made an application for the interview, including the admission, to be excluded because of the breaches and the court agreed. The prosecution were therefore left with no evidence as to who had driven. A vital piece of the jigsaw had been removed.

In this case, perhaps the police officers deployed a certain degree of familiarity. But if they stray from the script, they play into the hands of the defence. And if they do so deliberately, say by tampering with paperwork, they should be subjected to criminal and disciplinary proceedings.

But what astounds me is that, on various occasions throughout my career, I've discovered mistakes that are so blindingly obvious that I simply can't imagine what was going through the perpetrator's mind.

In fact, even if an officer alters his account in a gesture of generosity, it can still net an acquittal. This happened when I was defending a biker who was allegedly caught doing well over 100mph. At the roadside a police officer gave him a Notice of Intended Prosecution, or NIP, informing him that he was likely to be hauled before the courts on a charge of dangerous driving – one of the more serious offences in motoring law. Back at the station doing his paperwork, the officer, it seemed, had had a change of heart. Perhaps, on reflection, he felt he'd been too hard on my client and decided to change the charge to the far lesser one of speeding. And, since this was a lesser offence, perhaps he took the view that my client didn't need to be informed of this.

Well, speeding may well have been a lesser crime. But that wasn't the point. The statute required my client either to be told at the roadside or to be given a written notice within fourteen days of the incident that he might be prosecuted for speeding. This is what I argued in court.

The prosecution didn't agree and argued that dangerous driving included speeding. All of which might sound like two grown men throwing their toys at each other. But the law is the law. I didn't make it up. There are procedures that have to be followed. And in this case they hadn't been. The notice didn't cover speeding. The magistrates agreed and threw the case out.

However, most of the editorial tampering I've exposed over the years was not triggered by charitable motives. Take the time footballer Lee Bowyer was accused of (and denied) speeding at almost twice the limit – allegedly peaking at 132mph in his Porsche in Northumbria.

When I received the disclosure, the police officer had made four different statements, each one slightly different. However, even in the face of this revelation, as a lawyer I don't decide what my client does next. My job is to explain the possible legal consequences of the options open to them, then leave them to make their choice. In a case like this a defence lawyer might point out what he thinks is the perilous state of the prosecution case and the likelihood of a successful not-guilty plea. On the other hand, he could explain that if his client did plead guilty they might be in a position to strike what is known as a 'plea bargain' – exchanging a lesser sentence for a lesser speed.

In this case the Crown agreed to let Lee plead to a lesser – much lesser – speed of 99mph. And he was banned for six weeks, and received no penalty points which, in the scheme of things, was considered to be a good result.

Think this was a one-off? Just a slip of the pen? Over to the case of Dwight York, who was pulled over by motorway police for allegedly driving his Mercedes Coupé at 102mph as he headed home through North Yorkshire from a training session. The officer who stopped him made *seven* subsequent changes to his statement. When he'd done the original he had left seven blanks. Revisiting it before the trial months later, he had filled in these blanks. Despite discrediting the officer, who was unaware that I was in possession of a copy of the original form with the blanks, the magistrates still convicted. Dwight was banned for fourteen days, though this was still a good result as it could have been so much more. I was able to persuade the courts to disqualify him for the offence rather than give him points, which, as the situation was a potential 'totter', would have led to a minimum mandatory six-month ban.

Stress or moments of ill-judgement can make any of us do stupid things. And I understand that being a police officer is about as stressful as it gets. Maybe that's why these mistakes happen. Sometimes, though, they are born out of no more than momentary forgetfulness, taking the eye off the ball. A good example is a drink-driving case I did in the north-east a few years ago. During the trial a point of law arose that needed to be discussed with the prosecutor. The police officer who was in the middle of giving his evidence was asked to leave the court while the legalities were sorted out. But, before he did, he was reminded not to discuss the case with anybody.

A few minutes later an expert I'd called for the case, and who was due to give evidence later in the trial, came rushing into court in a state of agitation. Breathlessly he explained that while he had been waiting outside he'd been listening to the conversation an officer was having with a colleague. One of the policemen was telling the other what had happened during the case so far. It seems the officers hadn't appreciated that the expert was a witness in the same proceedings (or that he was eavesdropping).

When I heard this I knew immediately it was a remarkable opportunity and I had to grasp it quickly. Why? Because I could argue abuse of process. I asked for the officer from our case to be brought back into court and I cross-examined him about the conversation alleged to have taken place outside in the corridor. My expert then gave evidence about what he'd heard – which the officer disputed. However, the court believed my expert and the case was thrown out.

You can't legislate for situations like this – though, as I mentioned in a previous chapter, one of my favourite sayings is 'Chance favours a prepared mind.' But what a stroke of luck! I chuckled to myself as I left the court. I shouldn't have been smug, but I couldn't help feeling pleased with myself.

Moments later, however, I was brought back to earth with a thud. Standing not far away was the officer who had just been discredited in the case. I could tell by the scowl on his face that he wasn't terribly thrilled with me. He walked slowly towards me, stopping only when his face lingered just a few inches from mine. Oh heck, I thought, he's going to hit me. With my knees shaking I decided to make a pre-emptive (though not literal) strike. I calmly pointed out that it wasn't me who had disobeyed the court order, it was him. And maybe in future he ought to think more carefully about what the magistrates had suggested. He narrowed his eyes, I held my breath, then, with a menacing glare, he turned on his heel and walked away, muttering insults at me as he went.

What amazes me about some mistakes is that they're obvious as soon as the paperwork from a case is available to both the police and the prosecution. They have the chance to rectify matters before they reach court. And still things get overlooked. A classic instance of this was a case involving two brothers whose Porsche had driven head first into an oncoming car. Thankfully the motorist they'd hit was only dazed. However, the two siblings – let's call them A and B – leapt out of their car and 'legged it'.

Fortunately it didn't take long for the police to catch the pair and both were marched to the station and duly breathalysed. Witness accounts confirmed that A had been the one behind the wheel when it smashed into the other car. He was charged with driving without due care, drink-driving, failing to stop and failing to report. B, who was the passenger, was charged with obstructing the police as well as a public order offence.

However, when I got down to the meat and potatoes of the police's case file I made the most remarkable discovery. They had confused the brothers' charges. A was hit with B's charge and vice versa. Incredible! This is bloody fantastic, I thought. It was pure human error; a mistake maybe anyone could make. The blunder could have been picked up by the prosecution and their legal team when they came to review the files. But they failed to spot it.

So there I had it. Two men, two charges, all set down the wrong way round. After having a chuckle over this wonderful nugget of mistaken identity, I set about fine-tuning my strategy.

The brothers were being tried separately, and what I decided to do was press ahead with B's trial first. These, after all, were the more serious charges. When the case came to court I detonated my find and at half-time was able to make a submission that my client was not the man who had committed the offence. Case dismissed.

And so to the other trial, the case against A, who had also

been wrongly charged. The Crown had six months as decreed by the statute from the date of the incident to notice their mistake and summons the defendant. They failed to do so. Therefore, when the second brother was tried, the wrong charges remained against him.

Now you might think that, in the light of what had happened with B, the Crown would marry up the mix-up with their case against A. If one was wrongly charged, the other one had to be too. There was still time to act and rectify the charges. But they didn't and went ahead with the trial – only, of course, for my client to be acquitted.

I don't take pleasure in reeling off such mistakes. I've always had a good working relationship with prosecutors, and the police too, helping both when I can.

I remember one cold Thursday winter's night when, having crawled into bed with a terrible cold, I was woken at 1.30am by a ring at the door. My wife, Steph, jumped out of bed and peered through the curtains. The darkened lane outside was illuminated by blue flashing lights. When she opened the front door she was greeted by a huddle of police officers, who explained that one of my clients had been holding a group of people hostage in an isolated house out on the moors. The client would only agree to surrender if I was there, because, without his lawyer present, he thought he might get shot. Could I go with them to break the siege?

It was like something out of the movies. I dragged myself out of bed, pulled on some clothes and clambered into the back of the squad car, which roared off at breakneck speed. But after a couple of miles I yelled for the driver to stop, pushed open the door and threw up violently at the side of the road. Exhausted from retching, I meekly asked to be allowed to travel in the front. If the hostage situation was the stuff of Hollywood, then having a car-sick lawyer throwing up his guts hardly added to the glamour. And this was before I had to try to pacify an armed client! What's more, the police took a wrong turning to the station, prolonging my agony.

When we arrived at our destination I chucked up again, this time on the steps of the police station. With my stomach lurching and my head throbbing, I gingerly made my way inside, where I was given a bulletproof vest. Then we were off again, now hurtling through the inky-black countryside in a police Land Rover. Eventually we pulled up at the foot of a hill. I stepped out of the car and swallowed hard. Then, flanked by some burly coppers, we jogged together across the moorland. Suddenly an isolated farm house loomed out of the mist. We stopped about a hundred yards from its front gate.

An officer then drew a loudhailer to his lips and boomed to my client: 'Mr Freeman is here, Now please come out with your hands up.'

My client came out peacefully. No one was hurt. Job done. I didn't want a knighthood. I just needed some Night Nurse. And to get home to bed.

On another occasion the police asked for my help in recovering a sawn-off shotgun that had been used in offences relating to a client who was already in custody. It could only help my client's case if he cooperated with the police and arranged for this weapon to be handed over. Which meant handing it over to me.

The venue for the handover was a fairly rough pub and when I walked in, my sharp suit and shiny shoes made me stick out like a sore thumb. Had armed police not been outside I think my knees might have given way. I stumbled to the bar and muttered the name of the contact I'd been given. I was directed to a thickset man, huddled in the corner, cradling a long object swathed in carrier bags. Not wishing to hang around or to hold onto the gun for a second longer than necessary, I took possession of the package, threaded my way back through the pub and gulped in the fresh air as I handed it over to the police. Mission accomplished. Or so I thought.

As I proffered the gun, I felt the force of a hard palm slap on my back.

'You're under arrest for being in possession of a firearm,' growled a copper.

Oh hell, I'd been set up! I was looking down the barrel of a gun. Literally.

Then the officers all fell about laughing. Gotcha! So much for doing the cops a favour. Though it did help my client's case.

So far I've talked about the all-too-human side of Crown cock-ups: the stress, the shame, the misjudgement. All the things that lead to mistakes. But what about all the gadgetry involved in modern policing? Surely that must limit the number of errors the constabulary make?

Take the speed camera. When these were introduced it was to deal with accident blackspots and so help the police catch drivers who were treating our roads and motorways like a Formula One circuit. But unfortunately, even if a machine is in perfect working order, there is still an element of human error if the operator doesn't use it properly. And there's the loophole.

Handheld devices are particularly tricky because – unlike fixed speed cameras – they're prone to move in the opera-tor's hand. To get round this the officer is supposed to target suspect speeders and then train the laser beam on their number plate for a few seconds. This doesn't always happen.

Take the time I acted for golfer Colin Montgomerie, who'd allegedly been recorded in his BMW X5 travelling at 37mph in a 30mph zone on the A69 near Carlisle. In Monty's case the Crown weren't able to show that the reading from the handheld speed camera was reliable and accurate because there was what's rather cutely known as 'slippage' – that is, an incorrect reading from the device showing the car travelling faster than it was. The operator had also broken the rules by targeting everything that went past, even recording a jogger doing 6mph as well as a dog! In fact I discovered that the camera operator had actually zapped around 390 cars in seventy-three minutes – one every eleven seconds.

Indeed video footage showed that Monty's BMW was the third of three cars targeted in only five seconds as the laser beam 'swept' across them. My man was acquitted. Not only that, but the judge at Carlisle Crown Court said that one of the other drivers who'd already pleaded guilty shouldn't have been convicted. He then gamely suggested that the prosecution authorities contact the guy, give him his money back and remove from his licence the points he'd incurred with the charge. Technically, this anonymous motorist was receiving free advice. (I never did find out who he was – not that I would have charged him!) But he was welcome to it.

Cases like this show how defence lawyers test the system and why it is important that they do. We do need to find a way to monitor speed and apprehend the law breakers. But that way has to be foolproof.

Talking of guidelines, one basic requirement of speeding devices is that the machine used is a Home Office-approved device. It's something the prosecution have to prove was done. Now, police officers often don't know the name of the device used and in one particular case, believing this to be the situation, I said to the prosecutor before we started, 'I don't want you leading the witness, particularly about the type of speeding device used. The information has to come from him.'

The prosecutor gave me an affable shrug and we trooped off into court, only for him to ask the police officer in question whether the device used was Home Office-approved. I was astonished at such duplicity. This was a critical part of the case, and effectively the prosecutor was putting in a piece of evidence. By doing so he had contaminated the whole case. It was an abuse of process. I leapt to my feet.

The fact was that this police officer hadn't known the name of the device. So how would he have known if it had Home Office approval or not? That would have been part of my defence. I argued the point and the case was thrown out.

One of my most memorable police foul-ups happened in a case involving footballer Jonathan Woodgate, who was summonsed for allegedly speeding after driving at 85mph in a temporary 50mph zone on the A66 in County Durham.

When I saw the word 'temporary' on the court papers, something flickered in my mind. As I showed earlier, one aspect of loophole hunting is asking questions that others may fail to pose. In this case, what length was the stretch of road affected by the temporary limit? Some detective work was called for. I got hold of a copy of the speed order and discovered the reduced speed limit spanned a distance of 405 metres. Yet the speed check on Jonathan's car had been carried out over 519 metres. Time, as our American friends say, to do the math. What this meant was that the speed check exceeded by 114 metres the stretch of road with a reduced speed limit. Therefore the whole check was invalidated. Case over, with victory thanks to a 114-metre loophole.

I recall one colleague, on hearing about this particular case, ringing me up and saying, 'C'mon, Nick, where on earth did that come from?' The implication was that while I'd produced a great result, perhaps there was something slightly mad about me too. I don't mind. Being this forensic about my investigations may seem a little crazy. But it stems from a few guiding principles, one of which is, check whether someone has done their job properly. Just because an officer says to me that he carried out his check over an accurate area, I'm afraid I don't accept it. I question it instead.

Speed devices have to be checked for their accuracy, and there are procedures in place for this too. Again, these aren't always followed. In the case of the late William Stobart, the joint boss of haulage firm Eddie Stobart, my client was allegedly clocked doing 116mph near Carlisle. But the prosecution failed to prove that the Vascar speed device – which measures speed between two points – had been checked properly. (It had to be checked before and after it is used.) The prosecution were unable to show that the measured mile over which these checks are conducted was, in fact, a mile. They needed to adduce evidence from a surveyor to certify this. So, sorry to nit-pick, but, though the officer had checked the device before and after the speed check, he hadn't measured the distance itself and therefore couldn't prove it was a mile. Had my client been convicted he would have been facing a lengthy ban, since, as reported in the newspapers, he already had nine points on his licence. That's machines for you.

But I think the biggest stumbling block for the police, and perhaps the cause of the greatest number of mistakes,

is the procedures they have to go through when dealing
with a drink-driving suspect. The forms they have to complete are wordy and complicated, often making the rules
appear jumbled and snarled. Personally I don't mind this.
But then I have a peculiar affection for spending my free
time devouring law books and guidelines as well as all the
drink-driving procedure forms. (I was probably the only
person on the beach at Cannes last year whose holiday
reading included a speed camera's instruction manual.
Strange perhaps but, in my view, it's worth the pitying
glances for the pay-off.)

Deciding whether a suspect is over the limit is the crux of
any drink-driving case. As ever there are protocols to follow
– all of which are strewn with landmines. For a start there's no
single test. Instead there are three ways the hapless drink-
driving suspect can be assessed to see whether he's had one
tipple to many: breath, blood and urine. In each area there are
countless rules and regulations that guide the way the police
carry out these tests. Throw in the fact that not all boozed-up
detainees have the nicest party manners and it's understand-
able why errors happen. However, I'm a defence lawyer and
it's my job to grab these to demolish the Crown's case.

There are many examples of a mistake stymieing a drink-
driving case, so I've focused on some of my most memorable
cases to create just a snapshot of the scope for error.

Anyone suspected of drink-driving is usually given a
breath test first. It may be enough to provide a conclusive
result. Or it may be that the recorded result demands or
gives the suspect the option of providing a blood or urine
sample. This is the case when the alcohol reading is between
40 and 50mg per 100ml of breath.

Breathalysing has the potential to provide a rich source
of legal defences. For example, when a suspect is

breathalysed they're supposed to provide two specimens of breath within three minutes. Occasionally the second reading will be higher than the first. That doesn't mean the alcohol in the body is on the rise. But police officers sometimes mistakenly believe the time delay is causing the reading to go higher and so say to their suspect, 'If I were you, mate, I wouldn't bother doing a blood test. As the second reading is higher, at this rate, by the time the doctor gets here, you may be off the scale.' And so if this is an 'option case' (40–50mg inclusive per 100ml of breath) and it is established that the police may have said this, it would cause the case to collapse because he has, in effect, dissuaded the suspect from providing.

Actually it's not easy to do the breath test. I've had a go myself on a couple of occasions, just to see how difficult it is. Despite all those press-ups I do, it was still hard work. The flow of air has to be continuous and the machine produces some resistance. Even when your head is as clear as a bell and you have your wits about you, it can be a bit of a struggle.

I remember defending a solicitor who was stopped in his vintage Bentley leaving Ascot and charged with drink-driving. One of my defences was that he was too drunk to blow. And indeed an audio cassette of the breath test validated that he was making every effort to blow into the machine. This was critical because normally when people are being deliberately difficult they make the minimum effort to blow. In my client's case you could hear him trying repeatedly, yet still the machine didn't record a reading. It was rather perplexing. So I argued before the district judge that my client was too drunk to blow into the breathalyser. But he didn't accept my argument, so I took it on appeal to the Crown Court.

What's interesting about this case is that by the time the date came round for the new trial, I'd decided to focus on a second defence, which also related to the breathalyser.

Quite simply the police hadn't retained the mouthpiece. Sometimes officers just chuck them out, even if their guidelines tell them not to. Yet, as an expert would corroborate for me, mouthpieces can sometimes be defective, which is why the police need to hang onto them. Otherwise how would we know whether or not there'd been something blocking the mouthpiece and stopping my client from doing the breath test. In this case, my expert said the mouthpiece might have been defective and the Crown couldn't prove that it wasn't – because they didn't have it! What they should have done was retain the mouthpiece as an exhibit, as the police form directs. This would have permitted it to be tested. That was the end of the case.

Another twist on this theme is highlighted by a drink-driving case involving a motorist who had hit a lamppost yards away from his home. The incident was witnessed by a passer-by, who immediately dialled 999, and seven minutes after the collision my client received a knock on his door from the boys in blue. He was arrested on the spot and subsequently charged with both drink-driving and driving while unfit through drink. When the police had breathalysed him the reading was clearly well over the limit.

However, my client maintained that in the seven minutes between returning home and the police arriving at his door, he'd knocked back a whole bottle of Scotch. Presumably to settle his nerves after the accident. Now, I know that sounds like an eye-watering amount of alcohol. But I saw this as an example of what is known as the 'hip-flask defence', when booze has been consumed after an incident has occurred but before the suspect has been breathalysed. I'm not saying my client had been teetotal before hitting the lamppost. He'd been out and had enjoyed a couple of glasses of wine during the evening. But he hadn't been over the limit when the accident happened. What pushed him over was the whisky he had drunk on arriving home.

But how to prove this? To me, the central issue was proving my client could drink that quantity of whisky in such a short space of time. So, to corroborate this, I got an expert not only to consider the minimal impact of two glasses of wine on my client's formidable constitution, but also to video the defendant downing a whole bottle of whisky in about five minutes. Just to prove it could be done. This seminal piece of film making was played in court. The magistrates were convinced and acquitted my client of drink-driving on the basis that most of the alcohol had been consumed after the accident.

That should have been the end of that. But here's the twist. In a bizarre adjudication, the magistrates also found that the two glasses of wine my client had consumed before the accident rendered him unfit to drive! So I appealed to the Crown Court – and failed. However, I pressed on, utterly convinced of the accuracy of my defence. Thankfully, the High Court agreed, overturned the verdict and my client was acquitted.

Machines – as already illustrated with speed cameras – are not foolproof. They can malfunction or break down. Breathalysers are no different. That's why it's imperative to keep an eye on whether they are working properly or not.

I vividly remember defending one woman on her fourth drink-driving charge. (She had previously been acquitted of the other three.) On this fourth occasion she dutifully attempted to blow into the machine. However the machine indicated a problem, either with the breathalyser itself or the specimen of breath. When I received the paperwork I looked at the printout produced by the breathalyser. Actually, I scrutinised it, as part of my working method is to study every full stop and comma until my eyes start to blur. As I dissected the document I spotted the words 'interfering substance' on the printout. What this means is that somehow the breath has been contaminated, perhaps by a trace of acetone in the air. Acetone is naturally produced by the human body as a result of normal metabolic processes. However, this organic compound is also a substance that can be falsely identified as mouth alcohol by some breath machines. Both dieters and diabetics can have very high levels of acetone in their body, which they then exhale into the atmosphere. And this is what the breathalyser might have detected.

This is all speculation. And anyway, that wasn't my client's concern. The fact was that those two words 'interfering substance' were explosive. It meant that the breath readings were legally unreliable – and so my client should have been required to provide a sample of blood or urine instead. But she wasn't. It's a minor detail, but one the police hadn't noticed and maybe that's why the prosecution hadn't noticed either. The devil is in the detail. And it doesn't matter how slight or inscrutable that detail is. It's enough to make a case collapse. Which it did here.

It's important for both justice and public confidence to know that machines are working properly. That's why checks exist. There has to be a sense of fair play. But it cuts both ways. If checks haven't been carried out, who's to say there's any accuracy in the reading a breathalyser pulls up. Every step of the way, the law needs to be tested.

Take a case I did involving a racing driver who was slapped with a drink-drive charge after a breath test allegedly revealed him to be three times over the legal limit.

My client disputed the reading, claiming he'd only consumed a small amount of alcohol – maybe just a drink or two. Scrutinising the paperwork, my instinct started to prickle as I read the statement by the officer who'd dealt with my chap. Despite such a high reading, the copper hadn't noted down any significant signs to suggest my client was bladdered: no glazed eyes, unsteadiness or slurring of his words.

Now, the breathalyser was supposed to have been working properly. Yet here we had a man of good character, a first-time suspected offender, who volubly protested that he hadn't been sloshed.

Time, I thought, to test the law. So I consulted an expert and asked him, under controlled observation, to give my client enough alcohol to take him to over three times the legal limit. My client duly submitted himself to this, downed the booze and became utterly smashed. He could barely stand up, let alone remember his own name. Clearly then, if he had knocked back that amount of drink on the night of the offence, there's no way a police officer would have missed the obvious signs.

What the test suggested was that the original reading had to have been wrong. Or at least that there was some doubt concerning the efficacy of the machine. Otherwise my client would have been blind drunk. Though we lost the case at the magistrates court, we won it on appeal at the Crown Court.

One of my most memorable defences involved a chap who crashed his Ferrari into a dry stone wall on an unlit country lane. My client was arrested at the scene, duly breathalysed and found to be over the limit. So far, so straightforward. But here's the flaw. For the breath reading to be valid, there usually has to be evidence of calibration checks on the device. The Crown didn't produce any evidence of this, so how could the court be satisfied that the machine was actually working properly? The simple answer was, they couldn't. Which is why I won the case.

As I mentioned earlier, depending on the reading produced by the breathalyser, it may well be that a drink-driving suspect will be offered or obliged to give a blood or urine sample. For example, in an alcohol breath test the legally prescribed limit is 35mg of alcohol in 100ml of breath, although the police don't usually prosecute readings under 40mg. The idea behind this is that the odds are stacked in favour of the motorist. It's a way of making absolutely sure that they are over the limit before the wheels of justice start to turn.

If a defendant nudges over 40mg, even producing a reading of up to 50 inclusive, the law says he has an option to have that specimen of breath replaced by a blood or urine sample. It's actually commendable that this option exists, since it allays the natural fear and suspicion of having a machine decide your fate.

I'm the first to admit that the statute governing what happens in these cases is slightly baffling because of complex procedures, and could well explain why on occasion police officers trip themselves up.

Taking blood itself can be fraught with difficulties. First of all when blood is taken, it is divided into two containers. One is for the police to send away for analysis. The other sample is available to the driver should he want to arrange his own independent investigation of the blood. Sometimes, though, in the fuss of all the form filling, the police fail to hand it over. By simply messing up on dishing out a thimbleful of blood, if the defendant asks for it, the police kneecap their own case.

Meanwhile, the police sample has to be stored, labelled, marked and then sent to the forensic laboratory. All of this is tracked by a paper trail which has to be consistent in terms of dates and time, for obvious reasons. The blood also has to be stored properly so that there is no scope for contamination. Get any of this wrong and the case may evaporate.

Already your eyes may well be glazing over. But it gets far more complex, I'm afraid. So much so that sometimes the police can actually mistakenly use the wrong words when taking blood from a suspect. And that can knuckle a case.

This is exactly what happened in the case of Paige Savage, the wife of Def Leppard drummer Rick Savage. Mrs Savage gave a lower breath-test reading of 43mg and so was entitled to an option of providing a sample of blood or urine instead, since this reading was below 51mg. But the problem here was that in obtaining the blood the police took the wrong approach. They dealt with the case as if she *had* to provide – rather than having the *option* to provide – and warned her that if she didn't she would be liable for prosecution. So simply because of incorrect wording, the blood sample she provided was inadmissible. The statutory procedure hadn't been followed and the Crown dropped the case.

I know a lot of my detractors, particularly road safety campaigners, are inflamed by this kind of scenario. After all, the defendant provided the specimen of blood and analysis of this put her allegedly over the limit. Why should she be acquitted? This clash of factual and lawful accuracy is something I'll come to later in the book. Suffice it to say here that in my own private thoughts, away from the courtroom, I sympathise with this view. But legal procedures have to be followed. It's the role of the lawyer to spot that what Parliament says must happen does happen when a drink-driving suspect is dealt with in custody – and when it doesn't.

Cases like this, of course, raise the question: what is the point of this legislation, and should it be more just? But justice and legal procedure can be mutually exclusive. Which is why someone undeserving of an acquittal can sometimes go free as a result of the complexities of the law, and it also means that those who ought to be acquitted have less chance of being convicted.

Incidentally, in Mrs Savage's case, I was able to win on this point because the prosecution hadn't noticed this police cock-up. Which suggests that perhaps the case had not been looked at as carefully as it should have been. Surely someone doing a thorough job – and bear in mind these cases take months to come to trial – should have thought, this is wrong, we can't prove this case. End of.

After the trial Mrs Savage was so grateful that as we walked out of court she grabbed me in a bear hug in front of the phalanx of press and joked, 'If I wasn't already married I would marry him.' (That picture of me bring gripped in her grateful embrace was splashed across the news pages.) The small matter of my already being a married man seemed to have passed her by. One loophole I certainly couldn't dodge. Still, I always appreciate the sentiment of a grateful client.

It's important to bear in mind that the state a suspect is in when they are pulled over or taken into custody can be the catalyst for a police error. There you have a motorist, terrified and mortified after having been brought into the station.

They record a breath-test reading of between 40 and 50mg inclusive of alcohol and a police officer starts talking about the tested person having the option to give a blood or urine sample instead.

How on earth can someone in this state make the right judgement? The frightened motorist may turn to the police officer and say, 'What should I do?' But it's vital that the officer doesn't offer any advice. His job is simply to explain the options. He mustn't do anything to influence the defendant. It's the motorist's call. If the police officer gives advice, he does so at his own peril – and in doing so he may demolish the Crown's case.

I remember one case like this where my defence was that my client had been dissuaded from providing a blood sample. The officer was emphatic that this hadn't happened and that, in effect, my client was making it up. What was interesting was that, unbeknown to the officer, I'd pulled in the custody record for the night in question. And on the document the sergeant had quite clearly marked that the defendant had been given the option and had been willing to provide a specimen of blood. Evidently then something must have happened to change my client's mind. The officer disputed that the defendant had ever willingly agreed to provide. Ah, but he didn't know I had a document that totally contradicted his version of events. That's why I always get the custody record and go through it with a fine-tooth comb. Often there are pointers there that are incredibly useful.

I pulled out this little hand grenade and asked the policeman to read the custody record out to the court.

'Perhaps you want to reconsider your statement that the defendant has never agreed to provide?' I suggested after he'd finished.

Clearly either the officer was wrong or the record taken by the custody sergeant at the time of the test was incorrect. The officer capitulated. He humbly suggested that something clearly had taken place, something he clearly couldn't recall, to affect the course of events. That was the end of the case.

The examples go on and on and by now I'm sure you can see a picture forming. So I'll offer just one example where urine testing was concerned. This case involved a very successful businessman who faced an allegation of drink-driving. My client had given a positive breath test at the roadside, but at the police station he had been asked to provide an alternative urine sample. The law says two specimens should be taken within an hour, and the alcohol test is carried out on the second one. It turned out it was an hour and a quarter before my client was asked to provide the second sample, so he was cleared of drink-driving.

But even I was out-loopholed here. The case was taken to the High Court by the prosecution, a place where the judges overturned the acquittal. One of the roles of High Court judges is to interpret the law that Parliament sets down in statute. In this case the statute – the Road Traffic Act 1988, specifically Section 7(5), which clearly states that two specimens of urine need to be provided within an hour of a request being made.

What could be clearer? Yet the High Court took the view that the extra fifteen minutes had no bearing on the case. That, to me, is the loophole – the disparity between what Parliament states and the judiciary's interpretation. (Incidentally, it's an issue that became abundantly clear with the emergence of the super-injunction.) But the High Court is a higher authority than the Crown Court and magistrates court. And, for lawyers, the High Court's decision is binding – unless overturned by a higher authority.

Actually, when urine samples are taken, the receptacle has to be washed or changed between each specimen, to minimise the risk of contamination. I remember getting a case thrown out in Ashton-under-Lyne on this very point. When I cross-examined the officer it seemed he'd flushed away the first sample, then got my client to pee in the same receptacle again. But how could he be sure there was nothing left of the first specimen before he took the second? He couldn't.

To my mind, in this kind of situation the law simply causes problems for itself. My view is that it would be so much simpler if a defendant was accompanied to a toilet and told to do his first pee there. Then to do his second sample into a receptacle. That way there's no fear of contamination. And yet it simply isn't always done.

In another case my client, who happened to be a lawyer herself, was told to produce her two urine samples together: she was asked to pee, stop, then pee again, all within the same time. What I argued was that the urine she produced was all part of the same specimen. The magistrates didn't agree and convicted her, though I won the case on appeal at the Crown Court.

So, you see, there is just so much for a police officer to absorb. Mistakes happen because we're human. In fact it requires almost superhuman effort to be alive to every single possible error that an officer might make. But if a defence lawyer is prepared to pore over the statutes and procedures, he may find the ammunition he needs to mount a successful defence.

As I mentioned earlier, the highly charged atmosphere of a busy police station can create the setting for mistakes. Take the case of a lady who escaped drink-driving charges after it emerged that an administrator working at that station, rather than an officer, had charged her. It's the kind of thing you simply can't predict and it was a detail that emerged unexpectedly during the case.

How would such a detail get flushed out? In this case I was beetling along, cross-examining an officer when I asked if he knew who'd charged the defendant. The name on the charge sheet didn't correspond with that of any of the prosecution witnesses. So who was this mystery person? I wondered aloud. It turned out that it was a clerical worker! And further investigation revealed that she didn't have the power to charge. My client was acquitted and awarded costs.

Of course, a key player in drink-driving cases is the defence lawyer. Yes, that's me. Everyone is entitled to a lawyer when they are brought into custody. This is enshrined in statute – yet it has been eroded by case law. It's become one of those 'we should do but we don't' situations. Consequently there have been many drink-driving cases where the rights of suspects have been overlooked. A terrible irony since the defendant is likely to be drunk and could self-incriminate. So, in my opinion, the vulnerable motorist should be afforded more protection, not less.

I had one case involving footballer Mark Kennedy, who arrived at Wilmslow Police Station in Cheshire on suspicion of drink-driving. As would emerge in court, the Wolves player asked for a solicitor, and since one wasn't forthcoming he refused to do a breath test. (Because time is of the essence in alcohol testing, sometimes police officers rush their detainee onto the breathalyser machine before they start busying themselves with the task of tracking down a lawyer.)

We lost the case even though I took it all the way to the High Court. However, at the appeal, the judge did make an important point. He said that once a defendant asks for a lawyer the police must, in certain circumstances, make every effort to find out if one is available – if it will cause little or no delay to the breath-test procedure.

Though I lost the Kennedy case, I mentally banked the judgment. I hate losing, and smart for ages afterwards. But I also try to push my ego aside in order to learn what I can from the result.

So, when I had a case at Cheltenham Magistrates Court involving England and Gloucester rugby player Henry Paul, I pulled out the Kennedy case from the corner of my mind. Paul also claimed he'd been denied representation in custody. So, during cross-examination, I asked the custody sergeant, 'Have you got the custody record? Do you recall this defendant asking for legal representation?'

'Well, it's marked down here, sir, so it must be right,' he replied earnestly.

'How did you respond to that request, Sergeant?'

'I did what we always do down here,' he replied, again earnestly.

'What's that, Sergeant?'

'I told the defendant that he could have a solicitor after he'd been on the machine.'

No defiance, no arrogance: just a clear account of 'how we do things down here'.

The judge and I exchanged startled glances, both trying to stifle our disbelief.

The prosecution looked deeply embarrassed too. I then made a submission that the effect of such an attitude was to deprive the defendant of any legal access at all. The Crown couldn't argue against this and my client was acquitted.

★ ★ ★

It's not just police who mess up. On many occasions prosecutors have handed me the case because there has been a failing in their legal duty. It's not easy being a prosecutor – as I said, I've been one myself. And you can't always have your hands on all the law all the time. But, then, that's their problem. Ever since being stung by a defence lawyer as a young prosecutor I've tried to make it my business to be totally *au fait* with every single aspect of my case.

It's like revising for an exam. If you put the time in, you give your client and yourself the best chance of success. If you try to be selective, or don't do the case justice, you can't really expect to get great results. Things can arise *ex improviso* (unexpectedly) during the proceedings, so, even if you've gone in with certain defences, you can react to something that happens during the trial if you know your law.

And when you know your law, you know when your opponent is being unlawful. Take the case of Tory MEP Timothy Kirkhope, who was due to stand trial at Sheffield Magistrates Court after he'd allegedly been clocked at 35mph in his Mercedes in a 30mph zone. My client had been coming back from a visit to researchers at Sheffield University when he was caught on the speed camera.

Just before the trial was due to start, the prosecution wanted to make what's known as a hearsay application – that's an application to admit evidence which wouldn't be otherwise permitted to be included. They planned to make their application on the day of the trial – which was too late to make such a move – and for no good reason. I knew this evidence was crucial to their case and I opposed it. There's a time frame for including evidence and that had elapsed. They should have acted much sooner. The district judge agreed. My client was acquitted because without the evidence contained in the hearsay application the Crown couldn't prove its case.

At the time my client already had nine points on his licence and, if convicted of speeding, he could well have been banned from driving for six months.

But this case has stayed in my mind for another reason too. At the time it was going on, the Chief Constable of South Yorkshire, Meredydd Hughes, had allegedly been caught driving at 90mph in a 60mph zone. The previous year Chief Constable Hughes had maintained that officers were becoming increasingly frustrated with lawyers who used legal small print to win acquittals for clients (though he did add that it was the police's responsibility to prosecute offences correctly). So I had him on my radar.

Now, it's not often that a Chief Constable is charged with speeding. So I wanted to take this case, even going on national television and offering to defend him for nothing. I felt that by working together in this way Chief Constable Hughes would appreciate some of the difficulties and shortcomings that his police officers encounter when dealing with offending motorists. In turn this would enable his force – and others – to tighten up their procedures. The net result of which would be safer roads.

Not a bad offer all in all. Particularly since Mr Hughes was only recently quoted in the *Yorkshire Post* as saying he was 'offered the services of a famous loophole lawyer but I decided to plead guilty even though there were a number of defects in the prosecution case'.

What's more, Chief Constable Hughes was also head of the Association of Chief Police Officers (ACPO), one of the roles of which is to offer guidelines on road policing issues.

Unfortunately the Chief Constable declined to take up my offer. What a wasted opportunity, since he could have used his elevated position to showcase the defects in the prosecution case and so focus the spotlight on the sort of legal blunders that I constantly highlight in my work.

A short time later I heard that Chief Constable Hughes had asked for his case to be adjourned to allow time for finding a legal representative. I renewed my offer but he declined again. And just as my client Timothy Kirkhope was being acquitted, this high-ranking police officer was disqualified for forty-two days and fined £350 by Wrexham magistrates. Oh dear.

What can make prosecuting a case very difficult is when the prosecution's witnesses don't show up or call in sick. But, unless this absenteeism is handled correctly, the Crown can play directly into the hands of the defence. Take the case I had involving a chap charged with driving without due care and attention and drink-driving. On the day of the trial the witnesses to the accident didn't appear. It meant the prosecution had no witnesses to prove the 'due care' offence and so agreed to bin that particular charge and just focus on the drink-driving charge.

In order to save time and disperse with the 'due care' charge, the prosecution, with my agreement, prepared written evidence to confirm that my client had been lawfully arrested. The prosecutor wrote down the facts, then I checked them and signed them. However, in setting down the list of facts, the prosecutor mentioned the defendant's name and what had happened, but failed to formally state that the defendant was the driver. I signed the document – it wasn't for me to point out the mistake. And I sat back and waited for the judge to spot this glaring omission. He did and the case was thrown out.

★ ★ ★

By revealing this litany of Crown cock-ups, I'm not trying to gloat or suggest that these officers of the court and constabulary are inept. But I think what I do is healthy and will ultimately make for better prosecuting authorities.

We're fortunate in this country that we don't have a police state. It is imperative that lawyers like me can test the system and reveal its flaws. That way we should have better policing and therefore safer roads. And that will benefit all of us.

8

Loophole: check the small print

I've been following the same morning routine for as long as I can remember – though I'm the first to admit it's probably not to everyone's taste.

As I've already told you, I drag myself out of bed around 6.30am, punish my barely conscious body with a selection of stretches, tummy tucks and press-ups, and then either go for a run or take the dog for a long walk. Back home, it's a cold shower – I read somewhere it stimulates the brain cells and I haven't been able to shake off that thought ever since – then I feel I've earned my breakfast. Like I say, not to everyone's taste, and at times not even to mine. But as I constantly tell myself, 'Fit body, fit mind, get on with it.' So I keep it up. I try to, anyway.

After such a flurry of activity, I relish the tranquillity of breakfast: as a lawyer racing around from court to court, I savour that calm, almost reflective, half-hour before the business of the day begins. I have my holier-than-thou pro-biotic yoghurt, plate of fruit and a nice cup of hot water and lemon while reading the paper. Very noble, perhaps. But also very relaxing.

And so it was one particularly bright autumn morning. The sunlight was slanting in through the kitchen windows as I sat back contentedly, blowing curls of steam from my morning cuppa. All was good with the world. That was until I opened my newspaper and was confronted by a screaming headline: 'Rooney Scores Hat Trick of Driving Convictions.'

Rooney? Wayne Rooney? The same Wayne Rooney who plays for Manchester United and who'd recently instructed me to defend him over, yes, three driving charges? I sat bolt upright in shock.

The case hadn't even reached court yet. How the hell could my client be tried and convicted? What on earth was going on? And what would the soccer star be thinking if he'd read the papers too?

I had to move quickly. I leapt out of my chair – nearly scalding myself with hot water and lemon – and ran to the phone. A few frantic calls – to my office, to Liverpool Magistrates Court and the CPS – and the fog of confusion slowly began to lift. In short, my client had been felled by an almighty clerical error.

Here's what had happened. Wayne had come to me after being stopped by the police at the wheel of his BMW X5 in Liverpool and asked to produce his driving documents. (By coincidence, at that time we also had an X5, our family 'bus'.) If you don't have your licence and insurance documents on you in situations like this, the police often give you seven days to produce them. Wayne missed the deadline and so was summonsed to court. That was the long and short of it.

The first thing I did on taking this case was to contact the court by fax as well as by first-class post, to ask for the matter to be adjourned so that we could take full instructions and get all the necessary paperwork ready for the first hearing. I wanted to see what the evidence was to warrant such accusations – not least because I find it amazing how often footballers, get pulled over by the police.

For some reason, however, our request for the adjournment didn't reach the magistrates. Instead, as I would later
discover, it languished unnoticed in the court's adminis-
tration offices. And since the court didn't marry our
request up with the relevant papers, there was nothing on
record to show that we were acting for Wayne Rooney. It
appeared, instead, that my client was simply ignoring the
wheels of justice. On this assumption, the court went
ahead with a trial in Wayne's absence and slapped him
with convictions for driving without insurance. All done
without the United star being there – which the court was
perfectly entitled to do.

Obviously the press devoured the story and it was duly
splashed across the papers. And that's how I splashed hot
water and lemon down my trousers. As I said, the first thing
I did – even before changing my trousers – was make a
flurry of phone calls. My most pressing task was to check
my firm had done their job properly. I called my loyal secretary to confirm that we had sent the papers in. I felt bad
querying this – Denise has been with me for years and is
amazingly efficient – but I had to make sure the problem
wasn't our mistake.

'Of course we did,' Denise replied evenly. 'Why are you
asking?' I should never have doubted her. I was enormously
relieved to be assured that whatever had triggered this mess,
we were not in any way responsible.

Next I rang the court and pleasantly (though inwardly
seething) requested that they investigate the matter.

Soon the jigsaw pieces fell into place. In an apologetic
phone call, I was told by the court that the trial had gone
ahead because our correspondence had been overlooked. I
have to admit I could feel a red mist scudding over me when
I heard this. I know I should strive to be more tolerant, but

I'm not blessed with a great deal of patience or an ability to take incompetence in my stride. I was furious. It was all so unnecessary. The letter hadn't been taken from the post and put with the court papers. It just sat around the administration office. That's why there was no record. This error caused unnecessary anxiety and upheaval, as well as messing up my whole day, as I had to cancel my morning appointments while I sorted out this pressing matter.

So those were the facts. However, I learnt many years ago that 'the art of cross-examination is not to examine crossly', which is why I always remain calm, composed and professional at all times (even if my head is swimming with swear words). So I bottled my irritation and got the case re-listed as quickly as possible.

Then I went back to court with all the perfect documentation in place to prove we had requested the adjournment and that Mr Rooney was lawful in everything he had done in relation to this incident – that is, he had provided the necessary paperwork. I then invited the court to set the conviction aside (which means that the case was put back into the state it was before the conviction – as if the person had not been convicted), which the law entitled us to do under Section 142 of the Magistrates Courts Act 1980, a section specifically designed to deal with administrative mistakes.

I then produced my client's licence and certificate of insurance, which were in good order, and the prosecution agreed to take no further action. Good day, everybody.

Situations like this more than add to my already fine collection of grey hair and to my dry-cleaning bill: it's just gratuitous stress which no one ever needs. But what's so infuriating is that all that anxiety and frantic activity could be avoided if mistakes like this didn't happen in the first place. Unfortunately they do and, in my view, it's down to one of the biggest bugbears of the legal profession: paperwork. Or rather mountains of paperwork.

I remember a journalist who once interviewed me in my office remarking that law seemed to be nothing but paperwork. It certainly sometimes looks that way. On that particular day there were bulging case files heaped up on desks and piled on cabinets. But the truth is that this reporter was right. Law generates a massive amount of paperwork. Every case snags in its wake a frightening paper trail. The relevant parties and authorities have to be kept in the loop. Correspondence, forms, summonses, NIPs – the list seems endless. There's simply rainforests of the stuff. And wherever you get paperwork, human error isn't lagging far behind.

But why are there *so many* administrative errors? Maybe it's because the CPS and the constabulary are under-resourced. Maybe it's the dizzying effect of looking at so many documents that causes the eyes to blur. Paperwork in my profession is like a beast that needs taming. It needs to be filed, presented properly, married up with relevant court papers. If that doesn't happen, then mistakes do. As I was once wisely told by an old colleague, when it comes to paperwork, 'File it, bin it or pass it on to the right person.'

For example, it's amazing the number of letters that go missing in the handling of a case. You can write three or four times to the CPS asking for this or that, and the requests can be ignored – or maybe they were never even received.

However, though I do get infuriated when administrative errors happen, there can be a net benefit. Sure, mistakes like the one in Wayne Rooney's case can quicken the pulse and bring stress. But these clerical errors can sometimes spell out in BIG letters a strategy for a potentially successful legal defence. The flow chart, as always, shows a connection between an error and a so-called loophole.

So what are typical errors? Well, when names are mis-spelt, or wrong addresses or dates are recorded, notices or summonses arrive after the allotted time for their dispatch has expired. It doesn't matter if these things (and more) happen at best in all innocence or at worst because of incompetence: a blameless bureaucratic blunder can still make all the difference between a conviction and an acquittal. It's that loose rivet that causes the machinery of court procedure to come crashing down.

Look, we're all human. I'm not saying I'm perfect – certainly my ex-wife, my kids and some of my pals wouldn't think I was either. In fact away from work I've been guilty of the odd administrative blunder of my own.

Last summer I was landed with a massive bill because I failed to read the small print on my pet insurance before I took my Staffie, Rocco, on holiday to the south of France. While we were out walking in the hills one bright morning, he suddenly collapsed. Frantic, I rushed him to a vet in Nice, who diagnosed him with an auto-immune condition. The treatment involved blood transfusions and an extensive stay in an animal hospital. I assumed the medical bills, which ran into thousands of pounds, were covered by my policy. But when I called the insurers they said I should have told them about the trip before I left and duly paid an additional £100 for Rocco to be covered. I hadn't. And I ended up being much more seriously out of pocket. I just hadn't got round to reading the policy.

In work, however, I wouldn't dream of doing this (and since it happened I've tried to avoid it out of the office too). But, as I say, we're all human. However, what I find astonishing about administrative sloppiness in my profession is that, by and large, we're dealing with legal documents.

These have to be precise. If they're not, they can tip a case on its head.

The trick then is to be able to spot such errors. There's no real skill here – just a laser-like focus. Though in my case, as I said at the beginning of this book, I seem almost incapable of ignoring tiny details. Things just leap out at me, and not only at work. I remember once noticing a tiny dent on my wife's car. Since the car was due to have some more extensive repair to a wing, I suggested she get this dimpled bit of bodywork sorted out at the same time. When she brought the car home the following day, the dent was still there. Neither she nor the garage had been able to find it. Yet when she parked up I saw it straight away!

It's as if my eyes are in overdrive and I don't know how to make them take a more neutral view of the world. However, this often works to my advantage in practising law. Marry an over-active eye for detail with evidence of basic bureaucratic carelessness, throw in a slack-eyed prosecutor and, bingo, your nose twitches at the strong scent of a possible victory.

Sometimes my defences can amount to nothing more than proofreading. For if the prosecuting authorities don't bother to check documents, they often leave the field wide open for me to win. And so, when I first receive all the evidence relating to a case, I have a checklist in my head as I sift through the statements and legal notices. Such as:

Have police officers filled in the right statements?
Have they got the right dates and the right days?
Have they got the right road, the right car, right name, right number plate.

To name but a few. I'm rooting out any possible errors with which to attack the Crown's credibility. For example, there's nothing like my old friend Mr Spelling Mistake to dish up a potential oven-ready defence. Names are critical in law since they relate precisely to an individual. If the authorities misspell a name on a Notice of Intended Prosecution – the form sent out when you've been flashed by a speed camera – then, to me, it raises an interesting point.

On the back of the NIP – where the Section 172 is normally printed – the recipient is required by law to provide information about who was driving the car at the time of the offence. If the addressee's name isn't spelt correctly, then, in my opinion, *potentially* there may be no legal obligation to fill in the Section 172 (though a lawyer would have to make that judgement on a case-by-case basis rather than as a unilateral ruling). And I take the view that it has the potential to be a defence. After all, who should sign the form?

The legal obligation to fill in the Section 172 rests solely with the person to whom the notice is addressed. If the spelling is fine and dandy, the issue doesn't arise. But if it isn't? Well, as I say, every case has to be assessed individually. But I did use this legal argument successfully when representing the polar explorer Sir Ranulph Fiennes. Sir Ranulph was sent a speeding summons after he was allegedly snapped by a speed camera driving at 50mph on a 40mph road, but the Section 172 notice – the requirement for the registered keeper to identify the driver at the time of the alleged offence – was sent to the wrong address.

Not only was it sent to the wrong house, but it was addressed to Ralph Fiennes, the famous film actor, who is my client's distant cousin. (Had someone at central ticket office been watching a re-run of *The English Patient* or *Schindler's List*?)

Regardless of the reason, Sir Ranulph failed to respond

to the notice – a potentially far more serious offence, for which he was due to be hauled before magistrates in Northwich, Cheshire. Meanwhile he was sent another letter notifying him of this, and while this one got his first name right, his surname was misspelt! If it could even be said to be his surname!

What I found astonishing was that the mix-up with Ralph Fiennes came two years after another speeding case against Sir Ranulph, this time in Market Drayton, Shropshire, was scrapped for similar reasons. On that occasion, my client had been summonsed to appear before magistrates after allegedly failing to provide information about the driver of a Land Rover snapped by a speed camera on the A41 Whitchurch bypass. However, the initial notice was addressed to a Mr Ran Flens – who doesn't exist. A reminder was sent to this same, non-existent person who was later contended to be the client.

Faced with this nonsensical typo, the prosecuting authorities would have to ask themselves how my client could be identified in terms of full name and date of birth if the name on the document was incorrect. This was something the great explorer needed me to explore. I did and the case was discontinued. As was the one which was to follow.

Not all administrative blunders are down to office staff who are too busy eating their Pot Noodles or moonlighting on Facebook to take care over what they're doing. At times it can be a matter of not getting the right document to the right place on time. I can almost imagine these various bits of paper strewn around desks just waiting for someone to muster enough strength and enthusiasm to make the trek to the postroom down the corridor.

A lot of legal documents are time-sensitive. When a speed camera or a handheld device snaps its prey, in some cases the resulting NIP has to be sent out so that it can arrive at the address of the vehicle's registered keeper within four-teen days of the incident. Any later and it may be fatal to the case. Surely, you'd think, with so many speeders on the road, the courts would have got this simple technique off pat. Or rather off to Postman Pat. It seems not.

Take the case of cricketer Andrew Flintoff, who eventu-ally received a summons for speeding. The incident was captured on camera, the car allegedly travelling at 87mph in a 50mph zone on 1 July. Critically the first NIP was sent to the registered keeper so that it arrived on 19 July. By my brilliant mathematical skill (well, counting on my fingers) I calculated that this was five days beyond the fourteen-day time limit. Howzat!

When the prosecutor at Liverpool Crown Court was made aware of this fact just before proceedings started, he conceded that there was no case to answer. We trooped into court only for the case to be dropped in a matter of moments. Even I was a little, excuse the pun, bowled over by the breathtaking pace of the turn of events.

Afterwards a reporter came up to me and said, 'Mr Freeman, that took forty-one seconds to get thrown out – I timed it.'

I grinned and replied, 'Timing is everything! Was it really that long? I'll have to try and do better next time.' A bit of victory bravado as I haven't yet managed to live up to it.

Aside from the sheer speed of the proceedings, the memory of that case has lingered in my mind for other rea-sons. Next morning I read with some satisfaction that it had made front-page news. As I browsed through the rest of the paper I found another law story buried in the inside pages: it seemed that on the day of Andrew Flintoff's court victory, the Court of Appeal freed four alleged Al Qaeda terrorists. It was a brutal reminder of the commodity of celebrity and why my loophole cases would continue to make the news. I could have wrung my hands at the sheer triteness of it all.

Of course, my client's case was important to him and it was important that the law was upheld. But should it really have overshadowed a case involving allegations of international terrorism? So, although I was pleased to win my case, the priority its newsworthiness was given left a sour taste in my mouth.

Timing, then, is a vital component in defending cases. But what happens when the reason for a delay in the receipt of documents isn't because somebody in the postroom is nursing a hangover or because a wad of papers falls down the back of a filing cabinet? What happens when the postal service itself is to blame or, more precisely, the workers who decide to down tools and go on strike?

It's worth pointing out what you should do should another wave of discontent wash over Royal Mail. If there is a postal strike and you receive an NIP after being flashed by a camera for speeding, keep the envelope and ideally get a witness, if possible the postman, to confirm when the letter was delivered. It is a good idea to keep a diary as well, to provide further proof. But you mustn't ignore the notice, even if it arrives late – that is, more than fourteen days after the incident. As I said earlier, the keeper of the car has a legal duty to say who was driving at the time of the offence. Once the Section 172 has been filled in and sent back, the driver will eventually receive a summons for speeding. And he will be found not guilty, since the NIP for speeding arrived late. This loophole will not apply if there has been an accident.

If, however, the keeper doesn't comply with his legal duty to name the driver he will be summonsed with the separate offence of failing to furnish. The fact that the notice arrives late will not afford him a defence as there is no requirement here for an NIP to be served within fourteen days.

Postal strikes aside, NIPs are normally sent out by first-class post, the presumption being that it reaches its destination.

But what about that old chestnut 'I never received it – it must have got lost in the post'? Personally I think the prosecuting authorities could sidestep this perpetual problem by considering the use of recorded delivery. Pricey, I know, but when you think of taxpayers' money being squandered on court cases that fail because of postal problems, you'd think it might be worth the authorities sticking their hands into the public purse.

So much for a sluggish postal system. Nevertheless, time-frames for legal documents are enshrined in statute. The clock ticks as soon as there's an allegation of an offence and the paper trail stirs into life. Yet it amazes me how administrators for the Crown can get their calendars in a twist. Which is why checking and rechecking dates of offences, dates marked on documents, dates franked on envelopes, is a critical part of my work.

When legendary musician Van Morrison was alleged to have been driving his BMW at 36mph in a 30mph zone, the court papers revealed that the prosecuting authorities had served them late. In this case it was a summons to appear before magistrates.

Now, in most driving cases the information must be laid (that is, prepared by the court and ready to be sent) within a maximum period of six months from the incident. But what happens if it arrives after the six months? Then it's a case of how long is a piece of string and the law becomes uncertain and inconsistent. I've lost count of the number of times this has happened. And believe me, six months is one hell of a long time in law, so why leave it to the last moment?

In Van's case the summons was indeed printed just before the end of the statutory six-month period. But it wasn't actually issued until after the six months had elapsed – namely, six days afterwards. The Crown accepted that there was unnecessary delay and decided to discontinue the case.

I should point out that things seem to be changing a little and it seems to me that courts are, worryingly, becoming more flexible in their approach to fastidious timekeeping. When I represented the TV presenter Chris Tarrant, my defence had been this same abuse of process: that is, that the summons didn't reach my client until after the six-month time limit. In fact there was a delay of about two months before the court sent out the documents in the post. (Chris's 155mph Mercedes-Benz CL500 had allegedly been clocked doing 17mph above the 30mph speed limit in Upper Bucklebury, Berkshire.)

Now, my view and my argument was that the spirit of the legislation was designed to ensure that people were notified that they were being prosecuted within a maximum of six months. That is, the summons should be prepared by the courts, sent and received within a six-month period. If, for one reason or another, the paperwork languished in an office for an additional two months, that should in my opinion constitute an abuse of process. But in this case the Crown argued that the information was laid (prepared) a day before the end of the six months, so it didn't really matter. I just don't accept this. Six months is more than ample opportunity to inform a defendant of the offence for which they are being prosecuted.

Though it's a personal view, I cannot understand this arbitrary approach – even though there's a substantial amount of case law that goes against my argument. (Mind you, many lawyers believe that case law is too pro-prosecution.)

But I think the statute and interpretation need to be much clearer. The spirit of the legislation was intended to show that defendants would know within a specific period of time if they were to be prosecuted. To my mind, that should be a finite period of time that would be strictly adhered to. It shouldn't be extended even for a day. Otherwise, when does a late document matter? A notice that is one, two or ten years late? How overdue does it need to be before it is an abuse of process?

I'll admit, I'm still smarting from the Tarrant case. But different prosecutors deal with things in different ways. One can see two months as being barely a smudge over the deadline; another can think six days is too long.

It's fair to say that legal paperwork isn't terribly sexy or inviting. Many film and television dramas play on the glamour of the legal profession, but they rarely train the lens on the mountains of documents we lawyers almost drown in, day in and day out. Why would they? Paperwork is dull. It doesn't whet the appetite or coax the receiver into soaking up every luscious detail. Indeed because legal documents are, by their very nature, tedious to read, it's easy to overlook misprints. Unless, like me, you weather yourself for the tedium and take a microscope to every comma and semi-colon.

Sometimes, though, an error can happen at the most seminal stage of court procedure. Let me take you back to early 2000 and one particular magistrates court in the north of England, where a monumental administrative glitch flung the doors open for countless motorists to secure an acquittal.

Just to remind you, when a driver is flashed by a speed camera, he or she then receives a notice of intended prosecution (NIP). It's an important document as it's an essential element in a case of speeding where no accident has taken place. The NIP is usually sent out with a Section 172 form – normally printed on the reverse – which demands that the registered keeper of the car supplies details, if known, of who was driving the vehicle when it was zapped.

Once instructed, a defence lawyer should receive a copy of the NIP, with the completed Section 172 form, from the prosecuting authorities. That way, if the evidence is agreed with the prosecution, it saves the bother of having to call 'live' witnesses (that is, real people, rather than their written statements being read out to the court).

Around this time, in early 2000, a lot of speeding cases were being funnelled through this particular magistrates court. But for some reason, when the prosecuting authorities bundled all their paperwork together for each case (and then copied it for the defence lawyer), the NIPs with the Section 172 on the back weren't attached. Now, this was a pretty lethal error. Why? Because inscribed on the NIP are the hallowed words, 'Sent by or on behalf of the Chief of Police.' This phrase is sacred, because it's a statutory requirement and it confirms the authority of the correspondence.

However, if there's no Section 172 notice, then there's no vital wording. No wording, then no complying with what is demanded in law. Without this critical document, the prosecution's evidence is fatally flawed.

Every time I received my bundle of papers from the prosecution I'd spot this glaring omission. Then I incubated it. It wasn't for me to point out the Crown's problems. Well, not, at least, until the prosecution presented their evidence in court. Then I'd ignite my defence. Without the correct paperwork, the case would be thrown out. And not just one case. Case after case was junked because the lumbering, monolithic court system didn't have a handle on the problem. Every time I took one of these to court the prosecution would bin it. I can't begin to tell you how many clients were acquitted on this point. It took years for someone to finally crank up enough enthusiasm to rectify the error.

But there was a darker side to this legal loophole, and this came to light one morning when I was defending a client in a road-traffic case. As usual, the evidence provided by the prosecution didn't contain the Section 172. Winning was going to be as easy as slicing a warm knife through soft butter. But then something happened which took the edge off my victory. While the magistrates retired to debate my submission, I chatted to the court clerk.

'We had fourteen cases like this yesterday, Mr Freeman,' he told me cheerily.

'Really?' Clearly someone else had spotted the get-out clause too. 'All those acquittals, eh?'

'No, we potted the lot of them,' affirmed the clerk enthusiastically.

'I don't get it,' I said.

'They were all found guilty.'

I still didn't understand what he was saying.

'But how? If there was no Section 172, they should have been acquitted.'

The clerk gave a dismissive shrug. 'Simple, they were all unrepresented.'

I looked at him in astonishment.

'Hang about, how could you do that? The cases were all legally defective. You're the legal adviser. You should know that, and you're supposed to be advising magistrates of the law.'

The clerk gave another helpless shrug. 'I know that. But it's all about stats.'

It was a shameful admission. Whoever was responsible had allowed defendants who either hadn't shown up or who didn't have any legal representation, to get slapped with a fine and points on their licence as there was no one to contest this particular issue.

Another solicitor happened to be listening to the conversation, and she and I exchanged a look of horror. People were being convicted when clearly they shouldn't have been. Everyone realised that the Crown couldn't prove each case, because of the administrative error.

But if the defendant didn't come to court, or was defending himself and so didn't know the law, then the Crown obviously thought, we'll clobber him with a conviction. In my view, this episode proves that you should always get legal advice. Of course, my clients did have legal representation and so were able to take advantage of this administrative error.

In a similar blunder in Essex, the police force faced paying back £20 million in speeding fines after a gaffe meant that tickets were issued illegally. The error involved the part of the Road Traffic Offences Act 1988 which says that any civilian worker sending out penalty letters must have signed legal authority from the Chief Constable. It emerged that an employee at Essex Police's enforcement office may never have received authorisation from Chief Constable Roger Baker. At the time I was asked to comment on this and I said that if the error was proved to be true it could open the floodgates to motorists who pleaded guilty having their convictions quashed. Their fines would be reimbursed and their points removed. And that's just for starters. Imagine people who have lost their jobs because of their punishment and its financial implications. Another reason why it's always wise to get legal representation.

There is, of course, a gut-wrenching feeling when that crisp envelope cradling a speeding notice drops onto your doormat. I admit I've had it once myself, and I know how much your heart can sink as you ease open the letter and see words such as 'Greater Manchester Police' nudging over the horizon of the envelope.

Actually some people are so eager to deal with their brush with the law that, in their alacrity, they can unwittingly make administrative errors of their own. These should, of course, be picked up by the prosecuting authorities when the forms are returned. But if they don't spot them, the driver can find himself unexpectedly acquitted.

This is what happened to the wife of former Manchester United footballer Paul Ince. Claire Ince had allegedly been clocked doing 100mph on the M56 in Cheshire by a policeman using a handheld camera. The Mercedes CL600 sports car was actually registered in her husband's name. So he was the car's registered keeper, as the law puts it. For this reason Paul received the notice.

However, as Claire was driving, she thought – as she would explain in court – that she needed to fill it in. This she did, quite innocently, keen to take responsibility for the matter. But such noble intentions collide with what the law actually requires: which is for the registered keeper to fill in the form. And if they weren't the actual driver, as was the case here, it is the registered keeper's legal obligation to say who was driving. So, resplendent with Claire's neat handwriting, the form went winging off to Cheshire Police. She was then summonsed for speeding.

As I would explain to magistrates, since Claire rather than her husband – the registered keeper – had provided information, the document was inadmissible: she was being prosecuted on the basis of an admission she had made on Paul's notice. In court I argued that, by law, what the police should have done was give Claire her own form to complete before charging her. But they hadn't followed the correct procedure, and this unnoticed error paved the way to her acquittal.

After the case, various road safety commentators, including a spokesman for the AA, expressed their horror at how such a basic administrative mistake could happen. 'The police cannot afford to be so slipshod,' thundered one particularly angry voice. I completely agree. But if they are, and their actions are unlawful, then they provide a perfectly legitimate defence. And situations like this keep on happening.

In an almost copycat situation, Meg Matthews, the then wife of Oasis star Noel Gallagher, was due in court over the allegation that she drove her Porsche at 103mph in a 70mph zone near Thetford, Norfolk. However, the car had been registered in the name of a football club. Indeed the notice was addressed to someone at the club and, with careless splendour, this name was typed on the same line as the first line of the club's address – as if this was part of her title. So this 'person' didn't actually exist!

That, however, was a side issue. The original NIP/Section 172 went to the football club, and was allegedly filled in and signed by Meg Matthews. The day before she was due to stand trial the case was discontinued.

Let me point out that the Section 172 form states *very clearly* that it can only be completed by the addressee. To deliberately do otherwise could constitute a serious criminal offence.

★ ★ ★

All these paperwork blunders do make you wonder what's actually happening in the administrative heartlands of our legal system. Do things get sent out? Do they go to the correct addresses? Are the right bits of paper pushed into the right envelopes?

That's why I always suggest that anyone in receipt of any paperwork regarding allegations of an offence should keep or copy every bit of it, including the envelopes. And copies of any letters you write to the court.

Which is precisely what another client, *Top Gear* presenter and ex-Formula One racing driver Tiff Needell, had the foresight to do. Tiff was allegedly filmed driving at 91mph in his BMW 550i Sport on the M4 near Pontypridd. Yet he insisted he had never received a NIP from the police. Meanwhile they dashed off a reminder to him.

Before instructing me, as I would go on to explain in court, Tiff had actually written to the court, when he received his second notice, to say he hadn't received the previous one and so this was his first notification of the offence.

Aside from being startled to receive a reminder about a speeding allegation he'd never had, Tiff had another challenge: since his job was to test cars and he was always driving different vehicles, he couldn't remember who was driving at the time – particularly since weeks had passed since the date of the alleged offence.

When I looked over the paperwork, I immediately felt a tingle of anticipation. The second notice sent to Tiff didn't, in my view, actually comply with the legal requirements of Section 172: namely it had to state that it was being 'sent by or on behalf of the Chief Officer of Police'. You see, this second notice wasn't in fact a formal notice but a letter sent out by the prosecuting authorities. Normally they re-send a copy of the first notice. In this case they just sent a letter asking for the information, making reference to the fact there had been a previous notice but not including a copy of it.

The whole thing appeared terribly messy. You had notices going astray, letters that didn't comply with statute and the not insignificant problem of discussing an offence that had allegedly happened months before.

So the defence was twofold. When Tiff received what he regarded as his first notification it was actually a reminder to the first one, which he hadn't received. What's more, since several months had passed he honestly didn't have a clue who had been driving.

Confused? It was like a dizzying game of chess.

When the prosecutor carried out his cross-examination, he asked Tiff if there was a possibility that he had put the first letter to one side and not dealt with it.

'No,' my client replied earnestly. 'As soon as the following one came up I went straight for legal advice.'

In fact Tiff added that he'd actually received a speeding notice four years earlier which he had immediately responded to and for which he was given three penalty points on his licence.

He told Pontypridd Magistrates Court, 'I never received the original letter from the police and months later I was told I had failed to comply. I am a man of good character and I find it insulting to my character to suggest I didn't deal with the letter when it arrived. I just never received it and I have no idea who was driving that car on the day it was photographed.'

I was highly impressed with Tiff's account. But, as I sat and watched, I was thinking, what would I do if *I* were a magistrate listening to this?

Then came the trump card. Tiff produced his letter of instruction to my firm, explaining, among other things, that he'd never received the first notice.

Now, this was private correspondence, a privileged document between client and lawyer, so I'd never dream of asking a client to show or exhibit this to me in court. But in this case it was vital to our defence, and Tiff happily obliged. It corroborated to some extent the veracity of what he was saying.

Clearly the magistrates accepted that my client was being truthful, and that was the end of the case.

Situations like this aren't necessarily complex. As I say, it can save a lot of time, money and legal hot air in court if, as the defence lawyer, you can home in on the crux of the matter. But you also have to consider how to manage the information you have and deploy the right tactics. Getting Tiff to show the court the letter he had sent to me was a strategy that worked.

In another case former Stone Roses frontman Ian Brown was told that he was 'free to go' by Waltham Forest Magistrates Court in London after being charged with failing to name the driver of a car, registered in Brown's name, which was flashed doing 65mph in a 50mph zone on the A40 near RAF Northolt.

Brown did fail to respond to both the Section 172 and the reminder – though this was because he had moved from the address that these were sent to. So a summons was issued. However, this was defective, in my opinion, as the date of the alleged offence on it was incorrect. Had he been found guilty, Brown's licence would have automatically been endorsed with six points or he would have been disqualified.

In another case I defended a man who had two summonses for speeding, which really confused the system. Both offences allegedly took place on the same road, at the same time of day, and were flashed by the same camera – but happened two days apart, namely, on 17 and 19 May.

Before these alleged offences occurred my client already had six points on his licence and on the face of it was going to get another six points. So he was looking down the barrel of a ban.

However, someone at the central ticket office came up with the time-efficient idea of dealing with both matters on the same date. Very cost-effective too. Except that in doing this they hadn't thought about the consequences of the calendar. They prepared the information for the second offence on the last day of the six-month deadline, forgetting that it would take them over the valid six-month period for the first offence – by two days. Case dismissed.

Time and time again I'm astonished that these details – so small and yet so potentially deadly – are overlooked. Maybe we need to train our police and prosecutors to take a more eagle-eyed approach? That's not, of course, for me to say. But the catalogue of cases which highlight their inability to read the small print perhaps speaks for itself.

None more so than a case I had involving a client who received a speeding notice after he was zapped driving over the speed limit on the M1. Yes, the time and date were correct. And indeed he had been on that motorway at that particular moment. The only problem was that he had been travelling towards London in a southbound direction, whereas the notice stated he was driving the other way!

Now this raises a very interesting issue. We have a notice which states the right road, time and place. But if the police accuse my client of travelling in the opposite direction, when he wasn't, then, to my mind, there is no case. After all, how can my client furnish information if the police think he was hurtling towards Manchester when in fact he was on his way home to the capital? He can't provide evidence for a place he wasn't even in! Someone had made a sloppy mistake. But it was a critical mistake. 'Here's the notice, you're the registered keeper,' say the police. 'So we want to know who was driving northbound in this car at this time.' But hang about. Nobody was. This was the other side of the carriageway. So how do you deal with it?

The client decided not to furnish information because he hadn't been travelling northbound on that particular day. Of course, this needed to be corroborated. But as soon as I looked at the police officer's statement I saw that it clearly described an incident which was contrary to information available in the summons. So the proceedings were dropped.

I do know how critical it is when you get directions wrong. I remember once coming out of Penrith Magistrates Court after defending a fairly involved case. It was lunchtime, so I stopped and got a sandwich before hitting the motorway home. Deep in thought about what had happened that morning, I suddenly noticed a sign that said 'Lockerbie'. That isn't near Manchester, I thought. For reasons I can't explain I had gone right up the M6 heading north, instead of south to Manchester, which is why I found myself on the Scottish borders. Lovely scenery. But it completely screwed up my day. I had an afternoon jammed with four different client appointments and here I was, winging my way to the Highlands!

Perhaps the worst administrative error of all is when nothing happens. No dates, no spelling mistakes, no wrong bits of paper. Just silence. I remember being approached by another high-profile sporting celebrity after he'd received four notices relating to four separate occasions when his car was flashed through a speed camera. He filled in the Section 172 forms – which places a legal obligation on the registered owner to name the driver – and on each one he claimed his girlfriend was behind the wheel.

When the paperwork came through to my office, it was accompanied by a photo of the car at the time it was supposed to be speeding. And there, clear as a bell, was a snapshot of my client – behind the wheel. No surprise, then, that he'd been approached by the central ticket office, asking if he wanted to reconsider the way he had filled in his forms. He requested a fresh set of notices in order to correct the error and send them back. After which ... well, precisely nothing happened. And, incredibly, we heard nothing further. To this day I've no idea why.

Sometimes, though, when information isn't forthcoming, it's tantamount to a potentially devastating blunder. I remember getting a speeding case against comedian Jimmy Carr dropped over a error in the paperwork. I'd driven all the way to Feltham Magistrates Court after my client was accused of breaking a 30mph while driving his Bentley in west London. But when I arrived I was shocked to discover that there was no sign of my case on the court list. No one, it seemed, was expecting me. The court had moved the case to another date without my knowledge. The ushers and clerk in the general office knew nothing about it. It had, in fact, been adjourned to another day.

I was furious and immediately asked to see the chief court clerk. As he emerged, I said, 'Good morning, sir, we appear to have a slight problem. I am here to defend Jimmy Carr, who is summonsed with speeding and the trial date is today.' The chief clerk looked at me apologetically, embarrassed that such legal musical chairs were occurring on his watch. He'd only just been made aware of what was going on and was sympathetic to my situation. 'Am I on record?' I politely asked. He nodded again. 'Because it doesn't appear that anybody had notified myself, my firm or my client that this case has been adjourned. Furthermore, when was this application for an adjournment made and why weren't we advised?'

The chief clerk shook his head and was clearly embarrassed. It wasn't his fault but it happened in his court and I sensed he was keen to get the matter resolved quickly.

'OK,' I continued, spotting the gleam of an opportunity, 'the adjournment was unlawful and I would like to restore the status quo. I would like, as planned, to proceed with the case today and disregard what has happened. It's "void *ab initio*" – as if it never took place. The trial is supposed to be today. I'm here, it's not my fault there's no prosecutor, no witnesses and no files. Can we now get the case called on, please.'

The clerk nodded sympathetically. He could see I had a point. And I wasn't about to relent. 'I don't wish to seem rude,' I added, 'but if we don't get this show on the road today, I think we are both aware of the view that the High Court will take about this.'

And the clerk agreed. After all, the whole situation was an utter disgrace. Shrinking a little, and clearly keen to make this whole mess go away, he said, 'Look, Mr Freeman, give me some time and I'll see what I can do.'

It transpired that the court had written to Jimmy Carr a few days before about the adjournment. However, they accepted that the letter could not possibly have arrived in time because of the way their internal postal system operates.

The local CPS lawyers send all speeding cases to a specialist team in Marlowe House, their headquarters in Sidcup, Kent. But this court had unlawfully changed the date without notifying either my client or myself. I challenged the basis of this decision. I explained that the new date had been unlawfully fixed and asked for the papers to be brought before the court that day, so that a lawful judicial decision could be made there and then.

After consultation between all parties, the CPS decided to withdraw the case. An unexpected win and my client even got costs.

This had been one occasion where I wasn't going to seek redress by paperwork. What was the point in writing a letter of complaint? I was there and I was determined that this case would go ahead one way or another. Which, thankfully, it did. I'd turned a hopeless situation into a win. I'd gone there with no particular expectations and within an hour it had been thrown out. That, I suppose, is what the art of the loophole is all about. Dealing with the unexpected.

Of course, with so much paperwork in circulation, mistakes happen because bits of paper go astray. Manchester City legend Asa Hartford walked free from a drink-driving charge after the police lost all vital papers showing the results of a breath test. The assistant manager at City was charged with driving with excess alcohol and driving an uninsured vehicle. But the trial collapsed because prosecutors could not produce evidence that the machine used to carry out the breath test at Blackburn Police Station had been properly calibrated. The police had taken two printouts of the test, but both original copies were missing from the file and custody sheet. A third copy should have been given to Hartford, but he claimed that it wasn't.

In court, police officers from the motorway policing unit claimed that they spotted my client driving a Peugeot weaving between lanes on the M65. They said they used a breath-test machine for the test, which was alleged to have shown that Mr Hartford had 68mg of alcohol in 100ml of breath. The legal limit is 35mg. The court heard that three copies of the result were printed, one for the custody sheet, one for police files and one for Mr Hartford. But, despite a delay at the start of the court case to allow the officers to make further enquiries, they could only produce a photo-copy of the results. The court also heard that a form used to question suspects had not been filled in completely.

In my view, the missing forms meant that it was difficult for the prosecution to show that the machine had been properly calibrated before breath specimens had been pro-vided during the test. End of the case.

It's not just the prosecuting authorities but the adminis-tration relating to the state of our roads that can also cause a case to fold. One motorist I defended after being involved in a fatal collision walked free from court after the accident was blamed on substandard road markings.

My client had been driving on the wrong side of the road and collided head on with a motorcyclist, in the mistaken belief that she was using a one-way street. The broken white lines had worn away and there weren't any signs indicating two-way traffic. She was charged with driving without due care and attention.

I contacted the relevant local authority and discovered that, four weeks before the accident, an order had been made to replace the markings. The work should have been completed by the time my client found herself driving down this road. But it wasn't.

My client was quite rightly acquitted. But this was a par-ticularly shocking case and a needless tragedy, triggered by slapdash local governance. In my view, the administrators have blood on their hands. We drown endlessly in paper-work. And in this case it wrecked the lives of two families.

And so, case after case, year after year, acquittals happen because of a bureaucratic breakdown in the legal process.

Every time my client walks free, thanks to a rogue letter, a wrong number or a misspelling, I assume that the courts will sit up and take notice. Paperwork is the scaffolding which supports so much of our statutory procedures. It's there for a purpose. But its structure remains as flimsy as a house of cards.

Take one bit away, deploy a little loophole hunting and the rest simply collapses . . . .

9

Tying up loose ends and loose loopholes

The collision caused carnage, leaving behind a trail of destruction that would devastate a family and condemn a young father to a wheelchair for the rest of his days. Did these people deserve to suffer in this way? Of course not. Their only 'crime' was to be in the wrong place at the wrong time. They had been lucky to escape with their lives. But the lives they escaped with were broken, shattered.

The family had been struck by a lorry which swerved to avoid a car being driven at speed by a man who was almost twice over the legal alcohol limit. And I was the lawyer representing the drink-driver who stood accused of causing the smash and triggering this nightmare.

I'll spare you the finer details of the appalling mental and physical injuries suffered by the family in question. But even condensing their experience into a bleak snapshot of human torment, who wouldn't rage at the random devastation a drink-driver can unleash? In this case the entire family could have been wiped out. The torment probably haunts them to this very day. Is it any wonder that society's collective instinct and primal desire for justice cries out for the accused to be tossed into prison?

But none of this takes into account one critical factor: the law. Or rather, what the law says. So, what, as a lawyer, is expected of me? As Nick Freeman the human being, I feel deeply for anyone who has suffered this way and in this case was appalled by what had happened. I'm a father myself. I abhor drink-driving. Believe me, when I receive the papers concerning cases like this, they make for solemn reading. My private response is biblical. I fully understood why people might feel the need for retribution, for the Old Testament's 'an eye for an eye'. And I'm sure that my client, like any other drink-driver, would never expect or indeed foresee that their motoring may result in bloodshed and tragedy. But then what is the price that should be paid?

Yet what I feel inside in situations like this – and I've had experience of them many times – is irrelevant. It is my duty as a defence lawyer to focus exclusively on the law. When I uncover loopholes, however calamitous the facts of a case, that's my only guiding principle.

And so it was when I began to assess this particular case in terms of the law. I began to read through the documents and within minutes a loophole – or rather, a police error – leapt out at me. I knew immediately that, because of what I'd spotted, the prosecution case could be brought to its knees and my client would be likely to escape conviction. There couldn't be a moral dilemma, a struggle with my conscience. I couldn't turn down the case in the hope that a less observant lawyer might miss the mistake and so prevent an acquittal. I had been instructed to take the case and it was my job to defend my client.

So what was the tiny rivet that was about to bring the legal edifice crashing down? In short, it was that old prosecuting foe, the procedural error.

Here's what had happened: after the collision my client had agreed to be breathalysed after being taken to the nearest police station. Yet when he did the test, he didn't produce enough breath for a valid reading. There was no medical reason for this. He just didn't deliver. Perhaps he simply wasn't blowing hard enough. But when the officers asked him to try again, he refused point-blank. I've no idea why.

With no breath test to rely on, the police then gave my client the opportunity of doing a blood or urine test instead. When my client opted for a blood test, the officer trotted out a flawless rendition of the statutory warning about taking such a test. The results revealed that my client was over the limit.

So far, so good? One devastating collision, one drunk in custody, one positive blood test. What more would the Crown need to win their case and throw the book at this guy? It might have seemed this way to everyone who had reviewed the files, including the police and the CPS. But not to me. As soon as I read the papers I immediately realised that the police had committed a monumental blunder. Here's why.

The law says that when someone, as my client did, wilfully refuses to provide a breath specimen, then they should immediately be charged with the offence of 'failing to provide'. They should not be given the opportunity to do a blood or urine test instead. But my client was. So the reading – however high it was – was unlawfully taken.

I've no idea why the police made such a basic error. Perhaps, in the light of such a cataclysmic accident, they wanted to be sure that they had proof my client was over the limit. They couldn't rely on a breath test because my client was too 'bladdered'. Perhaps in their noble determination to get a reading, to secure justice for this terribly tragedy, they lost sight of the correct procedures and were instead propelled by a moral imperative (the very opposite of my approach as a lawyer). Whatever the reason, they got it wrong.

For the law, as I've said repeatedly, is the law.

And in this case that blood test was unlawful and so

should not have taken place. What the police officers should have done after my client refused to repeat his breath test was charge him with 'failing to provide', for which he would probably have been convicted and gone to prison. Instead he was charged with driving while over the limit – an assessment based on that unlawful sample. The police had cocked up. They had conducted the wrong procedure and they had charged him with the wrong offence. What this blunder meant was that my client now had a legal defence.

The case went to court and was then adjourned for various administrative reasons such as setting the date for a trial. Each time there was an adjournment it handed the CPS another opportunity to review the charges before the case went back to court. Not one single prosecutor spotted the error. Each one missed an opportunity to alter the charges.

So, despite the horrifying ramifications of the collision, my client walked free.

After the case, the press had a field day. No one focused on the blunders of the constabulary or the CPS. Instead I became the focus of society's target practice. I was, it seemed, the courtroom chancer who had handed back the keys to another dangerous driver. Discussing the case in one newspaper, one campaigner against drink-driving described me as a 'brilliant lawyer'. However, his caveat was that it was a pity I didn't deploy this so-called 'brilliance' for more worthy causes.

Road safety campaigners were further inflamed after it emerged that my client had also been convicted of drink-driving nearly a decade earlier and then banned for three years. When a person is ordered off the road for three years, this length of ban means that either the defendant has had two convictions in ten years or that they gave a very high reading on a previous offence. Either way, the three-year ban suggested that the courts were dealing with someone who had a predilection for drink-driving and yet had remained immune to any lesson he could learn from previous punishment.

Meanwhile the thrust of the accusation levelled against me was that so-called dangerous drivers shouldn't be allowed to escape justice just because, as one commentator pointed out, 'they can hire an expensive lawyer who can find a loophole'. But it is not down to me to make that judgement. I'm not the one doing the acquitting. That's what magistrates and judges have the power to do. I'm the lawyer putting forward a legal argument. It's for the court to decide whether they agree with it or not. More importantly, it's for the prosecution authorities to get it right. In this case the court had no choice but to acquit.

If the police had followed the correct protocol my client would have been convicted. It was because of this error – this loophole – that he walked free. The prosecution threw their hand in. There was nothing they could do. The case was fatally flawed.

Of course, I understood the sheer scale of the reaction and even the bitterness of the criticism. An alleged drink-driver destroys a family and walks away a free man. One of his victims never walks again. Where's the justice in that?

Take the law out of it and there is no justice. He was driving and he was drunk. But my clients are entitled to the best legal advice I can give – without moral judgement. If there is a legal defence I argue it, even though in cases like this a person may inflict unimaginable tragedy on an innocent family. And though I may sound like a parrot, or even someone who is protesting too much, believe me I'm not when I say that the law is the law. And the law often seems to obstruct the morality of the situation. But, without it, there would be vigilantism and kangaroo justice. Is that what society really wants?

A few weeks later, I was working in my office when the phone rang. A television company asked if I was prepared to meet the family, on camera, to discuss their case with them. I'd never had a request like this before and it startled me. I felt enormous sympathy for the appalling suffering of these people. But I had to do my job as a lawyer. After turning it over and over in my mind, I realised this was an opportunity to explain that to them. And so I agreed. I felt I had no real choice. I suppose I didn't want them to blame me. I wanted them to understand that my client had been acquitted because other people had failed to do their job properly. I knew I wouldn't be able to persuade them of the rightness of this. But at least I could clarify how something that they felt was an 'injustice' had come to pass.

The meeting was arranged for the following week and when the day dawned I didn't actually feel nervous about meeting the family. I was more concerned about maintaining a tight leash on my emotions. Underneath all that courtroom bravado I feel things very deeply and I felt so terribly upset for their suffering. They were decent people, innocent victims.

In the event only the parents came to the meeting, the father wheelchair-bound and clearly a broken man. Their questions were predictably salted with disbelief and anger.

'How could you do this? How could you defend that man?' the wife persisted, as the cameras recorded everything. 'He has ruined our lives. My husband will probably never work again. Yet thanks to you he went free.'

It was absurd, I agreed. Absurd that the law was structured in a way that allowed flawed legal procedure – the botched breath and blood tests – to ride roughshod over the facts. But that wasn't, I pointed out as clearly but gently as I could, 'down to me'.

'If this was judged on just the facts, then, yes, you could say it was a miscarriage of justice,' I explained carefully. 'But when procedures aren't followed correctly they provide a legal defence.'

'But how do you live with yourself?' the wife continued bitterly.

'As a defence lawyer you have to. You have to trust and believe in the law,' I replied truthfully.

Indeed, even in that tense, emotional atmosphere, even with the living proof of two damaged lives, I felt comfortable with my argument. It didn't mitigate the sorrow I felt for this couple. But I wanted them to know that my work involved playing by the rules. Not my rules. The laws of this land.

The interview drew to a close and with admirable dignity and composure the wife wheeled her husband from my office, clearly unconvinced by my words. If they had hoped for closure, it pains me to say, they wouldn't be able to get it from me. Though I imagine these brave and stoic people will never be at peace. To them the law had robbed them of justice.

That's why loopholes aren't really loopholes. They're the law. And this tragic episode so clearly demonstrates this. Defendants can be accused of horrendous offences, but they are entitled to a defence. Part of being a defence lawyer is testing whether the Crown have done their job properly. And if they haven't, that can have devastating consequences which are totally disproportionate to the errors they have made.

Indeed, even the High Court recognises the fact that 'unmeritorious defendants can sometimes be acquitted'. (It's mentioned in the landmark case DPP v Murray 1993 RTR

209, for those who wish to read around the subject.) This leads us to the nub of the issue. A serious offender can side-step justice because a court has to uphold the rule of law.

As a lawyer I have to believe that these so-called loop-holes have been put in place for a reason. And truth be told, there are times when I find it desperately hard to under-stand the rationale of the law myself. I mean, what difference does it make whether or not a warning has been given, says the lay moralist, if a defendant still provides a specimen that shows he's over the limit?

So the question I ask myself, and which others frequently put to me, is whether being a successful defence lawyer means I am the architect of constant miscarriages of justice. In the legal sense I'm not. But in the moral sense, well, it's not so clear-cut. Factually clients such as the one I mentioned are guilty. But it is not only a court of fact. It is a court of fact and law. And there is a presumption of innocence.

And this leads us to the biggest loophole of them all. Law and justice can be mutually exclusive. They're not bedfel-lows. Not even live-in lovers. More like an estranged couple who each fail to understand the value of the other. How do you reconcile that with the true justice of the situation?

This relationship between law and justice bleeds into all areas of criminal law. It means that alleged terrorists can walk away because of a glitch over what is perceived to be their 'yuman rights', or that prisoners may well get to vote. In 2011, Sharon Shoesmith, the director of Children's Services for the London Borough of Haringey and the woman felt to be 'responsible' for the failings that led to the death of 'Baby P', challenged her dismissal successfully and netted a huge payout. Her sacking was unlawful in the eyes of the courts. Ed Balls, at the height of 'Baby P' hysteria in December 2008, had hastily sacked Shoesmith without compensation by her employers, Haringey Council. The appeal judges ruled in 2011 that she had been unlawfully dismissed and 'summarily scapegoated'.

There was a legal process that should have been undertaken. Mr Balls should have been aware of that. But he dealt with Sharon Shoesmith summarily, ignoring the due process of law. Cynics suggested that this was a political sacking. But as soon as it happened, I knew that it was going to cost taxpayers a fortune, because Shoesmith had a legal defence. It angered me that politicians, the very people who make the law, could behave in such an autocratic way. Even though there is a baying public thirsting for justice, there can never be an excuse to subvert the rule of law.

And so Shoesmith got her pay-off. A box wasn't ticked, a 't' not crossed, an 'i' not dotted. Procedure had trumped the big picture, as a contributor to one national newspaper's letters pages wrote in anger.

In cases like this the question is raised whether we should simply have courts of fact. In my view, the answer is an unequivocal no. We need courts of law. That's the only way the Crown can be tested. The law is there to make sure that everyone does their job properly. It gives the defence lawyers teeth. Otherwise we'd have nothing to argue with. We'd basically be screwed. And the defendant would have to throw himself on the mercy of the court.

The law enables knowledgeable lawyers to take advantage of shortcomings in procedure. It may skew the ethical justice of the situation. But that's not our fault. It is the fault of every representative of the Crown who messes up. If there are loopholes, it's the Crown, not the defence, who ensure that they are ripe for the plucking.

Remember, the upholding of the law is vital for the sake of the innocent too. In some cases it has demonstrably saved what appeared to be a doomed but genuinely innocent client from being found guilty or has led to that person's conviction being overturned. Even if, as in the case of, say, Stefan Kiszko, the Rochdale man wrongly convicted of the sexual assault and murder of eleven-year-old Lesley Molseed, it takes an appalling sixteen years for a verdict to be overturned.

So you can see why, in all my years of loophole hunting, I have become a thorn in the side of so many police officers and prosecutors. But I don't make big pals of my clients either. They come to me as a lawyer and on the whole I keep them at arm's length.

I do always try to speak to my clients after every acquittal. Not to slap them on the back but precisely because I don't like the idea of people getting away with it. I tell them to drive carefully, that they should reflect on what has happened, that I don't really want to have to see them again. Maybe, just maybe, I think they have learnt a lesson and realised how bloody lucky they've been. And there are people who never pass through my office door again. Unfortunately, though, there are still the repeat offenders too. For example I have secured three consecutive drink-drive acquittals for not one, but three clients, and another client of mine has been acquitted four times. Again, it's not my call to wonder whether I have a serial drink-driver on my hands. I look at each offence with a fresh pair of eyes. It's what the law asks me to do.

I remember successfully defending one chap over two separate drink-driving cases a few years apart. After the second one, in which, like the first, he had been awarded costs, he turned his attention to prosecuting me. Phoning me up out of the blue, he asked how much the court costs were. When I told him he said, 'How do I know that's all the money the court have given to me?'

I prickled with irritation at his outrageous question. 'What are you suggesting?' I asked him. 'That I've kept some for myself?'

He wasn't convinced, and I told him to phone the court, who confirmed that the money he'd received was the exact amount he'd been entitled to.

It's pretty grim to be accused of dishonesty by a client. But I put the man's behaviour down to experience and set it aside in my head. And when he phoned me three years later, asking me to defend him, I did so again. Even though the memory of his unfounded suspicion lingered in my mind.

As I say, I look at each offence with a fresh pair of eyes. And I won his case again. This time, however, my client didn't say a word about court costs.

If we overlooked procedural errors or had better-trained police officers or prosecutors, would loophole hunting be wiped out? Probably. But in the interim it's a long reach to blame lawyers. Why don't those who complain petition MPs and get Parliament to change or tighten the system? But without lawyers scrutinising the law, we're simply a police state, and we hurtle towards a system of kangaroo justice where there is simply no justice at all.

Take the time I defended a woman who collided with another car on the motorway. The other vehicle was being driven by an elderly couple and the wife, who had been sitting in the passenger seat, was killed on impact. Again, it was one of those horrific twists of fate, of being in the wrong place at the wrong time. In one moment, a life had been snuffed out.

My client was charged with causing death by careless driving, which carries up to five years in prison. The prosecution suggested that she had been driving too quickly. But when I read over the statements I saw that my client had said that as she was driving along her car suddenly 'aquaplaned'. This, as I know from personal experience, can be terrifying. You lose all control of the vehicle and are at the mercy of force, gravity and the other road users hurtling past.

Aquaplaning happens when a layer of standing water – caused by heavy rainfall – builds between the surface of your tyres and the road surface beneath. The car effectively skates on the water, causing the driver to lose control. When this happened to me I was on the M1 driving back to Manchester after doing a trial in London. It had been raining hard and as I drove steadily in the outside lane, the suspension on my Range Rover suddenly dropped, I lost traction and found myself sliding towards the central reservation. Utterly helpless, I slapped on my hazard lights and jammed on the horn as huge lorries thundered past on the nearside. I felt like a deep-sea diver as everything floated by in a strange twist of slow motion.

It felt like an eternity before the car swung across the middle lane and I began to regain control. As I slowly nosed my car back into position, I was shaking like a leaf. Any of the lorries and cars that had been coming up behind me could have hit me broadside. I limped a few miles to the nearest service station, parked and stumbled across the car park and into the café, where I bought myself a strong coffee. I sat there for ages, my whole body shuddering. It may sound melodramatic. But anyone who has gone through something like this, who has been inches away from facing their mortality, will know how I felt. Only when I had finally regained my composure did I get back in my car to continue my journey home.

So when I discovered that my client had experienced exactly the same thing, my private self understood exactly how helpless she must have been. However, I had to park that empathy. Instead, I used my personal experience to focus on the case as a lawyer since it gave me an opportunity to argue that the accident had happened because of the road and weather conditions. And once I put this on the table – backing it up with a report by an accident reconstruction engineer and evidence about the shocking weather on the day – it was up to the Crown to negate my argument. They couldn't and the case was discontinued before it even got to court.

I rang my client afterwards to tell her the news. Though she was relieved to have avoided jail, it was clear that she was a broken woman. The accident had shattered her mental health and well-being. Even though she hadn't been in any way at fault, even though there was nothing she could have done, she couldn't rest. She would never be the same again.

If that's a note of sympathy you're detecting, well, you may be right. I did feel sorry for her. Particularly since I knew how terrifying it was for a driver to aquaplane. But I also felt grievously sorry for the man whose wife had died. This couple had done nothing wrong. There was no contributory negligence. Yet an innocent woman had been killed. It was one of those 'there but for the grace' moments. And it could have happened to anyone. There were no winners. Just a terrible, terrible situation.

Again, as with the other tragic case, I didn't buckle under the emotional weight of the facts. I can't. I practise law dispassionately and remotely. I detach myself from the personal issues involved and that makes it easy to focus on the legal issues. I want to concentrate on the things that are important to the case and upon which, ultimately, it will be decided. Trying to edit out personal emotion also makes it a damned sight easier for me. I haven't been instrumental in the tragedy. I'm there to focus solely on the law. That's why I don't get involved with clients unless I really need to. And indeed in both of these cases I never met either of them before the case. It helps me to focus exclusively on the evidence and absolves me of any emotional burden.

I'm not saying I don't think about my clients afterwards. For months after the family's crash, an image of that poor father in his wheelchair would flash through my mind as I went out for my morning jog or drove off to work – every time I had the freedom to do whatever I wanted to do. Meanwhile it caused me to reflect from time to time, how this man had been denied a full family life. I had it all on a plate: including two lovely children. I knew better than most how life can turn on a dime. Yet, despite handling these cases, I could never really change the setting on my thermostat. It remained fixed on workaholic. In fact my wife used to joke that all she ever saw was my back. That's because my desk at home, where I predominantly worked, faced out onto the lawn and whenever she came in I'd be crouched over some papers or have a phone glued to my ear.

Now that my marriage is over and my children are grown, I sometimes think, should I have done things differently? But that's the thing about knowledge, success, loophole hunting, winning – it's all so addictive. And I embraced it.

When I was a law student I wasn't interested in what was going on off the page. I'd learn what I needed to learn off by heart. The detail didn't bother me. But once your brain is in training with intricate knowledge – and it is like training your brain for a marathon – it's impossible to slow it down.

However many marathons your brain runs, it will never really be able to deliver a single formula for why people break the law. Some do so deliberately. For others, nothing could be further from their minds – but they react to opportunism or temptation. If law and justice seem contradictory, sometimes that's because the law allows exploration of why people commit an offence. It can have bearings on the case and produce a loophole. That's why, if I do decide I need to talk to the client, I'll ask, 'Why did you do it?'

On the face of it, a case can seem to point to a guilty plea. But often there's still a lot you can achieve with your client. It's not a lost cause. Exactly this situation happened when former world boxing champion Naseem Hamed was stopped for driving without a full licence and driving without insurance.

Now, this was a man with a fairly bad driving record. The former WBA world featherweight champion was jailed in 2006 for fifteen months and disqualified from driving for four years after a crash which left another man with fractures to 'every major bone in his body'. Hamed's driving ban ended in March 2010 but he hadn't got round to retaking his test – hence the charges.

So what had made Naseem go back behind the wheel? Well, as I would explain in court, having been housebound caring for his young son who had been seriously ill with asthma, he was tempted out one evening by a friend who told him he needed a break. My client decided to go, and went out in his wife's car. He quickly decided he wanted to return to his home in Surrey, after receiving a call to say his son had taken a bad turn again.

Surely any parent would have felt the same? As a father myself I knew I would have just wanted to get back to be with my child. The situation would have clouded all judgement and reason. I told the court that my client had 'thrown caution to the wind, the gale-force power of parental instincts kicked in. He was stopped two minutes from his home.' And it was this human element – the fact that he just wanted to get back to his son – which I think struck a chord with the magistrates and formed the backbone of the mitigation.

Naseem wasn't denying he'd done wrong. Indeed he readily acknowledged he should have taken the test and shouldn't have driven. But he had a reason for both going out and coming back. Consequently he was fined £1000 for driving without insurance and six penalty points were ordered to be added to his licence. He was fined £150 for driving without retaking his test and was ordered to pay £43 costs and a victims' surcharge of £15. A great result as he could have been disqualified.

Even in the face of a pretty dismal history or set of circumstances, even when all the odds are stacked against the client, I have a goal. To me, it's the key to finding the loophole. I think, what do I want here? What is my aim? Is it a not-guilty verdict? Do I want to avoid custody? Do I want to avoid disqualification? Or do I simply want to obtain the lowest number of penalty points?

It's about exploring, investigating the allegation, then searching for corroborative evidence so you can attach credibility to it. If someone told me they needed to keep their licence because their business would suffer, I'd say, 'Fine, let's get a letter from your accountant.' If someone says, 'I do a lot of charity work', then we'll get a letter from the organisation in question. I always try to corroborate what I say. It's not a legal requirement but I feel I need it to do the job properly.

I once represented a lorry driver accused of driving without due care and attention – a cyclist had been killed after being caught in the nearside wheels of my client's HGV.

The biker had drawn up beside my client at a set of red lights. When these changed to green, they both turned left at the same time.

The cyclist's death was a terrible tragedy, but in my opinion unavoidable since it had happened in my client's blind spot. He had no idea that the biker was there as he took the corner. It was the fulcrum of the case, but one I felt could best be explained through actions not words.

And so the judge was invited to sit in the cabin of the lorry to understand for himself how it would have been impossible for my client to have seen the cyclist, let alone have the opportunity to stop.

Like I say, a tragic case. But my client was not to blame. By being thorough and working off the page in preparation of his defence, it meant this lorry driver avoided the terrible stigma of being blamed for something that wasn't his fault.

So loophole hunting is as much about what goes on off the page as what's there in front of you.

England footballer Joe Cole was able to avoid an immediate ban following a speeding conviction after I told the court that his wife, Carly, had been the victim of a carjacking incident and had not driven since, so needed her husband to be mobile. I told the court that she was 'severely traumatised' after being dragged from her car by 'eight thugs on motorbikes' and that the stolen car had not yet been recovered. I pointed out that the situation was 'compounded' by the fact that Cole and his wife had moved up to Merseyside since his switch from Chelsea to Liverpool FC.

Mrs Cole and her five-month-old baby would not be able to use public transport if her husband was banned, because of their 'profile', and so would be reliant on my client, I added. The court agreed and Cole avoided a totting-up ban – that is, a ban of a minimum of six months. He was in fact disqualified for the offence itself for fifty-six days, which was suspended on appeal. This enabled Mrs Cole to overcome her fear of driving and the trauma of being car-jacked.

There are those who will never be convinced by the way I practise law. Indeed, what's to stop every single defence lawyer in the country using loopholes to secure an acquittal for a client who has more alcohol sloshing around their system than a barmaid on her hen night? Is the law eroding and destroying any vestige of residual justice? Is there something rotten at the heart of the justice system?

No, I don't think so. I think that if there is a rot, it's down to lack of training and preparation, especially among the police. The knock-on effect of jousting with people like me in court should be to ensure that training is improved. Arrogant as it may sound, I would wager that if every police officer in the land knew they were going to be questioned by me when they gave their evidence, you could be damned sure they would carry out every single procedure perfectly.

Of course, to say that operating this way hasn't done much for me in terms of popularity is a bit of an under-statement. People feel I have a responsibility to the general public. That they are shareholders in what I do. They want to make my work a matter of social conscience. And they love to hate the idea of me – because they presume that the benefits of what I do are for me alone, not for society. They think I simply pocket a fat cheque, leap into a flash car and race off to my next trial. And actually I do all those things (though the cheques are not as fat as some people think, and I never race behind the wheel). But I do it because it's my job and I win because of the law. I think part of the dif-ficulty many have with my loophole approach is that being judgemental is part of human nature. Morality can have a polarising effect. It's black or white, good or bad, hot or cold. But practising the law can be grey or tepid or morally ambiguous.

Does it bother me when I hear of the criticisms and sometimes even venom poured over my work? Well, I am only human. Honestly. But I also learnt at an early age to encase myself in a ring of steel. Probably because I was shipped off to boarding school, where I quickly had to learn to suppress my emotions and stand on my own two feet. Particularly, as I mentioned when discussing nicknames at the beginning of the book, since I had to deal with a stream of anti-Semitic abuse. (Believe me, when you're repeatedly called such names from a fairly tender age, it doesn't half build you!)

To be honest, I can take the criticisms about how I practise law. Everyone has a right to an opinion. I have mine and you have yours. I wholeheartedly believe in the professional credibility of what I do. I certainly didn't set out as I embarked on my career to be Mr Nice or Mr Nasty, a hero or a villain.

But I'll admit that when the comments get personal, it does sting a little. When I'm asked how I'd feel if a member of my family was mowed down by a drink-driver, it does hurt. Badly. I would never wish such a tragedy on anyone. But, as I say, when I practise law, I have to do so in a vacuum, hermetically sealed from any emotional fallout.

From time to time, when I have a moment, I indulge in a little self-flagellation. Though forget leather and whips. It's a far greater form of self-torture to look at readers' comments in online newspaper reports. At times it feels as if there are those who want to rip open your very soul. A lot of the time, as I say, it's personal. I'm called oily or slippery. I wonder to myself whether I'm using too much of that metrosexual moisturiser (because I'm worth it!)? Maybe my suits have a dash of the game show host? OK, so I'm hot on the self-grooming. If I ever went on Radio 4's *Desert Island Discs*, my luxury item would be a trouser press that also dispenses shoe polish. But I see that the comments suggest there is a devil-may-care vanity in my approach to my work. To my appearance? Perhaps. But to my work? Never.

Even so, there probably isn't an insult that hasn't, over the years, been lobbed my way. It doesn't matter whether such brickbats are hurled by media hacks or the man in the street. The message is usually the same. They accuse me of being a courtroom chancer, the man who puts speeding celebrities and A-list drunks back on the road. That there's one law for the rich and one for the poor.

Above all I'm told I'm a menace to society.

I don't expect anyone to feel sorry for me – even if I occasionally feel sorry for myself. Everyone has a right to an opinion. But sometimes, as I field yet another volley of criticism, the boy inside me who decades before dreamed of being a lawyer and who, in his pubescent innocence, regarded these officers of the court as romantic heroes, wonders again and again, how did I end up being the villain of the piece?

Let me share a few comments from online reports of my cases, to demonstrate the feelings some have about my work:

'It's time this "friend of the criminal" was curbed. He actually admits to being a hypocrite. There is NO EXCUSE for break-ing ANY law on the road. By so doing he is in fact a criminal himself.'

'This vile man is happy to ensure that these people who are a danger to us all remain behind the wheel. And he does it all for money. If people like this then go on to kill somebody whilst

*behind the wheel then, in my view, Freeman is responsible for
their death.'*

*'How does he sleep at night knowing people who are guilty
are being let off on technicalities? He is more greasy than a
greasy spoon.'*

As I have said, everyone has a right to an opinion. But if
there is an art to the loophole, there has to be a defence to
the loophole.

So what is the alternative? Do people seriously expect me
to turn my back on the law? Should it work like this instead?
A client comes to see me, very depressed after discovering
his wife is leaving him and moving abroad with their children. He tells me that this was the reason he got blind drunk
and then got in his car before being subsequently stopped
by the police. I look at the papers and realise the police have
messed up in, say, the drink-drive procedure. That should
be the end of the case.

But, in this alternative scenario, just to keep the public
happy, I will phone the prosecution and say, 'Have you
looked at PC Smith's statement? He hasn't used the right
phraseology when he obtained a specimen of breath, so the
reading is going out of the window. So I tell you what,
charge him for driving while unfit rather than drink-driving. Then you can throw the book at him.'

'That's a good idea,' says the copper.

'Glad to help,' I say.

After having executed this flawless own goal for my client,
should I then go back to him and say, 'Sorry about this but
I've had a chat with the prosecution to tell them what they
need to do to sort you out. You would have been found not
guilty, except now, thanks to me squealing to the Crown,
you'll probably go to jail. And you can't have your money
back. Good day'?

Is that seriously what the public expect me to do? Or am I entitled to look after a client who has come to me, charged by a State that has cocked up?

Every day lawyers defend rapists, murderers, terrorists. Sometimes the defendant's acquittal hinges on a loophole, or it is down to a police error. Perhaps these cases don't always get the same amount of prominence because their lawyers don't have my profile. But the principle remains the same.

There are lines I won't cross. But this is more about a client's attitude than whether a case has merit. During the Strangeways Prison riots in 1990 I was instructed to defend one of the four prisoners who had been charged with murder. The first thing my client said when I met him for the first time was, 'Where are my trainers?' Or rather he barked it at me. I told him that I was there to give him my very best legal attention, but that didn't extend to being his personal shopper. He told me that if I didn't buy him his trainers I was 'out of there'.

I stood up, shook his hand and left a case that would have netted a significant amount of money. At the time I was still with a large criminal law firm – I'd yet to set up on my own – and my partners weren't best pleased. The guy was convicted and then asked me to handle his appeal! I declined.

And yet when I was asked to defend a man who had fatally stabbed his girlfriend to death in front of their child because she had been cheating on him, I took the case. The attack had been frenzied, my client's reaction disproportionate to what had happened. The child, no doubt, has been mentally scarred for life.

Why didn't I have any qualms about representing this man? Well, my client accepted that he'd killed his girlfriend. But, in his eyes, that hadn't been murder. He wanted to plead guilty to manslaughter on the grounds of diminished responsibility. I didn't feel in this case that I was dealing with pure evil, but rather a man who had spectacularly lost control. The law comfortably allowed me to argue this, though I lost the case and he was found guilty of murder.

There's one final point to make about loopholes. Law and justice may at times seem to clash. But there are many occasions when loopholes do ensure a moral victory, as well as a legal one. When people genuinely don't deserve to be accused and the law enables them to be acquitted.

So many cases illustrate this, but here's just one of mine. It involved two chaps who were driving down a road when their cars were splattered by some children who were throwing berries at the passing traffic. They pulled in, and before the kids all scampered off, the men managed to corner one lad, who was about thirteen, and took him back to his parents nearby to tell them what had happened.

So who's the guilty party?

You've got two people driving along, minding their own business, when something peppers their windscreen, obscuring their view with a purple mush. Just random, mindless thuggish behaviour which could have caused a fatal accident had the car spiralled out of control. Yet the finger of blame was pointed not at the teenage perpetrator but at the two men in the car who'd taken him back to his parents. They were charged with common assault.

The case came to trial, during which time a deal was struck with the prosecution: the driver would get off and the other man would plead guilty.

As I was mitigating on behalf of the passenger's sentence, the judge intervened and said, 'Mr Freeman, as this is road rage, you are aware of the sentencing guidelines for road rage – which is immediate custody.'

Road rage is defined, many believe, as aggressive or angry behaviour by a motorist. But that's not quite true. And so my response came to me in a flash: 'Sir, this is not road rage, as it doesn't involve two separate vehicles – which is how the law, in my view, defines the circumstances surrounding this conduct. In this case the alleged altercation took place between the driver/passenger of one vehicle and someone who had nothing to do with the car. The situation, in my view, sir, is therefore no different from you sitting at home in your conservatory when someone starts throwing berries at the glass. You then set off in hot pursuit and get hold of them.'

My description was simply an appeal to logic. Road rage has never been defined by statute, as far as I'm aware. My view is that it involves two people getting out of their respective cars and one remonstrating with the other. How did I come up with this? I live the situation and put myself in the defendant's shoes. It never occurred to me that it would be road rage. Or that a judge would consider it to be road rage either. When he did, I had to think on my feet. Quickly.

The judge adjourned to consider what I'd said and decided to punish the defendant with an order to pay compensation to the boy. If the judge had sentenced my client on the basis that this was road rage, he would have been sent down.

So loopholes may help so-called unmeritorious defendants evade 'justice'. But they are also there to make sure people who don't deserve to be punished go free too.

There are those who will never be convinced by the rightness of the loopholes in law. And if there is a big enough swell of opinion, why doesn't the Government do more to close the loopholes? At one stage I went on record in the press saying that I was very happy to offer to help Parliament review road-traffic law and I have been approached by the government of a Caribbean island wanting me to advise on road-traffic law. I wouldn't say I know the law better than our government but I'm at the coalface every day, rather than in a Whitehall tower.

Among my recommendations to make our roads safer would be cutting the drink-driving limit. The Government has been cautious about backing a reduction in the limit from 80mg of alcohol per 100ml of blood to the standard of 50mg in many European countries. I find this unfathomable. Statistics have shown that the prospect of having an accident at this higher level increase four times. What greater evidence do they need?

I also think we should have a flexible speed limit – with an upper limit of 90mph – governed by weather and traffic conditions, rather than restricting our motorways to a unilateral maximum speed of 70mph. (That astonishing symbol of high-speed motoring, the Ford Anglia, has long gone.) There should also be a driving retest every ten years for motorists over the age of seventy. And then every five years for those over eighty. And the driving test itself should include motorway driving and a speed awareness course. So, plenty of thoughts to share with the Government. I never got the call.

As for loophole closing, what we need is a working party comprising a group of decent prosecutors, defence lawyers, court clerks and judges to sit down and thrash out a system that could cure all the ills in the statutory process. I am merely showing the courts the pothole in the road. I am not the guy with the asphalt. It is not my job to fill it in. I just say

it's there – now do something about it. I am hardly conceal-
ing its existence. But the point is, I'm as vocal as I can be
about the loopholes I unearth. Indeed, if I operated under
the radar I would be doing far more damage to road safety
campaigns by letting people do what they want. Once you
have put it out there you're highlighting it.

Certainly something needs to be done – and soon. For
while loopholes test the law, they leave the legal system in a
state of confusion. What we have at the moment is ostensibly
an adversarial system. Essentially, it works like an organised
prize fight. It's a case of two sides going into battle and, well,
may the best man win. I have no difficulties with that – except,
in practice, this is not quite what happens.

The defence, for example, are now obliged to disclose the
general issues they are going to argue in court. The High
Court has stated that the law is not a game, that the idea of
criminal proceedings is to convict the guilty and acquit the
innocent. But how can that fit with the fact that as a defence
lawyer I have to reveal my hand, show the prosecution where
their case may fail, in order to fight my client's corner?
Imagine sitting an exam where some of the candidates have
been told the main questions well in advance. Is that fair?

A lawyer has a duty to the court – because he is an officer
of the court – but his primary duty is to his client. At present these can be mutually exclusive, and this situation can
create tremendous conflict. When a client comes to me and
I notice, for example, several serious flaws in the prosecution case, under the present system I am then obligated to
disclose these issues to the court and the prosecution. In
doing so I not only put the Crown on notice but also provide them with the opportunity to rectify these mistakes.
Since to forewarn is to forearm, in effect I diminish my client's prospects of success. So, not a prize fight after all.

The alternative is to resort to what is known as an inquisitorial system, practised in European countries such as France and Germany. In this situation a judge, aided by two lawyers, considers the case. Should the UK Government choose to take this road, however, the system should also strip away the so-called loopholes, the legal technicalities, that have been the source of my success for so long, and concentrate more on the facts. And so, if a motorist is over the limit – regardless of any glitches in breathalysing him or taking a blood specimen – then, under this system, he would be convicted.

After all, we all want a crime-free society, a place where the innocent go free – or, better still, aren't even charged – and the guilty are convicted. But are we sure the system allows that at the present moment? And would we be better off with an alternative?

As I said, I strongly believe in loopholes as the law currently stands. They test that the prosecuting authorities are doing their job properly and that the letter of the law has been complied with. I've won over 2000 cases by showcasing fundamental flaws in legal procedure. This has happened because the law is crammed with legal intricacies which have paved the way for such victories.

If the Government should choose to adopt the inquisitorial system, it could only have any impact if lawyers worked hand in hand with the police, right from the beginning of the investigative process. A lawyer would need to be instructed immediately by the State to look over the procedural elements of the case and see if there were technical flaws that might otherwise cause a meritorious prosecution to collapse. Technical errors could be ironed out at an early stage, leaving the case to proceed on a largely factual basis.

As for financing this? Well, look at how much money is squandered on wasted hearings and unnecessary trials. Remove that element and it frees up the budget to provide more lawyers at an embryonic stage in the investigation.

If there is an appetite for serious change, the Criminal Justice System needs to decide what it wants to be and where it wants to go.

I began this book by talking about how my late father had guided me towards a career in law. He went on to become a magistrate, serving for twenty-five years, and so became especially interested in my work. I wanted him to be proud of me, but sadly he only got the chance to see me in action just the once. It was when I had a drink-driving case in my home town of Nottingham which involved, among other things, police assault and obstruction.

One of my defences hinged on the fact that my client had been put in handcuffs at the roadside and had been brought into custody still wearing them. There are Home Office guidelines regarding the use of handcuffs. They should only be slapped on if there is a reasonable fear of escape or violence from the suspect. So, to my mind, the handcuffs had been used unlawfully since there had been no evidence of a struggle to get my client to the station. I immediately began mauling the prosecution with my loophole.

At first I wasn't aware that Dad was in court, as he only managed to get there when the case was well under way. As soon as I caught sight of him, though, my heart started pounding and I began to sweat. Something that has never happened to me before or since. One moment I was my usual grounded self, the next I was quivering like a Victorian maiden.

It was ridiculous. I was perfectly comfortable with my

'loophole' and was on the way to destroying the officer's reliability. Yet having my father there catapulted me back to boyhood. I wanted to please my dad. Thankfully the court accepted my submission about the handcuffs, the police officer's credibility was crushed and I won the case. I was still shaking a little afterwards. Perhaps it wasn't such a bad thing that he only ever came to the one case.

Did Dad approve of such loopholes – both as my father and as a magistrate? Did the way I worked make him proud?

Actually he had no moral gripes about what I did. However, in his magisterial capacity, he'd wryly remark that my defences would never pass muster in his court. It was his little joke. He had no ethical grievances with me. He knew I needed to get on with my job.

And yet how ironic that the one time I didn't just go ahead and get on with my job – the one time I let my personal life trump my professional life – happened precisely because I am a father too. It occurred when my daughter Sophie, then nineteen years old, was caught speeding. She was driving back to Cheshire from our holiday apartment in North Wales when a speed camera recorded her doing 63mph in a temporary 50mph zone. She faced a £60 penalty and three points on her licence.

If Sophie had been a client, I'd have looked over the prosecution evidence, scoured all the relevant documents and may possibly have found a way to defend her, perhaps by spotting some procedural error. But, as she was my daughter, I decided not to even try. I reasoned that netting penalty points and a fine would help to teach her to drive safely. I wanted her to face the music. That's why I looked to the law. The offence had happened within two years of Sophie passing her driving test. If a motorist at this embryonic stage of their motoring career gets six points on their licence, then they are automatically obliged to take a retest. So, mushrooming insurance premiums aside, if Sophie got three points from this offence, then she'd have a sword of Damocles hanging over her. That, to my mind, would operate far better than anything else to ensure that she didn't do it again.

When I first told her this, Sophie initially failed to conceal her surprise. 'You're not serious, Dad. You're Mr Loophole, for goodness sake!' Carefully I explained my reasons for letting my own daughter take the rap without my intervention. Though I finished by adding, 'Sweetheart, you are free to go and see someone else if you want.'

To my immense pleasure, Sophie didn't hot-foot it down the high street in search of a willing motoring lawyer. Instead, she was gracious about it, accepting that she had done wrong, that she'd have to pay the price. In fact only recently she proudly came to tell me that she had completed her two years as a driver without getting any more points. The sword of Damocles had been lifted. My tactic had worked.

Hypocrite? Well, when the story hit the papers, that was the key charge levelled against me. One person even suggested that I'd refused to defend Sophie because I wouldn't be getting a fee. (You've no idea how much that girl costs me already!) But no, that wasn't the case. It's a father's prerogative to deploy a hypocritical tactic if he thinks it will ultimately benefit his own child. Call it a parental loophole. But I can't be a dad to all those other defendants out there. I can't be *in loco parentis* for the whole of society.

So what's next?

I've no idea what the future holds. Frankly, I have no desire to know, either. I never imagined as a young boy, that seven-year-old on the way home from Sunday school, that when I decided to be a lawyer, this is how it would pan out for me. It makes me realise that the best plan is not to plan. Anything is possible. As the Yiddish proverb goes, 'Man plans, God laughs.'

I remain as passionate and enthusiastic about practising the law – the way I practise the law – as I ever was. I'm still hungry for knowledge about the art of the loophole.

However, if there is an art to the loophole, then hopefully there will be a legacy to the loophole too. In criminal law, I profoundly hope that successive generations of defence lawyers will continue to put the Crown to proof on every single shred of evidence. This is the only way to test the system and ensure that we all practise law based on the law.

Though I never had any desire to be famous – or infamous – I've been told that some of my defences now crop up on law courses, that law students appraise my strategies and that my tactics are even taught in workshops. Meanwhile countless young lawyers still ask if they can come and watch me. It's all deeply flattering.

Having devoted thirty years of my life to building my career, soaking up the law and fighting to win, I feel that my way of giving something back is by teaching the next generation of lawyers whatever I can. And also by showing the ordinary man on the street what he should expect from the law should he ever be challenged by it.

In turn I hope prosecutors, the police and the system itself learn from the loopholes that trip them up so that our society becomes a safer place.

Meanwhile I've no intention of slowing down. I don't think I can.

When I'm tossing and turning at night, chewing over potential defences, I think of 'Man' by the seventeenth-century poet Henry Vaughan, who wrote:

> Man is the shuttle, to whose winding quest
> And passage through these looms,
> God order'd motion, but ordain'd no rest.

And I can't rest. I am that restless shuttle. And I won't rest until I know my work is done.

Even to me, the art of the loophole remains an expansive learning curve. As long as people want me to defend them, I'll keep on hunting through the law.

It's a crying shame when a defence lawyer fails to approach a case with the zest and enthusiasm that every client and every case deserves. My clients have been lucky. I've always wanted to win for me – and they have been the fortunate beneficiaries of my thirst for victory. And that thirst means you can never over-prepare, never think too much or read too extensively about the law. But you can fail to read into it.

What I can't understand is how any lawyer can have the temerity to appear before a court half prepared, advance half-baked arguments or miss fundamental points. Worse still, as I said at the very beginning, is any lawyer who takes the easy option of a guilty plea without first turning over every corner of the Crown case and considering his client's instructions. To haplessly enter a guilty plea on behalf of a client is a dereliction of duty and should have no place in any lawyer's brief.

Defending cases is about the pursuit of excellence. As far as I'm concerned, well, it's how I've always been, ever since scoring full marks in my times tables test. I want to be the best I can be. That's why I always keep in mind those words of Voltaire I quoted earlier: 'The best is the enemy of the [merely] good.'

There are plenty of good prosecutors and good police officers. But some are not so good.

When I first started out it was never my intention to do anything more than win my cases. I never intended to be some kind of moral crusader. However, I am convinced that if I carry on highlighting blunders in the system, society will benefit from even better prosecuting authorities, leading ultimately to safer roads.

The merely good will have become the best.